I0105352

Rhode Island Passenger Lists

RHODE ISLAND
PASSENGER LISTS

Port of Providence 1798–1808; 1820–1872

Port of Bristol and Warren 1820–1871

Compiled from
United States Custom House Papers

Maureen A. Taylor

Copyright © 1995
Maureen A. Taylor
All Rights Reserved.

Originally published by
Genealogical Publishing Company
Baltimore, Maryland
1995

Reprinted in paperback by
Genealogical Publishing Company
Baltimore, Maryland
2020

Paperback ISBN 9780806380148

CONTENTS

INTRODUCTION

This volume contains previously unpublished passenger lists from the ports of Providence, Bristol, and Warren, Rhode Island. The information was compiled using the U.S. Custom House Papers housed in the Manuscript Department at the Rhode Island Historical Society and the National Archives microfilm publication *Copies of Lists of Passengers Arriving at Miscellaneous Ports on the Atlantic and Gulf Coasts and at Ports on the Great Lakes*. There are three sections to this volume: passenger lists from the port of Providence, 1798–1808; passenger lists from the port of Providence from 1820–1872; and passenger lists from the port of Bristol and Warren from 1820–1871.

Alien Registration Lists 1798–1808

The Providence lists from 1798 to 1808 are actually Alien Registration lists that were federally mandated by the Alien and Sedition Acts of 1798–1799. Passenger documents from this period are extremely rare. The only other known lists are fragments from Beverly and Salem, Massachusetts.[1]

The Alien Act of June 25, 1798, stipulated that lists were to be kept of all non-citizens arriving at American ports of entry. Copies were to be sent to Washington. The Alien and Sedition Acts called for the recording of the name of each person, his age, the place of nativity, the country he came from, the nation he belonged to and owed allegiance to, his occupation, and a physical description. Individuals were sponsored, and the name of the sponsor appeared on the manifest. The forms used by local customs officials did not include space for a physical description of the individuals. The customs collector at the port of Providence, Jeremiah Olney, continued to maintain lists until 1808 even though an expiration date of two years from the date of passage was written into the original Act.

A separate notebook in the Custom House Papers at the Rhode Island Historical Society lists the aliens living in Providence from 1798 to 1808. It is difficult to ascertain whether this is a duplicate of the Alien Registration forms, since discrepancies and spelling variances exist, or whether this notebook was kept in compliance with another piece of legislation. An Act to Establish a Uniform Rule of Naturalization required that all white aliens register with their local customs official within six months of the passage of the Act, which took place on June

18, 1798. Olney wrote to the comptroller of the Treasury, John Steele, on September 27, 1798 for clarification of the word *white*. " In regard to the Naturalization Act, I also wish for your opinion—whether the term 'white' comprehends those Persons usually denominated *People of color*; some of whom, in a political view, or in point of Property, are of much more consequence than many *white* aliens."[2] The notebook entries start in early December of 1798 and include not just white travelers but individuals of color as well.

Customs Passenger Lists 1820–1872

The passenger manifests for 1820–1872 for Providence and Bristol/ Warren are a compilation of material found in the Custom House Papers at the Rhode Island Historical Society and the information on the National Archives microfilm. Customs collectors were required to obtain from vessels a passenger manifest that included the name of each individual; his age, sex, and occupation; country to which he belonged, country of which he intended to become an inhabitant, and whether that individual died on the voyage. Many of the manuscript manifests have a certificate of authenticity attached to them. The customs official would then submit copies of the manifests quarterly to Washington.[3]

The lists for 1820 to 1872, contained in the Custom House Papers at the Rhode Island Historical Society, are original passenger manifests. Michael Tepper, in *American Passenger Arrival Records*, outlines the criteria to ascertain whether passenger lists are originals or copies. The material at the Rhode Island Historical Society meets Tepper's criteria by indicating the name of each arriving vessel, the name of the port of embarkation, the name of the master, the date of arrival, and the port of arrival. Most of the arriving passengers' names are given in their entirety. Under the Works Progress Administration, several indexes were compiled using the Rhode Island Custom House Papers. In those instances the compilers stated in their introduction that copies in the National Archives in Washington were consulted whenever there were gaps in the material located in Rhode Island.[4]

The Rhode Island Custom House Papers

In 1790 the new federal government created the Rhode Island Custom House districts. The District of Providence was defined as "all the waters, shores, bays, harbors, creeks and inlets within the State north of the latitude of Conimicut point."[5] The District of Newport was designated as everything south of that. In 1801, the District of Bristol was created and defined as "all land and water within the following limits, viz. a line beginning at the middle of Mount Hope Bay between Mount Hope and Common Fence Point, running southwesterly through the middle of

Bristol Ferry to a point equidistant from the Island of Rhode Island to Prudence Island, from thence northeasterly on a straight line to the easternmost part of Nayatt Point, and from thence to the western shore of Bullock's Point."[6] Also that year, a section of the District of Providence was incorporated into the District of Bristol. Bristol was established as a port of entry with a customs collector.

The Rhode Island Custom House Papers were given to the Rhode Island Historical Society in two groups. Several years of effort by officers of the Rhode Island Historical Society resulted, in 1902, in the gift to the Society by the Treasury Department of records stored at the Providence Custom House. Ten years later, in 1912, additional material from the Rhode Island Custom District was transferred to Washington and on the verge of being destroyed when it was rescued by former Rhode Island senator Jesse Metcalf. Metcalf then purchased the papers and turned them over to the Rhode Island Historical Society. Detailed accession records for these gifts do not exist. Records for the District of Newport were not part of this material. [7]

References

1. They have been published in volume 106 (1952) of the *New England Historical and Genealogical Register.* For more background information on the Providence Custom House Papers see Earl C.Tanner's article " The Providence Federal Customhouse Papers as a Source of Maritime History since 1790," *New England Quarterly* (March 1953), 88–99.

2. Jeremiah Olney to John Steele, 27 September 1798, U.S. Custom House Papers. RIHS Library, Providence, RI.

3. Acts Regulating Passenger Ships, & c. U.S. Custom House Papers, RIHS Library, Providence, RI.

4. See Michael Tepper, *American Passenger Arrival Record*s (Baltimore: GPC, 1988), 66–67; Works Projects Administration *Ship Registers and Enrollments of Providence, R.I. 1773–1939.* (The National Archives Project, 1941), v.

5. Department of the Treasury. Inventory of Federal Archives in the States. Series III, No. 38. Rhode Island (National Archives Project, WPA), iv.

6. Ibid, v.

7. *Rhode Island Historical Society News Sheet*, October 3, 1902; Department of the Treasury. Inventory of Federal Archives in the States. Series III, No. 38, 241.

HOW TO USE THIS BOOK

Each section is arranged in alphabetical order by surname. The first line of data includes the name of each individual and his age, sex, occupation, place of birth, and date of arrival. On the line below, numbers are assigned for the other data. The key for the Alien Lists, for instance, is (1) Citizenship; (2) Residence; (3) Intended Residence; (4) Sponsor or Reporter's Name. For the lists from 1820 to 1872, the first line of data includes the name of each individual and his age, sex, occupation, and date of arrival. The information after the numbers differs from that of the Alien List, and includes (1) Country to which he Belongs; (2) Country of Which he Intends to Become an Inhabitant; and (3) Where taken on Board. A key appears on the verso of each section title page.

Note to the User

- The handwriting on these documents ranges from readable to illegible. Any information that is illegible is indicated by three dashes (---).
- Names without surnames appear first in each section.
- Names are spelled exactly as they appear in the records.
- Occupations and place names have been standardized whenever possible.
- Information missing from the passenger lists is indicated by a blank space between commas.

MATERIAL LISTED AS MISSING BY THE NATIONAL ARCHIVES

In 1964 the National Archives published microfilm publication M575, *Copies of Lists of Passengers Arriving at Miscellaneous Ports on the Atlantic and Gulf Coasts and at Ports on the Great Lakes, 1820–1873.* A list of missing records for each port appears with the passenger manifests. The following is a list of passenger lists located at the Rhode Island Historical Society that are listed as missing in the National Archives microfilm publication.

Port of Providence, 1820–1872

1820: November
1822: July, August, November and December
1823: July, August , September
1824: March, April, May, June, July, September, October, December
1825: April, June, July, August, September, October
1826: January, March, April
1827: July, August, September, October, November
1831: October, November
1832: November
1833: February, March, May June, July, August, September
1834: September
1835: March, April, May, June
1837: January, June, July, August, December
1838: February, March, May, June, August
1839: April, May, July, August
1840: February, April, May, June, August, October
1841: February, March, April, May, June, July, August, September
1846: October
1847: May, June, July, August, September
1853: May, July, August, September, October, November, December
1854: April, July, August, September, October, November
1855: May, June, July, August, September, October, November
1856: June, July, August, September, October, November
1861: October
1863: June, July, August, September, November
1865: July, September, October
1866: July, August, September
1867: May, June, July, August, September
1868: May, August, September, October
1869: May, August, September, November
1870: July, August, November
1871: April
1872: January, August, October, November

Port of Bristol and Warren, 1820–1871

1821: July
1822: July, August
1823: August, September
1825: January, April, May, June, August
1826: June

1827: April, May, June, July, August, September
1828: May, September
1829: May, July
1830: May, June
1831: June, August, October, November
1832: April, July, August, September, October
1833: June, July
1834: April, June, September
1835: April
1836: April
1837: February, April, May
1838: August
1839: August
1841: September, October
1844: April
1845: January
1846: January, March
1847: March, June, September
1857: May
1859: July
1861: July
1865: April

A GLOSSARY OF PLACE NAMES
MENTIONED IN THE PASSENGER LISTS

Aden: Ruled by the British from 1839–1937 as part of India.
  Currently part of Yemen.
Antigua: Part of the Leeward Islands.
Ardrossan, Scotland: Seaport on Firth of Clyde.
Arichat, Cape Breton: Village on Madeleine Island.
Barbados: Island in the West Indies.
Brewster: Town on Cape Cod Bay, Massachusetts
British America: Also known as British North America. Refers to
  Canada.
Buenos Aires: Capital of Argentina
Cape Haitien: Also spelled Cape Haytien, Haiti.
Cardenas: Seaport city in west central Cuba.

Castine: Town in Maine
Colchester: County in Nova Scotia
Cumberland, Nova Scotia: County in Nova Scotia.
Curacao: Island, part of the Netherland Antilles (Dutch West Indies)
Demerara: Region in North Guyana.
East Caicos, Turks Island: Also spelled East Caycos. Turks Island and
    Caicos Islands are British Colonies in the Bahamas.
Flores: Island in the Azores.
Frenchman's Bay: Located in Maine.
Gibraltar: British colony located on the south coast of Spain.
Goteborg: Also spelled Gotenberg and Gothenburg. Seaport in
    Sweden.
Halifax: Capital of Nova Scotia.
Havana: Capital of Cuba.
Madeira: Island off coast of Morocco.
Mariel: City in western Cuba.
Matanzas: City and province in west central Cuba.
Monrovia: Seaport capital of Liberia.
Mozambique: Located in southeast Africa.
Nassau, New Providence: Capital of the Bahama Islands.
North Kingstown: Town in Rhode Island.
Omoa: City in Honduras
Pawtucket, Mass.: Currently a part of Rhode Island.
Pictou: Town in Nova Scotia.
Ponce: Also spelled Ponca. City in Puerto Rico.
Port au Prince: Capital of Haiti.
Quilemaine: Also spelled Quillemaine. Seaport in Mozambique.
Remedios: City in west central Cuba.
San Miquel: Part of the Canary Islands.
Santiago: Also known as St. Jago. Seaport on south coast of Cuba.
Santiago de Chile: Capital of Chile.
St. Christopher: Part of the Leeward Islands.
St. Croix: Part of the Virgin Islands.
St. Helena: Island and British Colony in South Atlantic.
St. Martins: Part of the Leeward Islands.
St. Pierre, Martinique: Town on Martinique Island.
St. Thomas: Part of the Virgin Islands.
Sandwich Islands: Former name of the Hawaiian Islands.
Surinam: Country in South America.
Talcahuano: City in Chile.
Trinidad: Island in the West Indies.

ALIEN REGISTRATION LIST

❦

PORT OF PROVIDENCE 1798–1808

KEY: NAME, AGE, SEX, OCCUPATION, PLACE OF BIRTH,
      DATE OF ARRIVAL
      (1) CITIZENSHIP
      (2) RESIDENCE
      (3) INTENDED RESIDENCE
      (4) SPONSOR OR REPORTERS NAME

ANTHONY, 14, M, SERVANT, AFRICA, 03/18/1801
1. ENGLISH 2. PROVIDENCE 3. U.S. 4. ALEXANDER RUDEN

ANTONIA (BLACK), 14, M, SERVANT, AFRICA, 03/18/1801
1. AFRICA 2. 3. 4.

ARHONG, 31, M, SERVANT, CANTON, CHINA, 07/13/1803
1. CHINA 2. 3. PROVIDENCE 4. WILLIAM F. MEGEE

ARSIUS, 18, M, SERVANT, MACAO, CHINA, 07/29/1800
1. CANTON, CHINA 2. 3. PROVIDENCE 4. WILLIAM F. MEGEE

ARSOW, 25, M, SERVANT, CANTON, CHINA, 07/13/1803
1. CHINA 2. 3. 4. WILLIAM F. MEGEE

BATAVIA, 20, M, SERVANT, MALA KINGDOM, 12/17/1798
1. MALA KINGDOM 2. PROVIDENCE 3. PROVIDENCE 4. JOHN CORLIS

BEATRIX, 40, F, SERVANT, MARTINIQUE, WEST INDIES, 05/29/1805
1. FRANCE 2. 3. FRANCE 4. ROBERT TASCHER

BENEDICT, 40, , SERVANT, GUADALOUPE, , 08/04/1798
1. FRANCE 2. 3. 4.

ENOUGH, 1, M, SERVANT, PROVIDENCE, UNITED STATES, 12/14/1798
1. FRENCH 2. PROVIDENCE 3. PROVIDENCE 4. JOSEPH CHARIVITEAU

FELIX, 15, M, SERVANT, MARQUESAS ISLANDS, SOUTH PACIFIC, 05/26/1801
1. SAME 2. MARQUESAS IS. 3. PROVIDENCE 4. SCOTT JENCKES

FORTUNE, 9, M, SERVANT, BATAVIA, INDIA, 07/13/1801
1. DUTCH 2. PROVIDENCE 3. PROVIDENCE 4. SAMUEL SNOW

FRANCOIS, 16, M, SERVANT, MARTINIQUE, WEST INDIES, 05/29/1805
1. FRANCE 2. 3. NEW YORK 4. CHARLES RAUCE

JACK, 16, M, SERVANT, AFRICA, 07/01/1803
1. 2. 3. NEW YORK 4. SCHIOTTZ SCHIOTTZ

JUPITER, 14, M, SERVANT, MACASSAR, EAST INDIA, 04/30/1807
1. DUTCH 2. 3. AMSTERDAM 4.

LAMBO, 25, M, SERVANT, MALA KINGDOM, 12/17/1798
1. MALA KINGDOM 2. PROVIDENCE 3. PROVIDENCE 4. JN. CORLIS

LINDO, 22, M, IND. SERVANT, BENGAL, TABINGA, 12/17/1798
1. BENGAL 2. PROVIDENCE 3. PROVIDENCE 4. ELIZABETH NIGHTINGALE

LINDOR, 36, M, SERVANT, MARTINIQUE, WEST INDIES, 05/29/1805
1. FRANCE 2. 3. FRANCE 4. ROBERT TASCHER

LUC, 29, M, SERVANT, MARTINIQUE, 05/29/1805
1. FRANCE 2. MARTINIQUE 3. NEW YORK 4. MAYLOIRE BAILLARDEL

MARC, 50, M, SERVANT, MACOUBA, MARTINIQUE, 06/15/1805
1. FRANCE 2. 3. PARIS 4. AUGUST TRAVERSAY

PERO, 2, M, , SANTIAGO, CUBA, 05/01/1803
1. FRANCE 2. 3. NEW YORK 4. SUSANNAH MONPELLIER

PROVIDENCE, 13, M, SAILOR, HAWAII, SOUTH PACIFIC, 07/13/1803
1. HAWAII 2. 3. 4. WILLIAM F. MEGEE

ROLINS, 38, F, SERVANT, MARTINIQUE, WEST INDIES, 05/29/1805
1. FRANCE 2. 3. FRANCE 4. ROBERT TASCHER

SULLY, 16, M, SERVANT, MARTINIQUE, WEST INDIES, 05/29/1805
1. FRANCE 2. 3. NEW YORK 4. CHARLES RAUCE

TAREZE, 20, F, SERVANT, GUADALOUPE, FRENCH WEST INDIES, 12/14/1798
1. FRENCH 2. PROVIDENCE 3. PROVIDENCE 4. JOSEPH CHARIVITEAU

THUSTEEN, 20, F, SERVANT, AFRICA, 05/01/1803
1. AFRICA 2. 3. NEW YORK 4. SUSANNAH MONPELLIER

ABSTORF, JACOB, 40, M, CALICO PRINTER, MILHOUSEN, SWITZERLAND,
12/15/1798
1. GERMAN 2. PROVIDENCE 3. PROVIDENCE 4. JACOB ABSTORF

ADAMS, WILLIAM, 16, M, MARINER, ST. JOHN, NEW BRUNSWICK,
04/24/1805
1. BRITISH 2. 3. ST. JOHN 4. THOMAS RAWLEIGH

AMERINGE, MORRIS, 30, M, SUGAR REFINER, FRANKFORT, GERMANY,
12/17/1798
1. GERMANY 2. PROVIDENCE 3. PROVIDENCE 4. MORRIS AMERINGE

ANDERSON, ROBERT, 31, M, MARINER, KINCARDINE, SCOTLAND,
03/06/1804
1. BRITISH 2. 3. SCOTLAND 4. ROBERT ANDERSON

ARECHAGA, ANTONIO, 34, M, MARINER, BILBAO, SPAIN, 03/18/1800
1. SPAIN 2. PROVIDENCE 3. PROVIDENCE 4. ANTONIO ARECHAGA

ASTROF, JACOB, 46, M, CALICO PRINTER, MILHOMEN, SWITZERLAND,
12/07/1798
1. SWITZERLAND 2. PROVIDENCE 3. PROVIDENCE 4. JACOB ASTROF

AUBOYNEAU, P.L. ARMAND, 19, M, STUDENT RHODE ISLAND COLLEGE,
PETIT TROU, FRANCE, 12/17/1798
1. FRANCE 2. PROVIDENCE 3. NEWPORT 4. P.L. ARMAND AUBOYNEAU

AVICE, BERTRAND, 42, M, MERCHANT, PORT MALO, FRANCE, 12/26/1798
1. FRANCH 2. PAWTUXET 3. PAWTUXET 4. BERTRAND AVICE

BAADE, CHRISTIAN M., 15, M, SERVANT, AMSTERDAM, HOLLAND, 01/27/1808
1. DUTCH 2. 3. PROVIDENCE 4. JOS. N. COOK

BAILLARDEL, MARYLOIRE, 42, M, PLANTER, MARTINIQUE, 05/29/1805
1. FRANCE 2. MARTINIQUE 3. NEW YORK 4. MAYLOIRE BAILLARDEL

BARRE, MICHEL VICTOR, 57, M, MERCHANT, PARIS, FRANCE, 12/15/1798
1. ISLE OF BOURBON 2. PROVIDENCE 3. PROVIDENCE 4. MICHEL VICTOR BARRE

BARRE, MICHEL VICTOR, 57, , MERCHANT, PARIS, ISLE DE LA REUNION, 09/23/1798
1. FRENCH 2. 3. 4.

BERTRAND, J. BERNARDINE, 15, F, SEAMSTRESS, CAPE FRANCOIS, FRENCH WEST INDIES, 12/15/1798
1. FRANCE 2. PROVIDENCE 3. PROVIDENCE 4. STEPHEN LEWIS HUS DESFORGES

BESQUATE, MATTHEW, 23, M, SERVANT, CHESHIRE, ENGLAND, 10/03/1803
1. BRITISH 2. 3. BOSTON 4. ELIZABETH WAINWRIGHT

BIRCH, GEORGE, 15, M, GARDENER, LIMERICK, IRELAND, 12/15/1798
1. GREAT BRITAIN 2. PROVIDENCE 3. PROVIDENCE 4. JOHN BIRCH

BIRCH, JOHN, 49, M, GARDENER, WEXFORD, IRELAND, 12/15/1798
1. GREAT BRITAIN 2. PROVIDENCE 3. PROVIDENCE 4. JOHN BIRCH

BIRCH, MARY, 39, F, SEAMSTRESS, WEXFORD, IRELAND, 12/15/1798
1. GREAT BRITAIN 2. PROVIDENCE 3. PROVIDENCE 4. MARY BIRCH

BIRD, JAMES, 27, M, MARINER, IPSWICH, BRITAIN, 12/17/1798
1. BRITISH 2. PROVIDENCE 3. PROVIDENCE 4. JAMES BIRD

BIRD, SAMUEL, 1, M, , PROVIDENCE, U.S., 12/17/1798
1. BRITISH 2. PROVIDENCE 3. PROVIDENCE 4. JAMES BIRD

BIRD, JR., JAMES, 3, M, , PROVIDENCE, U.S., 12/17/1798
1. BRITISH 2. PROVIDENCE 3. PROVIDENCE 4. JAMES BIRD

BLACKBURN, ANN, 25, F, , SHIPLEY, ENGLAND, 10/03/1803
1. BRITISH 2. OLDHAM 3. PROVIDENCE 4. JOHN BLACKBURN

BLACKBURN, GEORGE, 4, M, , SHIPLEY, ENGLAND, 10/03/1803
1. BRITISH 2. OLDHAM 3. PROVIDENCE 4. JOHN BLACKBURN

BLACKBURN, HAND, 3, F, , SHIPLEY, ENGLAND, 10/03/1803
1. BRITISH 2. OLDHAM 3. PROVIDENCE 4. JOHN BLACKBURN

BLACKBURN, JOHN, 26, M, JOINER, SHIPLEY, ENGLAND, 10/03/1803
1. BRITISH 2. OLDHAM 3. PROVIDENCE 4. JOHN BLACKBURN

BONIN, FRANCOIS, 64, M, PLANTER, BOURGES, FRANCE, 05/29/1805
  1. FRANCE 2. 3. FRANCE 4. ROBERT TASCHER

BOS, HANCHIA, 10, F, SERVANT, AMSTERDAM, HOLLAND, 07/23/1804
  1. DUTCH 2. 3. PROVIDENCE 4. SYLVESTER SIMMONS

BOUNDY, WILLIAM, 19, M, SEAMAN, CORNWALL, ENGLAND, ENGLAND,
05/26/1801
  1. BRITISH 2. PROVIDENCE 3. PROVIDENCE 4. WILLIAM BOUNDY

BOUYER, ANTOINETTE MARGUERITE, 69, F, SEAMSTRESS, PARIS,
FRENCH, 12/15/1798
  1. CAPE FRANCIS 2. PROVIDENCE 3. PROVIDENCE 4. ANTOINETTE
  MARGUERITE BOUYER

BOUYER, PETER ANDREW, 69, M, M---, PARIS, FRENCH, 12/15/1798
  1. CAPE FRANCAIS 2. PROVIDENCE 3. PROVIDENCE 4. PETER
  ANDREW BOUYER

BROCKMEYER, HENRICK, 17, M, SERVANT, AMSTERDAM, HOLLAND,
01/27/1808
  1. DUTCH 2. 3. PROVIDENCE 4. THOMAS P. IVES

BROUSSARD-CADET, J.B., 38, M, MERCHANT, MARTINICO, 09/21/1801
  1. FRANCE 2. PROVIDENCE 3. NEW YORK 4. J.B. BROUSSARD-CADET

BROWN, JOHN, 32, M, ROPE MAKER, LUNENBURGH, GERMAN, 12/07/1798
  1. GERMANY 2. PROVIDENCE 3. PROVIDENCE 4. JOHN BROWN

BRUNEE, RENEE, 36, M, CABINET MAKER, LYONS, FRANCE, 12/07/1798
  1. FRANCE 2. PROVIDENCE 3. PROVIDENCE 4. RENEE BRUNEE

BRUNLE, RENEE, 36, M, CABINET MAKER, LYONS, , 12/17/1798
  1. FRENCH 2. PROVIDENCE 3. PROVIDENCE 4. RENEE BRUNLE

BRYAN, KELLEY, 40, , SAILOR, IRELAND, NEW SOUTH WALES, 07/29/1800
  1. BRITISH 2. 3. 4. KELLEY BRYAN

BURG, JOHN, 47, M, WEAVER, PERHERSETT, GERMANY, 12/07/1798
  1. GERMANY 2. PROVIDENCE 3. PROVIDENCE 4. JOHN BURG

BURG, PENELOPE, 7, F, , NEWPORT, U.S., 12/07/1798
  1. GERMANY 2. PROVIDENCE 3. PROVIDENCE 4. JOHN BURG

BURG, REBECCA, 15, F, SEAMSTRESS, NEWPORT, U.S., 12/07/1798
  1. GERMANY 2. PROVIDENCE 3. PROVIDENCE 4. JOHN BURG

CANNADY, JAMES, 21, , FARMER, COUNTY OF CLEAVE, IRELAND, NEW
SOUTH WALES, 07/29/1800
  1. BRITISH 2. 3. 4. JAMES CANNADY

CARSE, NANCY, 13, F, , PROVIDENCE, U.S., 12/15/1798
  1. U.S. 2. PROVIDENCE 3. PROVIDENCE 4. ROBERT CARSE

CARSE, ROBERT, 49, M, MARINER, FALKIRK, SCOTLAND, 12/15/1798
1. BRITISH 2. PROVIDENCE 3. PROVIDENCE 4. ROBERT CARSE

CHARIVITEAU, JOSEPH, 50, M, MERCHANT, GUADALOUPE, FRENCH
WEST INDIES, 12/14/1798
1. FRENCH 2. PROVIDENCE 3. PROVIDENCE 4. JOSEPH CHARIVITEAU

CHARIVITEAU, MARIE SOPHIE, 20, F, DAUGHTER, GUADALOUPE,
FRENCH WEST INDIES, 12/14/1798
1. FRENCH 2. PROVIDENCE 3. PROVIDENCE 4. JOSEPH CHARIVITEAU

CHAUVITEAUX, ELIZABETH, 46, F, SEAMSTRESS, GUADALOUPE,
FRENCH WEST INDIES, 12/15/1798
1. FRANCE 2. PROVIDENCE 3. PROVIDENCE 4. ELIZABETH
CHAUVITEAUX

CHEVALIER, A., 34, M, MERCHANT, MARTINICO, 09/21/1801
1. FRANCE 2. PROVIDENCE 3. NEW YORK 4. ALEX. CHEVALIER

CHRISTY, ADAM, 25, M, CLERK, LIMERICK, 05/25/1799
1. IRELAND 2. LIMERICK 3. UNCERTAIN 4. ADAM CHRISTY

CLARKE, WILLIAM, 26, M, MARINER, KINCARDINE, SCOTLAND, 03/06/
1804
1. BRITISH 2. 3. SCOTLAND 4. WILLIAM CLARKE

COQUIL, CHARLES, 22, M, MERCHANT, ISLE OF FRANCE, HITHER INDIES,
04/25/1804
1. FRENCH 2. 3. FRANCE 4. CHARLES COQUIL

CORDONE, EMANUEL, 52, M, MARINER, GENOA, 10/26/1804
1. GENOA 2. 3. GENOA 4. EMANUEL CORDONE

CRESTAN, DOMINGO, 45, M, MARINER, BIRCAYA, SPAIN, 09/04/1801
1. SPANISH 2. PROVIDENCE 3. UNCERTAIN 4. DOMINGO CRESTAN

CRITCHELL, RICHARD, 32, M, MARINER, ISLINGTON, ENGLAND,
PENTON VILLA, 05/12/1805
1. BRITISH 2. 3. 4. RICHARD CRITCHELL

CROW, JOHN, 27, M, BOOKBINDER, COLCRAINE, IRELAND, 12/14/1798
1. BRITISH 2. PROVIDENCE 3. PROVIDENCE 4. JOHN CROW

D.A. PUEYE, RAYMUNDO, 38, , GENTLEMEN, SPAIN, , 09/09/1798
1. SPAIN 2. HAVANNAH 3. 4.

DAVIS, ROWLAND, 19, M, CLERK, COVE OF CORK, IRELAND, 04/03/1802
1. BRITISH 2. PROVIDENCE 3. 4. ROWLAND DAVIS

DELACOSTE, J.C., 49, M, MERCHANT, STRASBOURGH, FRANCE, 08/03/1803
1. FRANCE 2. CAYENNE 3. PROVIDENCE 4. J.C. DELACOSTE

DEMADRELLE, DESGROTTE, 11, M, , MACOUBA, MARTINIQUE, 06/15/1805
1. FRANCE 2. 3. PARIS 4. AUGUST TRAVERSAY

DESANNEY, BARASM, 8, , IND. SERVANT, SEACO GAMBIA RIVER,
MONDENGO COUNTRY, 05/21/1799
1. KING OF BARRA 2. 3. 4.

DESFORGES, J.L. HUS, 38, F, SEAMSTRESS, BORDEAUX, FRENCH,
12/15/1798
1. FRANCE 2. PROVIDENCE 3. PROVIDENCE 4. J.L. HUS DESFORGES

DESFORGES, STEPHEN LEWIS HUS, 45, M, MERCHANT, BORDEAUX,
FRENCH, 12/15/1798
1. FRANCE 2. PROVIDENCE 3. PROVIDENCE 4. STEPHEN LEWIS HUS
DESFORGES

DESGROTTE, ROSEVILLE, 9, M, , MACOUBA, , 06/15/1798
1. FRANCE 2. 3. PARIS 4. AUGUST TRAVERS

DILLION, ALMY, 1, F, , PROVIDENCE, U.S., 12/07/1798
1. BRITISH 2. PROVIDENCE 3. PROVIDENCE 4. ANDREW DILLION

DILLION, ANDREW, 32, M, TAYLOR, BELLARAGGAT, IRELAND, 12/07/1798
1. BRITISH 2. PROVIDENCE 3. PROVIDENCE 4. ANDREW DILLION

DINGEMANS, C.P., 29, , ADMINISTERS PLANTATION, THE HAGUE,
HOLLAND, 09/03/1798
1. DUTCH 2. SURINAM 3. 4.

DONLEY, ABIGAIL, 1, F, , PROVIDENCE, U.S., 12/17/1798
1. U.S. 2. PROVIDENCE 3. PROVIDENCE 4. MICHAEL DONLEY

DONLEY, MARY, 6, F, , PROVIDENCE, U.S., 12/17/1798
1. U.S. 2. PROVIDENCE 3. PROVIDENCE 4. MICHAEL DONLEY

DONLEY, MICHAEL, 39, M, RUNS ROOMING HOUSE, WEXFORD,IRELAND,
12/17/1798
1. GREAT BRITAIN 2. PROVIDENCE 3. PROVIDENCE 4. MICHAEL
DONLEY

DRASAS, HENDRICK, 14, M, SERVANT, AMSTERDAM, HOLLAND, 07/23/
1804
1. DUTCH 2. 3. PROVIDENCE 4. SYLVESTER SIMMONS

DUBORG, PETER, 49, M, MARINER, CARTARET, FRENCH, 12/17/1798
1. FRANCE 2. JOHNSTON 3. PROVIDENCE 4. PETER DUBORG

DUCASSOU, JACQUES, 9, M, , MARTINIQUE, WEST INDIES, 05/29/1805
1. FRANCE 2. 3. NEW YORK 4. CHARLES RAUCE

DUFOUR, GUILLAUME, 43, M, PLANTER, JEREMIE, HISPANOLA, 06/15/1805
1. FRANCE 2. 3. BALTIMORE 4. AUGUST TRAVERSAY

DULINGO, JULIEN DAVID, 56, M, MARINER, MORLAIN, FRENCH, 12/15/1798
    1. MORLAIX 2. PAWTUXET 3. PAWTUXET 4. JULIEN DAVID DULINGO

DUPONT, LEON, 7, M, PLANTER, MARTINIQUE, WEST INDIES, 05/29/1805
    1. FRANCE 2. 3. FRANCE 4. ROBERT TASCHER

DURANS, FRANCIS, 14, M, INFANT, ISLE OF FRANCE, FRANCE, 12/17/1798
    1. ISLE OF FRANCE 2. TAUNTON 3. PROVIDENCE 4. JOHN INNES CLARK

DURANS, THOMAS, 12, M, INFANT, ISLE OF FRANCE, FRANCE, 12/17/1798
    1. ISLE OF FRANCE 2. CRANSTON 3. PROVIDENCE 4. JOHN INNES CLARK

FABREGAS, MAGUEL, 38, M, MARINER, CATALONIA, SPAIN, 03/18/1800
    1. SPAIN 2. PROVIDENCE 3. PROVIDENCE 4. MAGUEL FABREGAS

FARIER, ARTHUR, 45, M, COOPER, BELLY CASTLE, IRELAND, 12/15/1798
    1. GREAT BRITAIN 2. PROVIDENCE 3. PROVIDENCE 4. ARTHUR FARIER

FARIER, BETSEY, 4, F, INFANT, PROVIDENCE, NORTH AMERICA, 12/15/1798
    1. NO. AMERICA 2. PROVIDENCE 3. PROVIDENCE 4. ARTHUR FARIER

FARIER, NANCY, 39, F, SEAMSTRESS, CARRICKFERGUS, IRELAND, 12/15/1798
    1. GREAT BRITAIN 2. PROVIDENCE 3. PROVIDENCE 4. NANCY FARIER

FARIER, NANCY, 2, F, INFANT, PROVIDENCE, NORTH AMERICA, 12/15/1798
    1. NO. AMERICA 2. PROVIDENCE 3. PROVIDENCE 4. ARTHUR FARIER

FARIER, ROBERT, 15, M, MARINER, BELFAST, IRELAND, 12/15/1798
    1. GREAT BRITAIN 2. PROVIDENCE 3. PROVIDENCE 4. ARTHUR FARIER

FARIER, ROSELLA, 10 MTH, F, INFANT, PROVIDENCE, SOUTH AMERICA, 12/15/1798
    1. NO. AMERICA 2. PROVIDENCE 3. PROVIDENCE 4. ARTHUR FARIER

FARIER, WILLIAM, 11, M, INFANT, PROVIDENCE, NORTH AMERICA, 12/15/1798
    1. NO. AMERICA 2. PROVIDENCE 3. PROVIDENCE 4. ARTHUR FARIER

FARIET, MARY, 13, F, INFANT, PROVIDENCE, NORTH AMERICA, 12/15/1798
    1. NO. AMERICA 2. PROVIDENCE 3. PROVIDENCE 4. ARTHUR FARIER

FAULKNER, HENRY, 21, , PHYSICIAN, SHROPSHIRE, ENGLAND, NEW SOUTH WALES, 07/29/1800
    1. BRITISH 2. 3. 4. HENRY FAULKNER

FEUCHTENBERGER, GEORGE, 36, M, PLANTER, FURTH, PRUSSIA, 07/16/1804
    1. GERMANY 2. 3. SURINAM 4. GEORGE FEUCHTENBERGER

FOURBISSSEUR, LIDE, 38, F, SEAMSTRESS, MORSE, FRANCE, 08/03/1801
1. FRENCH 2. PROVIDENCE 3. UNKNOWN 4. LIDE FOURBISSEUR

GARDINER, JAMES, 48, M, INN HOLDER, MINTROS, SCOTLAND, 12/07/1798
1. BRITISH 2. PROVIDENCE 3. PROVIDENCE 4. JAMES GARDINER

GARDINER, NATHANIEL, 112, M, , PROVIDENCE, U.S., 12/07/1798
1. BRITISH 2. PROVIDENCE 3. PROVIDENCE 4. JAMES GARDINER

GARDINER, POLLY, 10, F, , PROVIDENCE, U.S., 12/07/1798
1. BRITISH 2. PROVIDENCE 3. PROVIDENCE 4. JAMES GARDINER

GEHRUNG, GOTTLIEB, 23, M, PAINTER, DUSSELDORF, GERMAN,
12/17/1798
1. GERMANY 2. PROVIDENCE 3. PROVIDENCE 4. GOTTLIEB GEHRUNG

GEOFFREY, ETIENNE JACQUES, 31, M, MERCHANT, PARIS, FRENCH,
12/15/1798
1. ISLE OF FRANCE 2. PROVIDENCE 3. PROVIDENCE 4. ETIENNE
JACQUES GEOFFREY

GEOFFREY, G. ETIENNE JACQUES, 31, , , MERCHANT, PARIS, ISLE DE
FRANCE, 09/23/1798
1. FRENCH 2. 3. 4.

GILLESFREY, NEPTUNE, 7, , IND. SERVANT, ISLAND DELOS, AFRICA,
05/21/1799
1. KING KENTOR 2. 3. 4.

GLAAN, C. BERNARD, 40, M, SHOPKEEPER, SENGINARDEN, GERMAN,
12/07/1798
1. GERMANY 2. PROVIDENCE 3. PROVIDENCE 4. C. BERNARD GLAAN

GUERDON, MICHAEL, 40, M, CARPENTER, ST. GENISSE, FRENCH',
12/15/1798
1. FRANCE 2. PROVIDENCE 3. PROVIDENCE 4. MICHAEL GUIDON

HAIG, JOHN, 30, M, MARINER, EDINBOURGH, SCOTLAND, 07/05/1803
1. GREAT BRITAIN 2. 3. QUEBEC 4. JOHN HAIG

HARDENBURGH, ANN, 10, F, , PROVIDENCE, U.S., 12/07/1798
1. U.S. 2. PROVIDENCE 3. PROVIDENCE 4. JACOB HARDENBURGH

HARDENBURGH, JACOB, 50, M, GARDNER, WEISSR, UNITED
NETHERLANDS, 12/07/1798
1. DUTCH 2. PROVIDENCE 3. PROVIDENCE 4. JACOB HARDENBURGH

HARDENBURGH, JOHN COOPER, 5, M, , PROVIDENCE, U.S., 12/07/1798
1. U.S. 2. PROVIDENCE 3. PROVIDENCE 4. JACOB HARDENBURGH

HARDENBURGH, JOSHUA, 8, M, , PROVIDENCE, U.S., 12/07/1798
1. U.S. 2. PROVIDENCE 3. PROVIDENCE 4. JACOB HARDENBURGH

HARVEY, JOHN, 16, , SEAMAN, BREST, FRANCE, , 09/09/1798
1. FRANCE 2. 3. 4.

HAWKES, PITTY, 29, M, STRAW HAT MAKER, ESSEX, ENGLAND, 03/06/1804
1. GREAT BRITAIN 2. 3. NEW YORK 4. PITTY HAWKES

HAWKINS, MARIA, 16, F, , SHROPSHIRE, ENGLAND, 10/03/1803
1. BRITISH 2. LIVERPOOL 3. NEW YORK 4. ELIZABETH WAINWRIGHT

HAYNE, FRANCIS, 12, M, , KINGS, IRELAND, 11/09/1807
1. GREAT BRITAIN 2. 3. UNCERTAIN 4. JOHN HAYNE

HAYNE, JOHN, 26, M, GENTLEMAN, LIMERICK, IRELAND, 11/09/1807
1. GREAT BRITAIN 2. 3. UNCERTAIN 4. JOHN HAYNE

HAYNE, JOHN, JR., 6, M, , KINGS, IRELAND, 11/09/1807
1. GREAT BRITAIN 2. 3. UNCERTAIN 4. JOHN HAYNE

HAYNE, MARY, 26, F, , LIMERICK, IRELAND, 11/09/1807
1. GREAT BRITAIN 2. 3. UNCERTAIN 4. JOHN HAYNE

HERSE, JAN FREDERICK, 15, M, SERVANT, AMSTERDAM, HOLLAND, 09/22/1801
1. DUTCH 2. PROVIDENCE 3. PROVIDENCE 4. EPHM. TALBOT

HIDDEN, TIMOTHY, 50, M, BLACK SMITH, KILKENNY, BRITISH, 12/07/1798
1. BRITISH 2. PROVIDENCE 3. PROVIDENCE 4. TIMOTHY HIDDEN

HINSON, EDWARD, 53, M, MERCHANT, BERMUDA, 07/05/1803
1. GREAT BRITAIN 2. 3. NEW YORK 4. EDWARD HINSON

HIORNS, CALEB, 23, M, MERCHANT, LONDON, ENGLAND, 07/29/1806
1. BRITISH 2. 3. ENGLAND 4. CALEB HIORNS

HOLMES, GEORGE, 31, M, MARINER, LIVERPOOL, ENGLAND, 04/24/1805
1. BRITISH 2. 3. ST. JOHN 4. THOMAS RAWLEIGH

HOWLAND, JOHN, 24, , MARINER, NEW BEDFORD, HOLLAND, 09/03/1798
1. U.S. 2. 3. 4.

HYSLOP, THOMAS, 21, M, BISCUIT BAKER, DUMFRIES, SCOTLAND, 05/17/1804
1. GREAT BRITAIN 2. 3. NEW YORK 4. THOMAS HYSLOP

IRWIN, MOSES, 26, M, COTTON SPINNER, CUMBERLAND, BRITAIN, 12/07/1798
1. BRITISH 2. COVENTRY 3. COVENTRY 4. MOSES IRWIN

IRWIN, MOSES, 26, , COTTON SPINNER, CUMBERLAND, BRITAIN, 12/17/1798
1. 2. COVENTRY 3. COVENTRY 4. MOSES IRWIN

IRWIN, STEPHEN, 1, M, , WARWICK, U.S., 12/07/1798
1. U.S. 2. COVENTRY 3. COVENTRY 4. MOSES IRWIN

IRWIN, STEPHEN P., 26, , SON, WARWICK, U.S., 12/17/1798
  1. 2. COVENTRY 3. COVENTRY 4. MOSES IRWIN

JUCKEN, PAUL, 20, M, SERVANT, TRANQUEBAR, HINDOOSTAN, 03/19/1799
  1. 2. PROVIDENCE 3. PROVIDENCE 4. JOHN BOWERS

JUILLET, ANTOINE, 29, M, PLANTER, LYON, FRANCE, 07/01/1806
  1. FRANCE 2. 3. NEW YORK 4. ANTOINE JUILLET

KELTIE, CATHARINE, 8, F, , LONDON, ENGLAND, 08/11/1806
  1. GREAT BRITAIN 2. 3. PROVIDENCE 4. SUSAN KELTIE

KELTIE, JOHN, 7, M, , LONDON, ENGLAND, 08/11/1806
  1. GREAT BRITAIN 2. 3. PROVIDENCE 4. SUSAN KELTIE

KELTIE, SUSAN, 28, F, VISITANT, LONDON, ENGLAND, 08/11/1806
  1. GREAT BRITAIN 2. 3. PROVIDENCE 4. SUSAN KELTIE

KELTIE, SUSAN, JR., 4, F, , LONDON, ENGLAND, 08/11/1806
  1. GREAT BRITAIN 2. 3. PROVIDENCE 4. SUSAN KELTIE

KOOPMAN, A.J., 48, , MERCHANT, SURINAM, HOLLAND, 09/03/1798
  1. HOLLAND 2. 3. 4.

LAIVON, JOS. JOHN BATES, 13, M, SERVANT, CAYENNE, COURT OF CAYENNE, 09/21/1807
  1. FRANCE 2. 3. PROVIDENCE 4. PETER DOUVILLE

LAMBERT, JAMES, 43, M, TRADER, PROVENCE, FRANCE, 05/01/1802
  1. FRENCH 2. 3. NEW YORK 4. JAMES LAMBERT

LANGEVETO, JOHANNA, 14, F, SERVANT, AMSTERDAM, HOLLAND, 01/02/1807
  1. HOLLAND 2. 3. PROVIDENCE 4. NATHANIEL PEARCE

LAROCHE, B., 4, M, , PROVIDENCE, UNITED STATES, 12/15/1798
  1. U.S. 2. PROVIDENCE 3. PROVIDENCE 4. BENOIT LAROCHE

LAROCHE, BENOIT, 45, M, MERCHANT, BORDEAUX, FRENCH, 12/15/1798
  1. FRANCE 2. PROVIDENCE 3. PROVIDENCE 4. BENOIT LAROCHE

LAWRENCE, ALEXANDER, 36, M, PLANTER, NEVIS, WEST INDIES, 11/12/1804
  1. GREAT BRITAIN 2. 3. NEVIS 4. ALEXANDER LAWRENCE

LAWRENCE, JAMES, 16, M, SERVANT, NEVIS, , 11/12/1804
  1. 2. 3. NEVIS 4. ALEXANDER LAWRENCE

LAWRENCE, MARY, 32, F, WF OF ALEXANDER, NEVIS, WEST INDIES, 11/12/1804
  1. GREAT BRITAIN 2. 3. NEVIS 4. ALEXANDER LAWRENCE

LAWRENCE, MARY, 14, F, SERVANT, AFRICA, , 11/12/1804
  1. 2. 3. NEVIS 4. ALEXANDER LAWRENCE

LEIRAC, L., 30, M, MERCHANT, CULLES, FRENCH, 12/15/1798
  1. ISLE OF BOURBON 2. PROVIDENCE 3. PROVIDENCE 4. L. LEIRAR

LEIRAR, LOUIS, 30, , MERCHANT, AULLE-LIMOSIN, ISLE DE LA REUNION,
09/23/1798
  1. FRENCH 2. 3. 4.

LEVY, JOSEPH, 44, M, MERCHANT, COPENHAGEN, DANISH, 08/03/1799
  1. DENMARK 2. PROVIDENCE 3. ST. THOMAS 4. JOSEPH LEVY

MANN, JAMES, 23, M, SEAMAN, NORTHUMBERLAND, ENGLAND,
05/26/1801
  1. BRITISH 2. PROVIDENCE 3. PROVIDENCE 4. JAMES MANN

MARIOL, CHARLES, 35, M, PLANTER, CLERMONT, FRANCE, 05/29/1805
  1. FRANCE 2. 3. FRANCE 4. ROBERT TASCHER

MASSON, NICHOLAS, 29, M, MERCHANT, LYON, FRANCE, 07/01/1806
  1. FRANCE 2. 3. NEW YORK 4. NICHOLAS MASSON

MCCANN, MARY, 7, F, SEAMSTRESS, NAUGHLIN BRIDGE, IRELAND,
12/07/1798
  1. BRITISH 2. PROVIDENCE 3. PROVIDENCE 4. PATRICK MCCANN

MCCANN, PATRICK, 45, M, MERCHANT, NAUGHLIN BRIDGE, IRELAND,
12/07/1798
  1. BRITISH 2. PROVIDENCE 3. PROVIDENCE 4. PATRICK MCCANN

MCCLOUD, SIMON, 18, M, MARINER, INVERNESS, SCOTLAND, 03/06/1804
  1. BRITISH 2. 3. SCOTLAND 4. SIMON MCCLOUD

MCGIE, JOHN, 40, M, MERCHANT, ABERDEEN, SCOTLAND, 09/09/1806
  1. GREAT BRITAIN 2. 3. PROVIDENCE 4. JOHN MCGIE

MCGLOCKLIN, PETER, 28, M, HAIR DRESSER, LONDON, BRITISH,
12/17/1798
  1. BRITISH 2. PROVIDENCE 3. PROVIDENCE 4. PETER MCGLOCKLIN

MCLANE, HECTOR, 38, M, COOPER, BELLY CASTLE, IRELAND, 12/15/1798
  1. GREAT BRITAIN 2. PROVIDENCE 3. PROVIDENCE 4. HECTOR
  MCLANE

MCLANE, JOHN, 9, M, SON, PROVIDENCE, UNITED STATES, 12/15/1798
  1. UNITED STATES 2. PROVIDENCE 3. PROVIDENCE 4. HECTOR
  MCLANE

MCLANE, MARYAN, 7, F, DAUGHTER, PROVIDENCE, UNITED STATES,
12/15/1798
  1. UNITED STATES 2. PROVIDENCE 3. PROVIDENCE 4. HECTOR
  MCLANE

MCLANE, NATH., 5, M, SON, PROVIDENCE, UNITED STATES, 12/15/1798
　　1. UNITED STATES 2. PROVIDENCE 3. PROVIDENCE 4. HECTOR
　　MCLANE

MCNELLY, CHARLES, 32, M, SAILOR, DUBLIN, IRELAND, 07/13/1803
　　1. BRITISH 2. 3. PEPPERELBOROUGH 4. CHARLES MCNELLY

MERLE, L., 22, M, MERCHANT, VALENCE, FRANCE, 04/25/1805
　　1. FRENCH 2. 3. FRANCE 4. L MERLE

MICHEL, JAMES, 21, M, MERCHANT, GRANVILLE, FRANCE, 07/01/1806
　　1. FRANCE 2. 3. NEW YORK 4. JAMES MICHEL

MIDDLETON, WM., 23, M, MERCHANT, LONDON, LONDON, 07/03/1807
　　1. ENGLAND 2. 3. PROVIDENCE 4. WM. MIDDLETON

MITCHENSON, THOMAS, 19, , SEAMAN, DURHAM, ENG., PORTUGAL,
03/18/1799
　　1. GREAT BRITAIN 2. 3. 4.

MITCHENSON, THOMAS, 20, M, SEAMAN, DURHAM, ENGLAND,
ENGLAND, 03/19/1799
　　1. ENGLAND 2. PROVIDENCE 3. PROVIDENCE 4. THOMAS
　　MITCHENSON

MOHRS, E.F., 28, , MERCHANT, AMSTERDAM, HOLLAND, 09/03/1798
　　1. DUTCH 2. 3. 4.

MOLONO, EDMUND, 22, M, MARINER, LIMERICK, IRELAND, 04/24/1805
　　1. BRITISH 2. 3. ST. JOHN 4. THOMAS RAWLEIGH

MONPELLIER, SUSANNAH, 50, F, TRADER, PARIS, FRANCE, 05/01/1803
　　1. FRANCE 2. 3. NEW YORK 4. SUSANNAH MONPELLIER

MORGAN, JAMES, 22, M, SERVANT, BENGAL, INDIA, 07/29/1806
　　1. BRITISH 2. 3. ENGLAND 4. THOMAS STEWART

MORIN, RENEE, 43, M, MERCHANT, PORT MALO, FRANCE, 12/14/1798
　　1. FRENCH 2. PAWTUXET 3. PAWTUXET 4. RENEE MORIN

MUENSCHER, CHRISTOPHER CHARLES, 5, M, SON, NEWPORT,
GERMANY, 12/17/1798
　　1. HESSE CASSELL 2. PROVIDENCE 3. PROVIDENCE 4. JOHN
　　MUENSCHER

MUENSCHER, HENRY, 10, M, SON, NEWPORT, GERMANY, 12/17/1798
　　1. HESSE CASSELL 2. PROVIDENCE 3. PROVIDENCE 4. JOHN
　　MUENSCHER

MUENSCHER, JOHN, 50, M, MUSICIAN, ---, GERMANY, 12/17/1798
　　1. HESSE CASSELL 2. PROVIDENCE 3. PROVIDENCE 4. JOHN
　　MUENSCHER

MUENSCHER, JOHN ERNST, 12, M, SON, NEWPORT, GERMANY, 12/17/1798
1. HESSE CASSELL 2. PROVIDENCE 3. PROVIDENCE 4. JOHN
MUENSCHER

MUENSCHER, WILLIAM, 2, M, SON, NEWPORT, GERMANY, 12/17/1798
1. HESSE CASSELL 2. PROVIDENCE 3. PROVIDENCE 4. JOHN
MUENSCHER

MURRAY, ELIZABETH, 25, F, WF OF JAMES, LONDON, ENGLAND,
07/29/1806
1. BRITISH 2. 3. ENGLAND 4. JAMES MURRAY

MURRAY, JAMES, 26, M, MILITARY, LONDON, ENGLAND, 07/29/1806
1. BRITISH 2. 3. ENGLAND 4. JAMES MURRAY

NOVION, GEORGE, 37, M, PROF. MATHEMATICIAN, LAON, FRANCE,
06/28/1800
1. FRENCH 2. PROVIDENCE 3. PROVIDENCE 4. GEORGE NOVION

OBRIEN, TERRENCE, 50, , PLANTER, IRELAND, , 08/26/1798
1. ENGLISH 2. TRINADADA 3. 4.

OGDEN, JANE, 31, F, HOUSE MAID, MANCHESTER, BRITAIN, 12/17/1798
1. BRITISH 2. PROVIDENCE 3. PROVIDENCE 4. JANE OGDEN

OWEN, HANNAH, 15, F, , NEWBURGH, U.S., 12/07/1798
1. BRITISH 2. PROVIDENCE 3. PROVIDENCE 4. WILLILAM OWEN

OWEN, MARY, 15, F, , NEWBURGH, U.S., 12/07/1798
1. BRITISH 2. PROVIDENCE 3. PROVIDENCE 4. WILLIAM OWEN

OWEN, SARAH, 13, F, , PROVIDENCE, U.S., 12/07/1798
1. BRITISH 2. PROVIDENCE 3. PROVIDENCE 4. WILLIAM OWEN

OWEN, THOMAS, 11, M, , PROVIDENCE, U.S., 12/07/1798
1. BRITISH 2. PROVIDENCE 3. PROVIDENCE 4. WILLIAM OWEN

OWEN, WILLIAM, 40, M, LABORER, LONDON, BRITAIN, 12/07/1798
1. BRITISH 2. PROVIDENCE 3. PROVIDENCE 4. WILLIAM OWEN

OWEN, JR., WILLIAM, 6, M, , PROVIDENCE, U.S., 12/07/1798
1. BRITISH 2. PROVIDENCE 3. PROVIDENCE 4. WILLIAM OWEN

PARRY, JOSEPH G., 32, M, MERCHANT, MARKET HARBRO,
LEICESTERSHIRE, 03/06/1804
1. BRITISH 2. 3. 4. JOSEPH G. PARRY

PEDEMONTE, EMILIO, 40, M, MARINER, LEGON, TUSCANY, 11/12/1804
1. TUSCANY 2. 3. TUSCANY 4. EMILIO PEDEMONTE

PERES, PEDRO PAULO, 17, M, SERVANT, GOAVA, PORTUGUESE, 12/17/1798
1. PORTUGAL 2. PROVIDENCE 3. PROVIDENCE 4. JN. CORLIS

PERROT, JACOB, 16, M, ILLEGIBLE, COPENHAGEN, DENMARK, 09/29/1804
1. DENMARK 2. 3. COVENTRY, RI 4. OLNEY POTTER

PERSELYN, CHRISTIAN, 15, M, SERVANT, AMSTERDAM, HOLLAND, 07/23/1804
1. DUTCH 2. 3. PROVIDENCE 4. HENRY OLNEY

PETERS, JOHN, 16, M, MARINER, COPENHAGEN, DENMARK, 12/15/1798
1. DENMARK 2. PROVIDENCE 3. PROVIDENCE 4. CHARLES SHELDON

PHILLIPS, JOHN, 30, M, SERVANT, CALCUTTA, BENGAL, 07/29/1806
1. BRITISH 2. 3. ENGLAND 4. JAMES MURRAY

PIETERRE, PIETER, 27, M, SEAMAN, HAMBURG, GERMANY, 03/19/1799
1. HAMBURG 2. PROVIDENCE 3. PROVIDENCE 4. PIETER PIETERRE

PINKNEY, BETSEY, 15, F, , LONDON, ENGLAND, 12/17/1798
1. GREAT BRITAIN 2. NO. PROVIDENCE 3. NO. PROVIDENCE 4. JACOB
PINKNEY

PINKNEY, ELIZABETH, 43, F, SEAMSTRESS, ESSEX, ENGLAND, ENGLAND, 12/17/1798
1. GREAT BRITAIN 2. NO. PROVIDENCE 3. NO. PROVIDENCE 4.
ELIZABETH PINKNEY

PINKNEY, ISAAC, 3, M, , CRANSTON, RI, U.S., 12/17/1798
1. GREAT BRITAIN 2. NO. PROVIDENCE 3. NO. PROVIDENCE 4. JACOB
PINKNEY

PINKNEY, JACOB, 50, M, FARMER, YORKSHIRE, ENGLAND, ENGLAND, 12/17/1798
1. GREAT BRITAIN 2. NO. PROVIDENCE 3. NO. PROVIDENCE 4. JACOB
PINKNEY

PINKNEY, JACOB, JR., 10, M, , LONDON, LONDON, 12/17/1798
1. GREAT BRITAIN 2. NO. PROVIDENCE 3. NO. PROVIDENCE 4. JACOB
PINKNEY

PINKNEY, JULIA, 6, F, , CRANSTON, RI, U.S., 12/17/1798
1. GREAT BRITAIN 2. NO. PROVIDENCE 3. NO. PROVIDENCE 4. JACOB
PINKNEY

PLACE, DANIEL, 38, M, MARINER, BERMUDA, 07/02/1804
1. GREAT BRITAIN 2. 3. BERMUDA 4. DANIEL PLACE

PLACE, JACK, 10, M, MARINER, BERMUDA, 07/02/1804
1. GREAT BRITAIN 2. 3. BERMUDA 4. THOMAS PLACE

PLACE, THOMAS, 34, M, MARINER, BERMUDA, 07/02/1804
1. GREAT BRITAIN 2. 3. BERMUDA 4. THOMAS PLACE

POIRIE, PETER T., 12, M, CLERK, GUADALOUPE, WEST INDIES, 11/09/1801

1. FRENCH REPUB. 2. PROVIDENCE 3. NEW YORK 4. EDWARD CARRINGTON

POIXEDON, PEDRO, 23, M, MERCHANT, CADIZ, SPAIN, 12/22/1806
1. SPAIN 2. PROVIDENCE 3. PROVIDENCE 4. PEDRO POIXEDON

POPPLE, ELIZABETH, 42, F, SERVANT, AMSTERDAM, HOLLAND, 12/22/1806
1. DUTCH 2. 3. PROVIDENCE 4. ALEXANDER RUDIN

PRATT, THOMAS, 40, , CARPENTER, LONDON, NEW SOUTH WALES, 07/29/1800
1. BRITISH 2. 3. 4. THOMAS PRATT

PRICE, CHARLES, 26, M, MERCHANT, DRAMMEN, NORWAY, 10/31/1807
1. DENMARK 2. 3. RETURN TO N.1ST 4. CHARLES PRICE

PRODOLLIET, LOUIS, 24, M, HUSBANDMAN, ST. LIVRE, PAYS DEVAUD, 08/03/1803
1. HELVETIC REPUB 2. 3. PROVIDENCE 4. LOUIS PRODOLLIET

RAUCE, CHARLES, 44, M, MERCHANT, PARIS, 05/29/1805
1. FRANCE 2. 3. NEW YORK 4. CHARLES RAUCE

RAUCE, CHARLES, JR., 9, M, , MARTINIQUE, WEST INDIES, 05/29/1805
1. FRANCE 2. 3. NEW YORK 4. CHARLES RAUCE

RAWLEIGH, THOMAS, 25, M, MARINER, TINMOUTHY DEVON, ENGLAND, 04/24/1805
1. BRITISH 2. 3. ST. JOHN 4. THOMAS RAWLEIGH

REVEL, JEAN, 12, M, HOUSE SERVANT, CALCUTTA, BENGAL, 12/17/1798
1. BRITISH 2. PROVIDENCE 3. PROVIDENCE 4. JN. ROGERS

RICE, BETSEY, 27, F, SEAMSTRESS, CARRICKFARGUS, IRELAND, 12/15/1798
1. GREAT BRITAIN 2. PROVIDENCE 3. PROVIDENCE 4. BETSEY RICE

RION, TURE, 14, M, CABIN BOY, AMSTERDAM, HOLLAND, 11/25/1803
1. DUTCH 2. 3. PROVIDENCE 4. WM SMITH

ROBEAN, LUREA, 30, F, SERVANT, CALCUTTA, BENGAL, 07/29/1806
1. BRITISH 2. 3. ENGLAND 4. JAMES MURRAY

ROBERT, CHARLES, 23, M, MERCHANT, PARIS, FRANCE, 07/01/1806
1. FRANCE 2. 3. NEW YORK 4. CHARLES ROBERT

ROBINSON, ANN, 56, F, WEAVER, MANCHESTER, GREAT BRITAIN, 12/17/1798
1. ENGLAND 2. PROVIDENCE 3. PROVIDENCE 4. ANN ROBINSON

ROBINSON, JANE A. B., 16, F, DAUGHTER OF ANN, DUBLIN, , 12/17/1798
1. 2. PROVIDENCE 3. PROVIDENCE 4. ANN ROBINSON

ROBINSON, JANET B., 16, F, DAUGHTER, DUBLIN, IRELAND, 12/17/1798
1. BRITISH 2. PROVIDENCE 3. PROVIDENCE 4. ANN ROBINSON

ROBINSON, MARY, 2, F, , PROVIDENCE, U.S., 12/07/1798
1. BRITISH 2. PROVIDENCE 3. PROVIDENCE 4. THOMAS ROBINSON

ROBINSON, RICHARD, 4, M, , PROVIDENCE, U.S., 12/07/1798
1. BRITISH 2. PROVIDENCE 3. PROVIDENCE 4. THOMAS ROBINSON

ROBINSON, THOMAS, 52, M, LINEN/COTTON MANUFACTUER, LURGAN,
IRELAND, 12/07/1798
1. BRITISH 2. PROVIDENCE 3. PROVIDENCE 4. THOMAS ROBINSON

ROCHETREAU, D., 20, , NONE, SURINAM, HOLLAND, 09/03/1798
1. DUTCH 2. 3. 4.

ROCHETREAU, ISAAC, 18, , NONE, SURINAM, HOLLAND, 09/03/1798
1. DUTCH 2. 3. 4.

RODRIGES, COSTODIO, 27, M, SEAMAN, LISBON, PORTUGAL, 12/17/1798
1. PORTUGAL 2. PROVIDENCE 3. PROVIDENCE 4. COSTODIO
RODRIGES

ROLLIARD, JAMES, 35, M, RIGGER, GUERNSEY, BRITISH, 12/07/1798
1. BRITISH 2. PROVIDENCE 3. PROVIDENCE 4. JAMES ROBILLARD

RONNING, FREDERIC, 19, M, CLERK, ELSINORE, DENMARK, 02/02/1808
1. DANISH 2. 3. UNCERTAIN 4. FREDERIC RONNING

RUDEN, ALEXANDER, 28, M, MERCHANT, AMSTERDAM, HOLLAND,
03/18/1801
1. ENGLISH 2. PROVIDENCE 3. U.S. 4. ALEXANDER RUDEN

RUYSSCH, HENDRIK ALEXANDER, 40, M, CAPTAIN OF NAVY, LUTSHEN,
HOLLAND, 04/30/1807
1. DUTCH 2. 3. AMSTERDAM 4. HENDRIK ALEXANDER RUYSCH

SACK, ALBERT, 40, M, GENTLEMAN, BERLIN, PRUSSIA, 07/03/1807
1. KING OF PRUSSIA 2. 3. EUROPE 4. ALBERT SACK

SAFFIN, G., 22, , NONE, SURINAM, HOLLAND, 09/03/1798
1. HOLLAND 2. 3. 4.

SCHELTER, F.W., 38, M, PLANTER, BREMEN, GERMANY, 07/16/1804
1. GERMANY 2. 3. SURINAM 4. F.H. SCHLUHTE

SCHIOTTZ, DAVID, 42, M, ATTORNEY, ---, NORWAY, 07/01/1803
1. DANISH 2. 3. NEW YORK 4. DAVID SCHIOTTZ

SCHMIDT, CHRISTIAN F., 30, M, PLANTER, GUSTROW, GERMANY,
09/01/1808
1. BRITISH 2. 3. PROVIDENCE 4. CHRISTIAN SCHMIDT

SCHOUTEN, J., 26, M, OFFICER DUTCH, BREDA, HOLLAND, 07/10/1804
1. DUTCH 2. 3. HOLLAND 4. J. SCHOUTEN

SCHUFFNER, G.E., 38, M, MERCHANT, DUISBURG, PRUSSIA, 07/16/1804
1. GERMANY 2. 3. SURINAM 4. G.E. SCHUFFNER

SCHWAB, PETER, 55, M, CALICO PRINTER, BIENNE, SWITZERLAND, 12/17/1798
1. GERMAN 2. PROVIDENCE 3. PROVIDENCE 4. PETER SCHWAB

SHAW, JAMES, 25, M, MARINER, ABROATH, SCOTLAND, 12/15/1798
1. GREAT BRITAIN 2. PROVIDENCE 3. PROVIDENCE 4. JAMES SHAW

SHEFFIELD, ELIZABETH, 21, F, T--- WORKER, CORK, IRELAND, 10/13/1801
1. BRITISH 2. PROVIDENCE 3. NEWPORT 4. ELIZABETH SHEFFIELD

SHLYNK, FREDERICK, 33, , SEAMAN, ALTONA, PORTUGAL, 03/18/1799
1. DENMARK 2. 3. 4.

SHLYNK, FRYEDERYK, 34, M, SEAMAN, ALTONA, DENMARK, 03/19/1799
1. DENMARK 2. PROVIDENCE 3. UNCERTAIN 4. FRYEDERYK SHLYNK

SLATER, JOHN, 26, M, WHEELWRIGHT, DERBYSHIRE, ENGLAND, 10/03/1803
1. BRITISH 2. DARBYSHIRE 3. NO.PROVIDENCE 4. JOHN SLATER

SMITH, GIDEON, 22, M, BLACKSMITH, WEST MORLAND, NEW BRUNSWICK, 06/27/1801
1. BRITISH 2. 3. 4.

SMITH, GIDEON, 22, M, BLACKSMITH, SACKVILLE, NEW BRUNSWICK, 08/27/1800
1. BRITISH 2. 3. TO RETURN 4. GIDEON SMITH

SMITH, JOHN, 27, M, , CARRON, SCOTLAND, 03/06/1804
1. BRITISH 2. 3. SCOTLAND 4. JOHN SMITH

SOMERS, CHARLES, 17, M, CLERK, LONDON, ENGLAND, 02/02/1808
1. BRITISH 2. 3. UNCERTAIN 4. CHARLES SOMERS

SPURR, JOHN, 36, M, PHYSICIAN, CHERTSEY, GREAT BRITAIN, 12/15/1798
1. GREAT BRITAIN 2. PROVIDENCE 3. PROVIDENCE 4. JOHN SPURR

ST. LAMBERT, JEAN, 22, M, PLANTER, MARTINIQUE, WEST INDIES, 05/29/1805
1. FRANCE 2. 3. FRANCE 4. ROBERT TASCHER

STEWART, THOMAS, 33, M, MERCHANT, LONDON, ENGLAND, 07/29/1806
1. BRITISH 2. 3. ENGLAND 4. THOMAS STEWART

STEYDING, JOHN WENDT, 39, , MARINER, SAXE GOTHA, , 09/27/1798
1. DUTCH 2. SURINAM/BARBAD 3. 4.

SUGDEN, ELEANOR, 6 MTH, F, , PROVIDENCE, U.S., 12/15/1798
1. U.S. 2. PROVIDENCE 3. PROVIDENCE 4. GEORGE SUGDEN

SUGDEN, GEORGE, 36, M, PAINTER, SKIPTON CRAVEN, GREAT BRITAIN, 12/15/1798
1. GREAT BRITAIN 2. PROVIDENCE 3. PROVIDENCE 4. GEORGE SUGDEN

SUMANDY, G., 37, , MERCHANT, MARSEILLES, , 08/04/1798
1. FRANCE 2. 3. 4.

SYDER, JOSEPH, 30, M, PLANTER, WYMONDHAM, ENGLAND, 10/26/1804
1. GREAT BRITAIN 2. 3. UNCERTAIN 4. JOSEPH SYDER

TALBOT, MARIE L., 33, F, SEAMSTRESS, PORT MALO, , 12/17/1798
1. FRENCH 2. CRANSTON 3. 4. MARIE L. TALBOT

TALBOT, MARIE LOUISE, 33, F, SEAMSTRESS, PORT MALO, FRANCE, 12/07/1798
1. FRANCE 2. CRANSTON 3. CRANSTON 4. MARIE LOUISE TALBOT

TASCHER, ROBERT, 66, M, PLANTERS, MARTINIQUE, WEST INDIES, 05/29/1805
1. FRANCE 2. 3. FRANCE 4. ROBERT TASCHER

TESTE, ALEXIS, 51, M, MERCHANT, GRENOBLE, FRENCH, 12/15/1798
1. LYON 2. PROVIDENCE 3. PROVIDENCE 4. ALEXIS TESTE

TESTE, LOUISA JULIE, 13, F, , PROVIDENCE, 2/15/1798
1. FRANCE 2. PROVIDENCE 3. PROVIDENCE 4. ALEXIS TESTE

TESTE, MARGUERITE COURLET, 45, F, , LYON, FRANCE, 12/15/1798
1. CAPE FRANCIS 2. PROVIDENCE 3. PROVIDENCE 4. MARGUERITE COURLET TESTE

THOMAS, GEORGE, 15, M, SON, PROVIDENCE, U.S., 12/07/1798
1. U.S. 2. PROVIDENCE 3. PROVIDENCE 4. GEORGE CHRISTIAN THOMAS

THOMAS, GEORGE CHRISTIAN, 47, M, TANNER, OLDENDORF, GERMAN, 12/07/1798
1. GERMANY 2. PROVIDENCE 3. PROVIDENCE 4. GEORGE CHRISTIAN THOMAS

THOMAS, MASON, 3, M, SON, PROVIDENCE, U.S., 12/07/1798
1. U.S. 2. PROVIDENCE 3. PROVIDENCE 4. GEORGE CHRISTIAN THOMAS

THOMAS, PHILIP, 12, M, SON, PROVIDENCE, U.S., 12/07/1798
1. U.S. 2. PROVIDENCE 3. PROVIDENCE 4. GEORGE CHRISTIAN THOMAS

THOMAS, WILLIAM, 25, , SAILOR, BRISTOL, NEW SOUTH WALES, 07/29/1800
1. BRITISH 2. 3. 4. WILLIAM THOMAS

THOMPSON, THOMAS, 27, M, MARINER, LONDON, ENGLAND, 10/26/1804
1. ENGLISH 2. 3. UNCERTAIN 4. THOMAS THOMPSON

TRAVERSAY, AUGUST, 43, M, PLANTER, SERRON, MARTINIQUE, 06/15/1805
1. FRANCE 2. 3. PARIS 4. AUGUST TRAVERSAY

TRAVERSAY, JULES, 10, M, , ST. MESSAN, FRANCE, 06/15/1805
1. FRANCE 2. 3. PARIS 4. AUGUST TRAVERSAY

TUCKER, PAUL, 20, , SERVANT/LEPOUAR, MADRAS, PORTUGAL, 03/18/1799
1. INDIES 2. 3. 4.

UELSEY, JOSEPH, 16, M, SERVANT, MARTINIQUE, WEST INDIES, 05/29/1805
1. FRANCE 2. 3. NEW YORK 4. CHARLES RAUCE

VAN BUTTEN, HERMENUS, 60, M, COOPER, PARAMARIBO, SURINAM, 04/08/1806
1. BRITISH 2. 3. PROVIDENCE 4. HERMENUS VAN BUTTEN

VAUCHER, JACQUES FRANCIS, 45, M, MERCHANT, SALIN, FRENCH, 12/15/1798
1. FRENCH 2. PROVIDENCE 3. PROVIDENCE 4. JACQUES FRANCIS VAUCHER

VAUCHER, JACQUES FRANCOIS, 45, , OFFICER ARMY, , ISLE DE FRANCE, 09/23/1798
1. FRENCH 2. 3. 4.

VIESELIUS, JUSTUS, 42, M, PHYSCIAN/SURGERY, RUTSBACK, HEDSAN DARMSTADT, 07/13/1801
1. GERMAN/LUTHERAN 2. PROVIDENCE 3. UNCERTAIN 4. JUSTUS VIESELIUS

VITTIMA, CARLO, 13, M, CABIN BOY, SPSARA, 11/12/1804
1. SPSARA/GREECE 2. 3. TUSCANY 4. EMILIO PEDEMONTE

WAINWRIGHT, ELIZA, 9, F, , LANCASHIRE, ENGLAND, 10/03/1803
1. BRITISH 2. 3. BOSTON 4. ELIZABETH WAINWRIGHT

WAINWRIGHT, JONATHAN, 11, M, , LANCASHIRE, ENGLAND, 10/03/1803
1. BRITISH 2. 3. 4. ELIZABETH WAINWRIGHT

WAINWRIGHT, PETER, 9, M, , LANCASHIRE, ENGLAND, 10/03/1803
1. BRITISH 2. 3. BOSTON 4. ELIZABETH WAINWRIGHT

WALSH, MARK, 7, M, , PROVIDENCE, U.S., 12/15/1798
1. U.S. 2. PROVIDENCE 3. PROVIDENCE 4. MARY WALSH

WALSH, MARY, 30, F, MANTUA MAKER, KARNGARA, IRELAND, 12/15/1798
1. GREAT BRITAIN 2. PROVIDENCE 3. PROVIDENCE 4. MARY WALSH

WALTER, JAMES, 9, M, , PROVIDENCE, U.S., 12/07/1798
1. BRITISH 2. PROVIDENCE 3. PROVIDENCE 4. JOHN WALTER

WALTER, JOHN, 43, M, RIGGER, YORKSHIRE, BRITISH, 12/07/1798
1. BRITISH 2. PROVIDENCE 3. PROVIDENCE 4. JOHN WALTER

WALTER, JOHN, 11, M, , PROVIDENCE, U.S., 12/07/1798
1. BRITISH 2. PROVIDENCE 3. PROVIDENCE 4. JOHN WALTER

WALTER, NANCY, 20, F, , PROVIDENCE, U.S., 12/07/1798
1. BRITISH 2. PROVIDENCE 3. PROVIDENCE 4. JOHN WALTER

WALTER, SAMUEL, 7, M, , PROVIDENCE, U.S., 12/07/1798
1. BRITISH 2. PROVIDENCE 3. PROVIDENCE 4. JOHN WALTER

WALTER, SARAH, 14, F, , PROVIDENCE, U.S., 12/07/1798
1. BRITISH 2. PROVIDENCE 3. PROVIDENCE 4. JOHN WALTER

WALTER, SOLOMON, 6, M, , PROVIDENCE, U.S., 12/07/1798
1. BRITISH 2. PROVIDENCE 3. PROVIDENCE 4. JOHN WALTER

WALTER, SOPHIA, 3, F, , PROVIDENCE, U.S., 12/07/1798
1. BRITISH 2. PROVIDENCE 3. PROVIDENCE 4. JOHN WALTER

WEATHERBE, SAMUEL, 44, , DRAYMAN, PROVIDENCE, , 12/17/1798
1. 2. PROVIDENCE 3. 4. SAMUEL WEATHERBE

WEBBER, PETER, 48, M, CORDWAINER, HANNAN, GERMANY, 12/07/1798
1. GERMANY 2. PROVIDENCE 3. PROVIDENCE 4. PETER WEBBER

WESTON, CHARLES, 27, M, PLANTER, ESSEX, ENGLAND, 10/21/1805
1. DENMARK 2. 3. 4. CHARLES WESTON

WETHEBE, SAMUEL, 41, M, DRAYMAN, PROVIDENCE, U.S., 12/07/1798
1. GREAT BRITAIN 2. PROVIDENCE 3. PROVIDENCE 4. EBENEZER
WETHEBE

WILSON, JOHN, JR., 4, M, , PROVIDENCE, U.S., 12/07/1798
1. BRITISH 2. PROVIDENCE 3. PROVIDENCE 4. SARAH WILSON

WILSON, MARY, 30, F, SEAMSTRESS, MANCHESTER, GREAT BRITAIN,
12/17/1798
1. GREAT BRITAIN 2. PROVIDENCE 3. PROVIDENCE 4. MARY WILSON

WINTHRIES, FREDERICK N., 12, M, GENTLEMAN, PARAMARIBO,
SURINAM, 04/08/1806
1. ENGLISH 2. 3. PROVIDENCE 4. SAMUEL WHEATON

WOOD, GEORGE, 14, M, APPRENTICE, GLOUCESTERSHIRE, ENGLAND, 05/16/1804
1. BRITISH 2. 3. PROVIDENCE 4. BENJAMIN C. SIMMONS

WORTHGEN, JAN GEORGE, 14, M, APPRENTICE, SURINAM, DUTCH W. INDIES, 12/17/1798
1. HOLLAND 2. SMITHFIELD 3. SMITHFIELD 4. JOHN JENCKES

YOUNG, ROBACK, 19, M, , PROVIDENCE, U.S., 12/07/1798
1. BRITISH 2. PROVIDENCE 3. PROVIDENCE 4. JAMES GARDINER

CUSTOMS PASSENGER LISTS

❦

PORT OF PROVIDENCE 1820–1872

KEY: NAME, AGE, SEX, OCCUPATION, DATE OF
      ARRIVAL
      (1) COUNTRY TO WHICH THEY BELONG
      (2) COUNTRY TO WHICH THEY INTEND TO
           BECOME INHABITANTS
      (3) TAKEN ON BOARD AT

ALIERT, , , , 12/30/1823
1. NEW YORK 2. TRINIDAD 3. PROVIDENCE

AUGUSTE, , , , 12/14/1823
1. PHILADELPHIA 2. GUADELOUPE 3. PROVIDENCE

DANICK, 32, M, , 03/20/1835
1. 2. 3. MARTINIQUE

FRANESISE, , , , 12/14/1823
1. NEW YORK 2. MARTINIQUE 3. PROVIDENCE

HENRY, 23, M, SERVANT (BLACK), 07/20/1826
1. MIDDLETOWN 2. CONNECTICUT 3. MATANZAS

JOAO ANTONIO, 25, M, MARINER, 08/28/1872
1. FLORES 2. CALIFORNIA 3.

JOHN, 14, M, SERVANT, 07/19/1833
1. AFRICA 2. SPAIN 3. HAVANA

JOSE FRANCISCO, 18, M, MARINER, 08/28/1872
1. FLORES 2. PROVIDENCE 3.

LOUISA, 20, F, , 06/09/1834
1. U.S. 2. U.S. 3. MATANZAS

MARIA JOSE, 12, F, SEAMSTRESS, 08/28/1872
1. FLORES 2. BOSTON 3.

MARIA JULIA, 23, F, SEAMSTRESS, 08/28/1872
1. FLORES 2. BOSTON 3.

MARIA LUCIA, 19, F, SEAMSTRESS, 08/28/1872
1. FLORES 2. PROVIDENCE 3.

MARIA MARGARIDA, 24, F, SEAMSTRESS, 08/28/1872
1. FLORES 2. BOSTON 3.

MARIA UGENIA, 20, F, SEAMSTRESS, 08/28/1872
1. FLORES 2. BOSTON 3.

MARIANA JULIA, 50, F, SEAMSTRESS, 08/28/1872
1. FLORES 2. BOSTON 3.

MARY, 36, F, SERVANT, 07/22/1822
1. CUBA 2. CUBA 3. HAVANA

SEUROLLE, 7, M, , 03/20/1835
1. 2. 3. MARTINIQUE

VICTOR, 25, M, SERVANT, 08/14/1820
1. U.S. 2. U.S. 3. SANTIAGO

YURIN, 14, M, SERVANT, 03/28/1838
1. CHINA 2. U.S. 3. CANTON

ZULINE, 24, F, , 03/20/1835
1. 2. 3. MARTINIQUE

---, ANTONIO, 33, M, MARINER, 08/28/1872
1. FLORES 2. PROVIDENCE 3.

---, FRANCISCO, 29, M, BARBER, 08/28/1872
1. FLORES 2. BOSTON 3.

---, FRANCISCO, 29, M, FARMER, 08/28/1872
1. SAN MIQUEL 2. BOSTON 3.

---, FRANCISCO C., 20, M, FARMER, 08/28/1872
1. FLORES 2. BOSTON 3.

---, JOAO, 18, M, FARMER, 08/28/1872
1. FLORES 2. BOSTON 3.

ABBOT, GEORGE, 37, M, MARINER, 06/18/1829
1. U.S. 2. U.S. 3. PUONAMBANO

ADAMSON, ANN, 9, F, LADY, 09/09/1844
1. ENGLAND 2. U.S. 3. PICTOU

ADAMSON, GRACE, 22, F, LADY, 09/21/1846
1. NOVA SCOTIA 2. BRITISH AMERICA 3. PICTOU

ADAMSON, HANNAH, 42, F, LADY, 09/09/1844
1. ENGLAND 2. U.S. 3. PICTOU

ADAMSON, HANNAH, 17, F, LADY, 06/27/1849
1. 2. 3. PICTOU

ADAMSON, HARRIET, 17, F, LADY, 09/09/1844
1. ENGLAND 2. U.S. 3. PICTOU

ADAMSON, MARY, 19, F, LADY, 09/09/1844
1. ENGLAND 2. U.S. 3. PICTOU

ADAMSON, SUSAN, 15, F, LADY, 09/09/1844
1. ENGLAND 2. U.S. 3. PICTOU

ADAMSON, WILLIAM, 55, M, SHIP WRIGHT, 09/09/1844
1. ENGLAND 2. U.S. 3. PICTOU

ADDEMAN, JOSHUA, 4, M, CHILD, 04/07/1845
1. ENGLAND 2. U.S. 3. NEW ZEALAND

ADDEMAN, MARY ANN, 34, F, LADY, 04/07/1845
1. ENGLAND 2. U.S. 3. NEW ZEALAND

ADDEMAN, MARY ANN, 2, F, CHILD, 04/07/1845
  1. ENGLAND 2. U.S. 3. NEW ZEALAND

ADDEMAN, THOMAS, 40, M, GENTLEMAN, 04/07/1845
  1. ENGLAND 2. U.S. 3. NEW ZEALAND

ADDISON, AMELIA S., 1, F, , 10/24/1842
  1. 2. 3. LIVERPOOL

ADDISON, ANN M., 4, F, , 10/24/1842
  1. 2. 3. LIVERPOOL

ADDISON, ELIZA R., 5, F, , 10/24/1842
  1. 2. 3. LIVERPOOL

ADDISON, HARRIET, 29, F, , 10/24/1842
  1. 2. 3. LIVERPOOL

ADDISON, HARRIET M., 7, F, , 10/24/1842
  1. 2. 3. LIVERPOOL

ADDISON, ROBERT, 39, M, SURGEON, 10/24/1842
  1. ENGLAND 2. U.S. 3. LIVERPOOL

ADDISON, ROBERT M., 2, M, , 10/24/1842
  1. 2. 3. LIVERPOOL

AGUSTA, EMILIA, 19, F, TAILORESS, 08/28/1872
  1. SAN MIQUEL 2. BOSTON 3.

ALCASA, BUENEVENTURA DE, 30, M, DIPLOMAT, 04/14/1828
  1. COLOMBIA 2. COLOMBIA 3. OMOA

ALEXANDER, THEO. R., 24, M, MERCHANT, 07/25/1826
  1. U.S. 2. U.S. 3. HAVANA

ALFORCACO, DOMINQUES, 25, , , 05/18/1868
  1. 2. 3. BRAVA

ALLEN, HERMAN B., 38, M, TRADER, 05/10/1824
  1. U.S. 2. U.S. 3. HAVANA

ALLEN, HERMAN B., 47, M, MARINER, 06/29/1826
  1. U.S. 2. U.S. 3. HAVANA

ALLEN, ISAAC JAMES, , , DISTRESSED SEAMEN, 01/16/1849
  1. 2. 3. NASSAU

ALLEN, JAMES H., 24, M, MERCHANT, 05/05/1829
  1. U.S. 2. U.S. 3. MATANZAS

ALLEN, MARIA, 26, F, SERVANT, 10/18/1836
  1. PICTOU 2. PROVIDENCE 3. PICTOU

ALLEN, NATHAN, 25, M, CARPENTER, 08/02/1827
1. NORTH KINGSTOWN 2. NORTH KINGSTOWN 3. MATANZAS

ALLEN, SAMUEL S., 28, M, MERCHANT, 07/12/1824
1. U.S. 2. U.S. 3. CANTON

ALLIN, JOHN, 62, M, SCHOOLMASTER, 06/11/1856
1. IRELAND 2. U.S. 3. PICTOU

ALLIN, MRS. JOHN, 53, F, HOUSEWIFE, 06/11/1856
1. IRELAND 2. U.S. 3. PICTOU

ALLIN, WM., 21, M, MERCHANT, 09/15/1827
1. U.S. 2. U.S. 3. MATANZAS

ALLISON, JOHN, 30, M, MINER, 10/13/1865
1. BRITISH AMERICA 2. U.S. 3. COW BAY

ALVES, MANUEL G., 34, M, MARINER, 08/28/1872
1. FLORES 2. PROVIDENCE 3.

AMEDA, JUAN BAPTISTA, 32, M, SERVANT, 07/02/1829
1. ST. DOMINGO 2. HAVRE DE GRACE 3. ST. DOMINGO

AMORY, JOHN, 19, M, SEAMAN, 07/20/1820
1. U.S. 2. U.S. 3. CANTON

ANDRADE, ANGELICA DE, 25, F, LADY, 10/17/1867
1. CAPE DE VERDE IS. 2. U.S. 3. FLORES

ANDRADE, JOSEPH DE, 6, M, , 10/17/1867
1. CAPE DE VERDE IS. 2. U.S. 3. FLORES

ANDRADO, MARIANNA, 19, , , 05/18/1868
1. 2. 3. BRAVA

ANDREW, JOSEPH, 47, M, MINISTER, 11/08/1859
1. GERMANY 2. U.S. 3. PICTOU

ANDREWS, A.L., 35, M, CABINET MAKER, 08/23/1845
1. U.S. 2. U.S. 3. PICTOU

ANDREWS, MRS., 22, F, LADY, 08/23/1845
1. U.S. 2. U.S. 3. PICTOU

ANDREWS, WILLIAM, 38, M, NONE, 06/11/1855
1. GREAT BRITAIN 2. U.S. 3. PICTOU

ANNER, MARK, 27, M, BLACKSMITH, 03/11/1859
1. U.S. 2. U.S. 3. MATANZAS

ANTHONY, EDMUND, 30, M, CARPENTER, 05/09/1832
1. U.S. 2. U.S. 3. MATANZAS

APPLETON, LUCY, 24, F, , 07/03/1851
1. BRITISH AMERICA 2. U.S. 3. PICTOU

ARAOZ, DIEGO, 30, M, SPANISH MILITARY, 04/14/1828
1. CUBA 2. MEXICO 3. OMOA

ARBUCKLE, ALEXANDRIA, 17, F, SERVANT, 08/23/1845
1. BRITISH AMERICA 2. U.S. 3. PICTOU

ARCHIBALD, JOHN H., 22, M, GENTLEMAN, 05/24/1848
1. U.S. 2. U.S. 3. COAST OF AFRICA

ARNO, JAMES, 46, M, MERCHANT, 02/24/1821
1. U.S. 2. U.S. 3. HAVANA

ARNOLD, G.T., 18, M, GENTLEMAN, 07/08/1853
1. U.S. 2. U.S. 3. ZANZIBAR

AROY, ANTONIO, 28, M, MERCHANT, 11/11/1828
1. SPAIN 2. SPAIN 3. HAVANA

ASH, GEORGE A., 2, M, , 08/19/1859
1. NOVA SCOTIA 2. U.S. 3. PICTOU

ASH, MARGARET, 32, F, DOMESTIC, 08/19/1859
1. NOVA SCOTIA 2. U.S. 3. PICTOU

ASH, ROBT, 1, M, , 08/19/1859
1. NOVA SCOTIA 2. U.S. 3. PICTOU

ASH, WM, 4, M, , 08/19/1859
1. NOVA SCOTIA 2. U.S. 3. PICTOU

ASKEW, ANNA, 22, F, HOUSEWIFE, 07/09/1860
1. NOVA SCOTIA 2. U.S. 3. PICTOU

ASKEW, EDWARD, 23, M, PRINTER, 07/09/1860
1. NOVA SCOTIA 2. U.S. 3. PICTOU

ATKINS, ZACHARIAH, 55, M, MERCHANT, 08/24/1839
1. CUBA 2. CUBA 3. MATANZAS

ATKINS, JR., L., 28, M, MERCHANT, 06/23/1830
1. BOSTON 2. BOSTON 3. MATANZAS

AUSTIN, ANN MARIA, , , , 12/14/1823
1. BOSTON 2. BARBADOS 3. PROVIDENCE

AUSTIN, ANNIE, 16, F, SERVANT, 07/01/1862
1. NOVA SCOTIA 2. U.S. 3. PICTOU

AUSTIN, MARIA, 21, F, , 08/01/1859
1. NOVA SCOTIA 2. U.S. 3. PICTOU

AUTOY, JANE, 21, F, HOUSEWIFE, 08/12/1853
1. NOVA SCOTIA 2. U.S. 3. PICTOU

AYER, JACOB, 24, M, SHOEMMAKER, 10/24/1854
1. GREAT BRITAIN 2. U.S. 3. GLASGOW

AYER, MRS. JACOB, 24, F, HOUSEWIFE, 10/24/1854
1. GREAT BRITAIN 2. U.S. 3. GLASGOW

AZEVEDO, LEOPOLD, 12, M, NONE, 08/21/1861
1. AFRICA 2. AFRICA 3. ZANZIBAR

AZZENDO, DOMINGO, 17, M, , 10/19/1858
1. AFRICA 2. U.S. 3. QUILEMANE

B---, ANTONIO I., 40, M, MARINER, 08/28/1872
1. FLORES 2. BOSTON 3.

BACON, EDMUND, 35, M, MACHINIST, 05/12/1835
1. U.S. 2. U.S. 3. HAVANA

BACON, ENOCH, 32, M, ENGINEER, 06/11/1845
1. U.S. 2. U.S. 3. CARDENAS

BACON, FRANCIS N., 35, M, ENGINEER, 06/11/1845
1. U.S. 2. U.S. 3. CARDENAS

BADGER, JOSEPH, 31, M, SHIP MASTER, 06/19/1824
1. U.S. 2. U.S. 3. LIVERPOOL

BADGER, MANIA, 24, F, WIFE OF JOSEPH, 06/19/1824
1. U.S. 2. U.S. 3. LIVERPOOL

BAILEY, CATHARINE, 21, F, NONE, 05/25/1858
1. NOVA SCOTIA 2. U.S. 3. PICTOU

BAILEY, DONALD, 52, M, MASON, 08/05/1856
1. NOVA SCOTIA 2. U.S. 3. PICTOU

BAILEY, ISABELLA, 45, F, HOUSEWIFE, 08/22/1861
1. U.S. 2. U.S. 3. PICTOU

BAILEY, ISABELLA, 21, F, NONE, 08/22/1861
1. U.S. 2. U.S. 3. PICTOU

BAILEY, JOHN, 54, M, SHOEMAKER, 08/22/1861
1. U.S. 2. U.S. 3. PICTOU

BAILEY, JOHN, 45, M, SHOEMAKER, 08/05/1856
1. U.S. 2. U.S. 3. PICTOU

BAILEY, MARGARET, 16, F, NONE, 08/22/1861
1. U.S. 2. U.S. 3. PICTOU

BAILEY, PABODIE, 32, M, HOUSE CARPENTER, 03/16/1821
1. U.S. 2. U.S. 3. HAVANA

BAILY, JOHN, 38, M, SHOE MAKER, 10/08/1849
1. BRITISH AMERICA 2. U.S. 3. PICTOU

BAIN, JOHN, 19, M, , 10/24/1860
1. NOVA SCOTIA 2. U.S. 3. PICTOU

BAIN, MARY ANN, 21, F, DRESSMAKER, 09/26/1859
1. NOVA SCOTIA 2. U.S. 3. PICTOU

BAKER, ANNA, 24, F, SERVANT, 08/22/1850
1. BRITISH AMERICA 2. U.S. 3. PICTOU

BAKER, CHRISTINE, 18, F, DOMESTIC, 08/19/1859
1. NOVA SCOTIA 2. U.S. 3. PICTOU

BAKER, DAVID, 27, M, CARPENTER, 10/27/1826
1. U.S. 2. U.S. 3. MATANZAS

BAKER, ELIZABETH, 17, F, DOMESTIC, 10/10/1853
1. GREAT BRITAIN 2. GREAT BRITAIN 3. PICTOU

BAKER, GILBERT, 27, M, MERCHANT, 08/29/1853
1. U.S. 2. U.S. 3. PICTOU

BAKER, SARAH, 20, F, WIFE OF GILBERT, 08/29/1853
1. U.S. 2. U.S. 3. PICTOU

BALDWIN, ELEAZER, 32, M, EXHIBITOR OF WILD ANIMALS, 06/29/1826
1. U.S. 2. U.S. 3. HAVANA

BALLIE, MARY ANNE, 18, F, DOMESTIC, 08/19/1859
1. NOVA SCOTIA 2. U.S. 3. PICTOU

BARCLAY, DANL, 18, M, MINER, 05/23/1857
1. NOVA SCOTIA 2. U.S. 3. PICTOU

BARCLAY, FREDERICK JAY, 37, M, GENTLEMAN, 05/16/1821
1. NEW YORK 2. NEW YORK 3. ST. CROIX

BARMILLA, ANTONIO, 22, M, MERCHANT, 09/11/1825
1. GUATEMALA 2. GUATEMALA 3. HONDURAS

BARNS, TIMOTHY W., 37, M, MARINER, 05/27/1823
1. U.S. 2. U.S. 3. L. BARTS

BAROTH, CHARLES, 31, M, MERCHANT, 05/28/1834
1. ENGLAND 2. ENGLAND 3. HAVANA

BARR, PATRICK, 28, M, MECHANIC, 09/20/1838
1. IRELAND 2. NEW YORK 3. PICTOU

BARRY, ANN, 27, F, HOUSEWIFE, 10/07/1857
1. GREAT BRITAIN 2. U.S. 3. PICTOU

BARRY, CATHARINE, 3 MONTHS, F, NONE, 10/07/1857
1. GREAT BRITAIN 2. U.S. 3. PICTOU

BARRY, DANL A., 21, M, CARPENTER, 08/28/1872
1. NOVA SCOTIA 2. U.S. 3. PICTOU

BARRY, JOHN, 4, M, NONE, 10/07/1857
1. GREAT BRITAIN 2. U.S. 3. PICTOU

BARRY, PATRICK, 12, M, NONE, 10/07/1857
1. GREAT BRITAIN 2. U.S. 3. PICTOU

BARRY, WILLIAM, 7, M, NONE, 10/07/1857
1. GREAT BRITAIN 2. U.S. 3. PICTOU

BARTH, FLOUDU, 28, M, MERCHANT, 07/16/1835
1. FRANCE 2. U.S. 3. MATANZAS

BARTHOLEMEW, THOMAS, 25, M, ENGINEER, 05/13/1839
1. U.S. 2. U.S. 3. MATANZAS

BARTON, ALFRED, 29, M, MARINER, 04/25/1820
1. WARREN 2. WARREN 3. HAVANA

BARTON, JOHN G., 30, M, MERCHANT, 10/12/1829
1. ENGLAND 2. U.S. 3. BRISTOL, ENGLAND

BARTON, LIZZIE TAYLOR, 11, F, NONE, 03/24/1858
1. U.S. 2. U.S. 3. ZANZIBAR

BARTON, MARY, 42, F, HOUSEWIFE, 03/24/1858
1. U.S. 2. U.S. 3. ZANZIBAR

BATON, ISABELLA, 25, F, SERVANT, 09/15/1856
1. GREAT BRITAIN 2. U.S. 3. PICTOU

BATY, GEORGE, 55, M, FARMER, 07/07/1851
1. NOVA SCOTIA 2. U.S. 3. PICTOU

BATY, JOSEPH, 14, M, FARMER, 07/07/1851
1. NOVA SCOTIA 2. U.S. 3. PICTOU

BATY, MARY, 45, F, LADY, 07/07/1851
1. NOVA SCOTIA 2. U.S. 3. PICTOU

BAYLESS, WILLIAM, 17, M, CARPENTER, 07/08/1867
1. BRITISH AMERICA 2. U.S. 3. PICTOU

BAYLEY, JAMES, 29, M, MERCHANT, 06/29/1833
1. U.S. 2. U.S. 3. MATANZAS

BAYNE, DANIEL, 32, M, SHIP CARPENTER, 06/08/1864
1. U.S. 2. U.S. 3. PICTOU

BAYNE, SUSAN, 31, F, , 06/08/1864
1. U.S. 2. U.S. 3. PICTOU

BAYNE, WILLIAM, 21, , BLACKSMITH, 06/08/1864
1. NOVA SCOTIA 2. U.S. 3. PICTOU

BEAL, SAMUEL, 35, M, CARPENTER, 07/16/1823
1. U.S. 2. U.S. 3. HAVANA

BEALE, HIRAM, 40, M, ENGINEER, 04/08/1854
1. U.S. 2. U.S. 3.

BEARS, JANE, 22, F, LADY, 08/18/1849
1. BRITISH AMERICA 2. U.S. 3. PICTOU

BEATHEN, MARY, 21, F, SERVANT, 09/29/1852
1. BRITISH AMERICA 2. U.S. 3. PICTOU

BEATON, ALEXANDER, 33, M, MECHANIC, 10/04/1848
1. BRITISH AMERICA 2. U.S. 3. PICTOU

BEATON, ELLEN, 35, F, LADY, 10/04/1848
1. BRITISH AMERICA 2. U.S. 3. PICTOU

BEATON, MARGARET, 20, F, SERVANT, 09/09/1844
1. NOVA SCOTIA 2. U.S. 3. PICTOU

BEATON, NANCY, 16, F, MISSES, 07/06/1846
1. NOVA SCOTIA 2. U.S. 3. PICTOU

BECK, ISABELLA, 22, F, , 11/04/1851
1. BRITISH AMERICA 2. BRITISH AMERICA 3. PICTOU

BECKWITH, WILLIAM, 23, M, MECHANIC/CARPENTER, 07/23/1828
1. U.S. 2. U.S. 3. SANTIAGO

BELL, ANDREW, 33, M, CARPENTER, 09/15/1854
1. NOVA SCOTIA 2. U.S. 3. PICTOU

BELL, ANNA, 28, F, HOUSEWIFE, 09/13/1859
1. NOVA SCOTIA 2. U.S. 3. PICTOU

BELL, ANNA B., 22, F, HOUSEWIFE, 10/01/1853
1. U.S. 2. U.S. 3. PICTOU

BELL, ELIZABETH, 63, F, NONE, 09/15/1854
1. NOVA SCOTIA 2. U.S. 3. PICTOU

BELL, ELIZABETH, 5, F, , 09/13/1859
1. NOVA SCOTIA 2. U.S. 3. PICTOU

BELL, GEORGE, 23, M, SHOE MAKER, 07/11/1850
1. U.S. 2. U.S. 3. PICTOU

BELL, GEORGE, 3, M, , 09/13/1859
1. NOVA SCOTIA 2. U.S. 3. PICTOU

BELL, GEORGE B., 35, M, MARINER, 11/16/1857
1. U.S. 2. U.S. 3. CARDENAS

BELL, JOHN, 32, M, SHOEMAKER, 09/13/1859
1. NOVA SCOTIA 2. U.S. 3. PICTOU

BELL, MARY, 2, , CHILD, 07/03/1851
1. BRITISH AMERICA 2. U.S. 3. PICTOU

BELL, MRS., 20, F, , 07/11/1850
1. BRITISH AMERICA 2. U.S. 3. PICTOU

BELL, ROBERT, 40, M, ENGINEER, 06/11/1840
1. U.S. 2. U.S. 3. MATANZAS

BELLY, STEPHEN, 40, M, TRADER, 01/06/1825
1. HAITI 2. HAITI 3. PUERTA PLATA

BELOTT, EUSTAU, 12, M, , 03/22/1837
1. CUBA 2. U.S. 3. HAVANA

BENNETT, ANTONIO, 16, M, NONE, 11/21/1855
1. CUBA, SPAIN 2. CUBA, SPAIN 3.

BENNETT, DOMINGO, 18, M, NONE, 11/21/1855
1. CUBA, SPAIN 2. CUBA, SPAIN 3.

BENOIT, J.T., 25, M, MERCHANT, 04/15/1824
1. MATANZAS 2. CUBA 3. HAVANA

BENTON, MARY, 19, F, , 07/17/1850
1. BRITISH AMERICA 2. U.S. 3. PICTOU

BERG, ERNST, 21, M, MARINER, 07/19/1850
1. DENMARK 2. DENMARK 3. EAST CAICOS, TURKS ISLAND

BERRYMAN, MARY, 24, F, , 10/20/1853
1. GREAT BRITAIN 2. GREAT BRITAIN 3. PICTOU

BETFORD, JANE, 22, F, NONE, 10/12/1846
1. PICTOU 2. U.S. 3. PICTOU

BETFORD, MARGARET, 1, F, , 10/12/1846
1. PICTOU 2. U.S. 3. PICTOU

BETHUNE, JERINIMA, 19, F, DOMESTIC, 08/19/1859
1. NOVA SCOTIA 2. U.S. 3. PICTOU

BETHUNE, MARGARET, 50, F, HOUSEWIFE, 08/14/1858
1. NOVA SCOTIA 2. NOVA SCOTIA 3. PICTOU

BETHUNE, MARGARET, 58, F, , 05/28/1861
1. PICTOU 2. U.S. 3. PICTOU

BILLET, JOHN, 35, M, MOULDER, 05/06/1867
1. U.S. 2. U.S. 3. ARDROSSAN

BISHOP, ANN, 13, F, NONE, 07/31/1857
1. NOVA SCOTIA 2. U.S. 3. PICTOU

BISHOP, C.W.P., , , , 12/30/1823
1. PROVIDENCE 2. DEMERARA 3. PROVIDENCE

BISHOP, ELIZA, 15, F, NONE, 07/31/1857
1. NOVA SCOTIA 2. U.S. 3. PICTOU

BISHOP, JOHN, 11, M, NONE, 07/31/1857
1. NOVA SCOTIA 2. U.S. 3. PICTOU

BISHOP, MARIE, 5, F, NONE, 07/31/1857
1. NOVA SCOTIA 2. U.S. 3. PICTOU

BISHOP, N.A., 29, M, MECHANIC, 06/22/1840
1. U.S. 2. U.S. 3. MATANZAS

BISHOP, NATHAN, 38, M, MECHANIC, 05/10/1842
1. U.S. 2. U.S. 3. MATANZAS

BISHOP, NATHAN, 39, M, COOPER, 07/22/1847
1. U.S. 2. U.S. 3. MATANZAS

BISHOP, NATHAN, 45, M, COOPER, 08/03/1855
1. U.S. 2. U.S. 3. MATANZAS

BISHOP, NATHANIEL, 2, M, NONE, 07/31/1857
1. NOVA SCOTIA 2. U.S. 3. PICTOU

BISHOP, RACHAL, 18, F, NONE, 07/31/1857
1. NOVA SCOTIA 2. U.S. 3. PICTOU

BISHOP, SARAH, 38, F, HOUSEWIFE, 07/31/1857
1. NOVA SCOTIA 2. U.S. 3. PICTOU

BISHOP, SARAH, 9, F, NONE, 07/31/1857
1. NOVA SCOTIA 2. U.S. 3. PICTOU

BISHOP, WILLIAM, 48, M, FARMER, 07/31/1857
1. NOVA SCOTIA 2. U.S. 3. PICTOU

BISHOP, WILLIAM, 7, M, NONE, 07/31/1857
1. NOVA SCOTIA 2. U.S. 3. PICTOU

BLACK, CHARLOT, 23, F, , 08/19/1836
1. PICTOU 2. PICTOU 3. PICTOU

BLACKEY, JANE, 20, F, SERVANT, 05/23/1857
1. NOVA SCOTIA 2. U.S. 3. PICTOU

BLACKWOOD, JAMES, 26, M, BLACKSMITH, 07/20/1844
1. NOVA SCOTIA 2. U.S. 3. PICTOU

BLACKWOOD, JAMES, 66, M, LABORER, 09/14/1858
1. NOVA SCOTIA 2. U.S. 3. PICTOU

BLACKWOOD, MARY, 22, F, LADY, 07/20/1844
1. NOVA SCOTIA 2. U.S. 3. PICTOU

BLAIR, JESSIE, 23, F, DRESS MAKER, 07/07/1851
1. NOVA SCOTIA 2. U.S. 3. PICTOU

BLAKE, ALEX, 44, M, CARPENTER, 11/02/1850
1. BRITISH AMERICA 2. U.S. 3. PICTOU

BLAKE, ANN, 17, F, , 11/02/1850
1. BRITISH AMERICA 2. U.S. 3. PICTOU

BLAKE, DANIEL, 25, M, MARINER, 05/27/1823
1. U.S. 2. U.S. 3. L. BARTS

BLAKE, ELLEN, 13, F, , 11/02/1850
1. BRITISH AMERICA 2. U.S. 3. PICTOU

BLAKE, MARGARET JANE, 10, F, , 11/02/1850
1. BRITISH AMERICA 2. U.S. 3. PICTOU

BLAKE, MARTHA, 40, F, , 11/02/1850
1. BRITISH AMERICA 2. U.S. 3. PICTOU

BLAKE, PETER GRANT, 4, M, , 11/02/1850
1. BRITISH AMERICA 2. U.S. 3. PICTOU

BLAKE, SUSAN, 7, F, , 11/02/1850
1. BRITISH AMERICA 2. U.S. 3. PICTOU

BLAKE, WILLIAM, 15, M, , 11/02/1850
1. BRITISH AMERICA 2. U.S. 3. PICTOU

BLANCHARD, ALFRED, 12, M, NONE, 09/02/1856
1. U.S. 2. U.S. 3. PICTOU

BLANCHARD, CHARLES, 10, M, NONE, 09/02/1856
1. U.S. 2. U.S. 3. PICTOU

BLANCHARD, N. G., 25, M, , 05/16/1821
1. U.S. 2. 3. MATANZAS

BLODGET, SUSAN, 30, F, LADY, 04/28/1842
1. U.S. 2. U.S. 3. MATANZAS

BLODGET, WILLIAM P., 33, M, MERCHANT, 04/28/1842
1. U.S. 2. U.S. 3. MATANZAS

BLOM, CHRISTIAN, 49, M, MARINER, 07/19/1850
1. DENMARK 2. DENMARK 3. EAST CAICOS, TURKS ISLAND

BOLANO, A.B., 27, M, MERCHANT, 06/10/1839
1. HAVANA 2. HAVANA 3. HAVANA

BONE, MARGARET, 9, F, SERVANT, 08/17/1853
1. U.S. 2. U.S. 3. PICTOU

BONILIA, JOSE MARIA DE, 20, M, SERVANT, 04/14/1828
1. CENTRAL AMERICA 2. U.S. FOR EDUCATION 3. OMOA

BOON, CHRISTOPHER, 27, M, CARPENTER, 05/05/1829
1. U.S. 2. U.S. 3. MATANZAS

BOON, ELIZA, 35, F, LABORER, 07/03/1839
1. U.S. 2. U.S. 3. MATANZAS

BOON, MRS. C., 18, F, , 05/05/1829
1. U.S. 2. U.S. 3. MATANZAS

BOOTH, WM, 33, M, MECHANIC, 03/22/1837
1. U.S. 2. U.S. 3. HAVANA

BORDEN, EPHRAIM, 72, M, MERCHANT, 07/08/1829
1. U.S. 2. U.S. 3. MATANZAS

BORDEN, GEO. C., 21, M, MARINER, 11/03/1835
1. U.S. 2. PROVIDENCE 3. PICTOU

BORRAS, MATHILDA, 19, , , 05/18/1868
1. 2. 3. BRAVA

BOSNOSDO, JOSE, 20, M, FARMER, 08/28/1872
1. FLORES 2. PROVIDENCE 3.

BOSS, MRS., 35, F, , 03/22/1837
1. U.S. 2. U.S. 3. HAVANA

BOTELHO, MANUEL, 23, M, FARMER,1872
1. SAN MIGUEL 2. PROVIDENCE 3.

BOTELHO, MANUEL, 23, M, FARMER, 08/28/1872
1. SAN MIQUEL 2. FALL RIVER 3.

BOWEN, ANN M., 10, F, CHILD OF ISAAC, 04/15/1824
1. U.S. 2. U.S. 3. HAVANA

BOWEN, ELIZA, 40, F, WF OF ISAAC, 04/15/1824
1. U.S. 2. U.S. 3. HAVANA

BOWEN, GEORGE, 32, M, MARINER, 09/20/1831
1. U.S. 2. U.S. 3. LIVERPOOL

BOWEN, ISAAC, 42, M, MERCHANT, 07/10/1821
1. U.S. 2. U.S. 3. HAVANA

BOWEN, ISAAC, 47, M, MERCHANT, 09/10/1824
1. U.S. 2. U.S. 3. HAVANA

BOWEN, ISAAC, 46, M, MARINER, 04/15/1824
1. U.S. 2. U.S. 3. HAVANA

BOWEN, ISAAC, 48, M, MERCHANT, 04/25/1826
1. U.S. 2. U.S. 3. HAVANA

BOWEN, MARIA, 8, F, CHILD OF ISAAC, 04/15/1824
1. U.S. 2. U.S. 3. HAVANA

BOWEN, NICHOLAS W., 46, M, MERCHANT'S CLERK, 05/19/1823
1. U.S. 2. U.S. 3. HAVANA

BOWEN, NICHOLAS W., 23, M, CLERK, 07/07/1827
1. U.S. 2. U.S. 3. HAVANA

BOWEN, JR., ISAAC, 46, M, MERCHANT, 05/19/1823
1. U.S. 2. U.S. 3. HAVANA

BOWMAN, HARKNESS, 23, M, ENGINEER, 06/28/1847
1. U.S. 2. U.S. 3. CARDENAS

BOWMAN, JOHN, 28, M, ENGINEER, 06/28/1847
1. U.S. 2. U.S. 3. CARDENAS

BRADFORD, HENRY, 11, M, BOY, 04/25/1840
1. U.S. 2. U.S. 3. MATANZAS

BRADFORD, MARY, 3, F, GIRL, 04/25/1840
1. U.S. 2. U.S. 3. MATANZAS

BRADFORD, MRS. J. G., 38, F, LADY, 04/25/1840
1. U.S. 2. U.S. 3. MATANZAS

BRADLEY, GEORGE, 35, M, MINER, 08/29/1845
1. BRITISH AMERICA 2. U.S. 3. PICTOU

BRADLEY, JAMES, 22, M, MINER, 05/23/1857
1. NOVA SCOTIA 2. U.S. 3. PICTOU

BRADLEY, JAMES, 3, M, , 05/23/1857
1. NOVA SCOTIA 2. U.S. 3. PICTOU

BRADLEY, JONATHAN, 45, M, FARMER, 11/08/1827
1. ENGLAND 2. U.S. 3. LIVERPOOL

BRADLEY, MACK, 18, M, SHIP MATE, 09/11/1837
1. IRELAND 2. UTICA 3. PICTOU

BRADLEY, MARY, 64, F, , 07/11/1850
1. BRITISH AMERICA 2. U.S. 3. PICTOU

BRADLEY, MARY, 9 MONTHS, F, , 05/23/1857
1. NOVA SCOTIA 2. U.S. 3. PICTOU

BRADLEY, MARY, 22, F, HOUSEWIFE, 05/23/1857
1. NOVA SCOTIA 2. U.S. 3. PICTOU

BRADLEY, MARY ANN, 27, F, , 07/11/1850
1. BRITISH AMERICA 2. U.S. 3. PICTOU

BRAINARD, JOSHUA, 29, M, SHIP JOINER, 05/08/1838
1. U.S. 2. U.S. 3. HAVANA

BRANCH, T.H.J., 23, M, MERCHANT, 11/08/1827
1. U.S. 2. U.S. 3. LIVERPOOL

BRASEVER, JOHN H., 35, M, COOPER, 08/06/1836
1. U.S. 2. 3. HAVANA

BRASTOW, HENRY B., 16, M, GENTLEMAN, 06/19/1844
1. U.S. 2. U.S. 3. LAGUIEVU, MEXICO

BRENNAN, CATHERINE, 18, F, , 07/27/1835
1. NOVA SCOTIA 2. FALL RIVER 3. PICTOU

BRENNAN, PATRICK, 20, M, COOPER, 07/27/1835
1. NOVA SCOTIA 2. FALL RIVER 3. PICTOU

BRENNAN, WILLIAM, 45, M, MERCHANT, 08/17/1831
1. NEW YORK 2. U.S. 3. SURINAM

BREWER, GEORGE, 1, M, NONE, 01/16/1849
1. U.S. 2. U.S. 3. SANDWICH ISLANDS

BREWER, H.B., 38, M, MISSIONARY, 01/16/1849
1. U.S. 2. U.S. 3. SANDWICH ISLANDS

BREWER, MARY, 37, F, MISSIONARY, 01/16/1849
1. U.S. 2. U.S. 3. SANDWICH ISLANDS

BREWER, SUSAN, 7, F, NONE, 01/16/1849
1. U.S. 2. U.S. 3. SANDWICH ISLANDS

BREWER, WALTER, 5, M, NONE, 01/16/1849
1. U.S. 2. U.S. 3. SANDWICH ISLANDS

BRIAN, SARAH C., 15, F, , 09/07/1838
1. GREAT BRITAIN 2. U.S. 3. PICTOU

BRIAN, WM. C., 21, M, FARMER, 09/07/1838
1. GREAT BRITAIN 2. U.S. 3. PICTOU

BRICE, JOHN, 30, M, CARPENTER, 04/12/1836
1. HARTFORD 2. MATANZAS 3. MATANZAS

BRITTO, D.S., 40, M, MERCHANT, 05/24/1822
1. SURINAM 2. SURINAM 3. CURACOA

BRITTO, GABRIEL S., 15, M, MERCHANT, 05/24/1822
1. SURINAM 2. SURINAM 3. CURACOA

BROSNATHAM, JOHN, 35, M, MARINER, 09/15/1827
1. U.S. 2. U.S. 3. MATANZAS

BROWN, ANN, 27, F, LADY, 07/20/1844
1. NOVA SCOTIA 2. U.S. 3. PICTOU

BROWN, ANN, 16, F, NONE, 07/07/1857
1. NOVA SCOTIA 2. U.S. 3. PICTOU

BROWN, CLARKE, 32, M, MARINER, 03/09/1829
1. U.S. 2. U.S. 3. SURINAM

BROWN, DAVID, 19, M, PAINTER, 08/24/1870
1. PICTOU 2. U.S. 3. PICTOU

BROWN, ELISA, 22, F, SERVANT, 07/02/1829
1. PHILADELPHIA 2. HAVRE DE GRACE 3. ST. DOMINGO

BROWN, ELLEN, 17, F, , 07/27/1835
1. NOVA SCOTIA 2. CRANSTON 3. PICTOU

BROWN, JAMES, 10, M, , 06/22/1840
1. U.S. 2. U.S. 3. MATANZAS

BROWN, JAMES M., 25, M, MERCHANT, 11/02/1820
1. AMERICA 2. AMERICA 3. BELIZE

BROWN, JAMES M., 23, M, TRADER, 06/16/1820
1. U.S. 2. NORWICH, CT 3. HONDURAS

BROWN, JAMES M., 22, M, JEWELLER, 02/21/1820
1. U.S. 2. U.S. 3. HONDURAS

BROWN, JAS., 14, M, , 06/22/1840
1. U.S. 2. U.S. 3. MATANZAS

BROWN, JOHANNA, 15, F, SERVANT, 07/01/1862
1. NOVA SCOTIA 2. U.S. 3. PICTOU

BROWN, JOHN, 28, M, SHIPWRIGHT, 08/16/1850
1. NOVA SCOTIA 2. U.S. 3. PICTOU

BROWN, JOHN, 26, , SHIP CARPENTER, 07/11/1850
1. PICTOU 2. U.S. 3. PICTOU

BROWN, JOHN, 30, M, SHIP CARPENTER, 08/20/1857
1. NOVA SCOTIA 2. U.S. 3. PICTOU

BROWN, MAY, 8, F, , 06/22/1840
1. U.S. 2. U.S. 3. MATANZAS

BROWN, MRS. E., 40, F, LADY, 06/22/1840
1. U.S. 2. U.S. 3. MATANZAS

BROWN, NATHANIEL, 25, M, MARINER, 10/13/1820
1. PROVIDENCE 2. U.S. 3. HAVANA

BROWN, NATHANIEL, 35, M, MERCHANT, 04/04/1825
1. U.S. 2. U.S. 3. HONDURAS

BROWN, SAML, 12, M, , 06/22/1840
1. U.S. 2. U.S. 3. MATANZAS

BROWN, THOMAS, 27, M, MINER, 08/29/1845
1. BRITISH AMERICA 2. U.S. 3. PICTOU

BROWNING, LYDIA, 24, F, HOUSE WIFE, 06/03/1857
1. NOVA SCOTIA 2. NOVA SCOTIA 3. PICTOU

BROWNING, WILLIAM, 28, M, SHOEMAKER, 06/03/1857
1. NOVA SCOTIA 2. NOVA SCOTIA 3. PICTOU

BROWNING, WM H., 1, M, , 06/03/1857
1. NOVA SCOTIA 2. NOVA SCOTIA 3. PICTOU

BRUCE, C, 23, F, , 07/11/1850
1. BRITISH AMERICA 2. CANADA 3. PICTOU

BRUCE, CATHARINE, 70, F, , 07/11/1850
1. BRITISH AMERICA 2. CANADA 3. PICTOU

BRUCE, CATHARINE, 27, F, , 07/11/1850
1. BRITISH AMERICA 2. CANADA 3. PICTOU

BRUCE, FLORA, 25, F, , 07/11/1850
1. BRITISH AMERICA 2. CANADA 3. PICTOU

BRUCE, HANNAH, 18, F, , 07/11/1850
1. BRITISH AMERICA 2. CANADA 3. PICTOU

BRUCE, JAMES, 3, M, CHILD, 07/11/1850
1. BRITISH AMERICA 2. CANADA 3. PICTOU

BRUCE, MASTER, 5, M, CHILD, 07/11/1850
1. BRITISH AMERICA 2. CANADA 3. PICTOU

BRYAN, FRANCIS, 21, M, LABORER, 11/02/1831
1. IRELAND 2. U.S. 3. SYDNEY

BRYANT, PATRICK, 22, , LABORER, 05/09/1837
1. IRELAND 2. NEW YORK 3. LIVERPOOL

BUCK, JAMES A., 17, M, WEAVER, 09/09/1854
1. U.S. 2. U.S. 3. PICTOU

BUCK, JANE W., 25, F, WEAVER, 09/09/1854
1. U.S. 2. U.S. 3. PICTOU

BUCKLEY, MARY, 20, , SPINSTER, 05/09/1837
1. IRELAND 2. U.S. 3. LIVERPOOL

BUCKLIN, JAMES, 23, M, CARPENTER, 04/26/1831
1. U.S. 2. U.S. 3. HAVANA

BUMPSTEAD, JERIMIAH, 21, M, CLERK, 06/05/1834
1. U.S. 2. U.S. 3. HAVANA

BUNKER, THOMAS G., 28, M, MARINER, 04/16/1821
1. U.S. 2. NEW YORK 3. LISBON

BUREL, JOHN, 12, M, , 08/29/1836
1. SCOTLAND 2. NEW YORK 3. PICTOU

BURGES, THOMAS M., 20, M, MERCHANT, 09/30/1826
1. U.S. 2. U.S. 3. GOTEBORG

BURGESS, JR., TRISTAM, 25, M, FARMER, 05/03/1841
1. U.S. 2. 3. MATANZAS

BURK, PATRICK, 26, , LABORER, 05/09/1837
1. IRELAND 2. NEW YORK 3. LIVERPOOL

BURLING, B. L., 25, M, MERCHANT, 08/14/1820
1. U.S. 2. U.S. 3. SANTIAGO

BURNES, MICHAEL, 50, M, CARPENTER, 07/27/1835
1. IRELAND 2. PROVIDENCE 3. PICTOU

BURNETT, JOHN, 20, M, MASON, 08/20/1844
1. NOVA SCOTIA 2. U.S. 3. PICTOU

BURNS, BRIDGET, 3, F, CHILD, 08/14/1852
1. BRITISH AMERICA 2. U.S. 3. PICTOU

BURNS, JANE, 35, , LABORER, 09/12/1842
1. ENGLAND 2. U.S. 3. LIVERPOOL

BURNS, JOHN, 30, M, COOPER, 08/14/1852
1. BRITISH AMERICA 2. U.S. 3. PICTOU

BURNS, JOHN, IN, M, CHILD, 08/14/1852
1. BRITISH AMERICA 2. U.S. 3. PICTOU

BURNS, MARY, 28, F, WIFE, 08/14/1852
1. BRITISH AMERICA 2. U.S. 3. PICTOU

BURNS, MARY, 7, F, CHILD, 08/14/1852
1. BRITISH AMERICA 2. U.S. 3. PICTOU

BURNS, NATHAN, 30, M, CARPENTER, 06/12/1838
1. U.S. 2. U.S. 3. HAVANA

BURNS, PATRICK, 2, M, CHILD, 08/14/1852
1. BRITISH AMERICA 2. U.S. 3. PICTOU

BURNS, ROBERT, 36, M, LABORER, 09/12/1842
1. ENGLAND 2. U.S. 3. LIVERPOOL

BURNS, SUSAN, 5, F, CHILD, 08/14/1852
1. BRITISH AMERICA 2. U.S. 3. PICTOU

BURROUGHS, JAS., 25, M, MERCHANT, 07/10/1821
1. U.S. 2. U.S. 3. HAVANA

BURROWS, WILLIAM, 30, M, MINER, 10/13/1865
1. BRITISH AMERICA 2. U.S. 3. COW BAY

BURTON, EDWARD, 53, M, GROCER AND DRAPER, 06/16/1828
1. ENGLAND 2. U.S. 3. LIVERPOOL

BURTON, HODGSON, 9, M, CHILD OF EDWARD, 06/16/1828
1. ENGLAND 2. U.S. 3. LIVERPOOL

BURTON, JABEZ A., 12, M, CHILD OF EDWARD, 06/16/1828
1. ENGLAND 2. U.S. 3. LIVERPOOL

BURTON, JAMES, 10, M, CHILD OF EDWARD, 06/16/1828
1. ENGLAND 2. U.S. 3. LIVERPOOL

BURTON, MARY, 19, F, CHILD OF EDWARD, 06/16/1828
1. ENGLAND 2. U.S. 3. LIVERPOOL

BUTCHER, AMOS, 23, M, CARPENTER, 08/05/1839
1. U.S. 2. U.S. 3. HAVANA

BUTLER, CARLOS ANTONIO, 5, M, NONE, 05/20/1837
1. CUBA 2. AMERICA FOR SCHOOL 3. MATANZAS

BUTLER, JUAN CARLOS, 7, M, NONE, 05/20/1837
1. CUBA 2. AMERICA FOR SCHOOL 3. MATANZAS

BUTLER, MARGARET, 16, F, MILLINER, 10/27/1834
1. NOVA SCOTIA 2. BOSTON 3. PICTOU

BUTLER, SAMUEL, , , , 05/16/1821
1. PROVIDENCE 2. 3. MATANZAS

BUTLER, SARAH, 40, F, NONE, 10/27/1834
1. NOVA SCOTIA 2. BOSTON 3. PICTOU

BUTMAN, JANE, 30, F, LADY, 08/09/1847
1. U.S. 2. U.S. 3. PICTOU

BUTMAN, MARY JANE, 2, F, CHILD, 08/09/1847
1. U.S. 2. U.S. 3. PICTOU

BYERRANO, JOHN, 14, M, SERVANT, 06/23/1834
1. SPAIN 2. SPAIN 3. HAVANA

BYRNE, EDWIN, 1, M, CHILD, 07/05/1849
1. GREAT BRITAIN 2. GREAT BRITAIN 3. ST. THOMAS

BYRNE, ROBERT, 26, M, LIEUT. BRITISH ARMY, 07/05/1849
1. GREAT BRITAIN 2. GREAT BRITAIN 3. ST. THOMAS

BYRNE, SARAH, 26, F, LADY, 07/05/1849
1. GREAT BRITAIN 2. GREAT BRITAIN 3. ST. THOMAS

CABALIERO, CARLOS L., 37, M, GENTLEMAN, 07/10/1854
1. HAVANA 2. U.S. 3. MOZAMBIQUE AND ST. HELENA

CAETANO, MANUEL, 27, M, MARINER, 08/28/1872
1. FLORES 2. BOSTON 3.

CAFFELY, PATRICK, 24, , LABORER, 05/09/1837
1. IRELAND 2. NEW YORK 3. LIVERPOOL

CAFFREY, ANN, 1, F, LADY, 07/08/1848
1. PICTOU 2. 3. PICTOU

CAFFREY, SUSAN, 27, F, LADY, 07/08/1848
1. PICTOU 2. PROVIDENCE 3. PICTOU

CAHILL, JOHN, 50, , MILLWRIGHT, 05/28/1869
1. IRELAND 2. U.S. 3. PICTOU

CAHOONE, CHRISTOPHER, 30, M, GENTLEMAN, 08/06/1836
1. U.S. 2. U.S. 3. HAVANA

CALDER, JAMES, 27, M, LABORER, 11/03/1835
1. PICTOU 2. FALL RIVER 3. PICTOU

CALDER, JANE, 27, F, MANTUA MAKER, 11/03/1835
1. 2. FALL RIVER 3. PICTOU

CALDER, WM., 2, M, , 11/03/1835
1. 2. FALL RIVER 3. PICTOU

CALDEVEN, PHILLIPE, 19, M, MERCHANT, 12/03/1824
1. SANTIAGO DE CHILE 2. SANTIAGO 3. LINTIN

CAMERON, ALEXANDER, 21, M, BLACKSMITH, 10/14/1842
1. PICTOU 2. U.S. 3. PICTOU

CAMERON, ALEXANDER, 30, M, CARPENTER, 08/17/1850
1. PICTOU 2. U.S. 3. PICTOU

CAMERON, ANN, 25, F, SERVANT, 07/01/1870
1. NOVA SCOTIA 2. U.S. 3. PICTOU

CAMERON, ANN, 18, F, SERVANT, 06/18/1850
1. NOVA SCOTIA 2. U.S. 3. PICTOU

CAMERON, ANNE, 16, F, , 07/29/1846
1. PROVIDENCE 2. PROVIDENCE 3. PICTOU

CAMERON, BETSEY, 19, F, LABORER, 10/14/1842
1. PICTOU 2. U.S. 3. PICTOU

CAMERON, CHRISTINA, 25, F, SERVANT, 07/12/1864
1. BRITISH AMERICA 2. U.S. 3. PICTOU

CAMERON, DANIEL, 20, M, LABORER, 10/14/1842
1. PICTOU 2. U.S. 3. PICTOU

CAMERON, HANNAH, 19, F, SERVANT, 06/03/1844
1. NOVA SCOTIA 2. U.S. 3. PICTOU

CAMERON, HUGH, 17, M, HOUSE CARPENTER, 09/13/1859
1. NOVA SCOTIA 2. U.S. 3. PICTOU

CAMERON, JAMES, 18, M, SHOEMAKER, 07/30/1846
1. PICTOU 2. U.S. 3. PICTOU

CAMERON, JAMES, 19, M, CARPENTER, 07/03/1851
1. BRITISH AMERICA 2. U.S. 3. PICTOU

CAMERON, JOHN, 27, M, TAILOR, 07/17/1850
1. BRITISH AMERICA 2. U.S. 3. PICTOU

CAMERON, MARGARET, 45, F, LABORER, 10/14/1842
1. PICTOU 2. U.S. 3. PICTOU

CAMERON, MARY ANN, 20, F, SERVANT, 07/30/1846
1. PICTOU 2. U.S. 3. PICTOU

CAMERON, PETER, 30, M, CARPENTER, 08/27/1846
1. PICTOU 2. U.S. 3. PICTOU

CAMERON, ROBERT, 23, M, CARPENTER, 10/14/1842
1. PICTOU 2. U.S. 3. PICTOU

CAMERON, ROBERT N., 31, M, CARPENTER, 08/17/1850
1. PICTOU 2. U.S. 3. PICTOU

CAMMELL, MARY A., 16, F, SERVANT, 07/31/1863
1. PICTOU 2. PROVIDENCE 3. PICTOU

CAMPBELL, ABBY, 3, F, , 08/17/1853
1. U.S. 2. U.S. 3. PICTOU

CAMPBELL, AMELIA, 9 MONTHS, F, NONE, 06/11/1856
1. U.S. 2. U.S. 3. PICTOU

CAMPBELL, ANN, 26, F, HOUSEWORK, 09/25/1854
1. PICTOU 2. U.S. 3. PICTOU

CAMPBELL, ANNA, 7, F, NONE, 06/11/1856
1. U.S. 2. U.S. 3. PICTOU

CAMPBELL, CATHARINE, 19, F, , 10/01/1850
1. BRITISH AMERICA 2. U.S. 3. PICTOU

CAMPBELL, CATHARINE, 27, F, HOUSEWIFE, 06/11/1856
1. U.S. 2. U.S. 3. PICTOU

CAMPBELL, CHARLOTTE, 5, F, , 08/17/1853
1. U.S. 2. U.S. 3. PICTOU

CAMPBELL, DAVID, 13, M, NONE, 08/17/1853
1. U.S. 2. U.S. 3. PICTOU

CAMPBELL, ELIZA, 19, F, MANUFACTURER, 07/30/1846
1. NOVA SCOTIA 2. NOVA SCOTIA 3. PICTOU

CAMPBELL, FLORA, 27, F, SERVANT, 07/12/1867
1. BRITISH AMERICA 2. 3. PICTOU

CAMPBELL, GEORGE, 20, M, WAITER, 01/03/1834
1. U.S. 2. U.S. 3. MATANZAS

CAMPBELL, ISABELLA, 26, F, SERVANT, 07/05/1864
1. NOVA SCOTIA 2. U.S. 3. PICTOU

CAMPBELL, JAMES, 21, M, TAILOR, 08/27/1846
1. NOVA SCOTIA 2. U.S. 3. PICTOU

CAMPBELL, JANE, 20, F, SERVANT, 06/03/1844
1. NOVA SCOTIA 2. U.S. 3. PICTOU

CAMPBELL, JANE, 35, F, SERVANT, 08/17/1853
1. NOVA SCOTIA 2. NOVA SCOTIA 3. PICTOU

CAMPBELL, JANET, 31, F, HOUSEWIFE, 08/17/1853
1. U.S. 2. U.S. 3. PICTOU

CAMPBELL, JOHN, 24, M, MACHINIST, 07/22/1844
1. U.S. 2. U.S. 3. PICTOU

CAMPBELL, JOHN, 3, , CHILD, 10/01/1850
1. BRITISH AMERICA 2. U.S. 3. PICTOU

CAMPBELL, JOHN, 14, M, BOY, 09/22/1851
1. BRITISH AMERICA 2. U.S. 3. PICTOU

CAMPBELL, JOHN, 10, M, NONE, 06/11/1856
1. U.S. 2. U.S. 3. PICTOU

CAMPBELL, JOHNSON, 9, M, , 08/17/1853
1. U.S. 2. U.S. 3. PICTOU

CAMPBELL, MARGARET JANE, 6 MONTHS, F, CHILD, 08/17/1853
1. U.S. 2. U.S. 3. PICTOU

CAMPBELL, MARY, 25, F, SERVANT, 06/03/1844
1. NOVA SCOTIA 2. U.S. 3. PICTOU

CAMPBELL, MARY, 20, F, SERVANT, 09/16/1858
1. NOVA SCOTIA 2. U.S. 3. PICTOU

CAMPBELL, MARY ANN, 11, F, , 08/17/1853
1. U.S. 2. U.S. 3. PICTOU

CAMPBELL, MICHAL, 27, M, LABORER, 03/22/1826
1. IRELAND 2. PROVIDENCE 3. LIVERPOOL

CAMPBELL, NEAL, 45, M, SHIP CARPENTER, 06/11/1856
1. U.S. 2. U.S. 3. PICTOU

CAMPBELL, NELSON, 32, M, MECHANIC, 10/21/1837
1. U.S. 2. U.S. 3. PICTOU

CAMPBELL, PETER, 22, M, LABORER, 06/24/1856
1. NOVA SCOTIA 2. U.S. 3. PICTOU

CAMPBELL, PETER, 25, M, FARMER, 08/16/1859
1. NOVA SCOTIA 2. NOVA SCOTIA 3. PICTOU

CAMPBELL, ROBERT, 7, M, , 08/17/1853
1. U.S. 2. U.S. 3. PICTOU

CAMPBELL, SUSAN, 16, F, SERVANT, 06/03/1844
1. NOVA SCOTIA 2. U.S. 3. PICTOU

CAMPBELL, SUSAN, 20, F, SERVANT, 08/22/1850
1. BRITISH AMERICA 2. U.S. 3. PICTOU

CAMPBELL, WITMAN CHARLES, 40, M, AGRICULTURE, 05/28/1836
1. U.S. 2. U.S 3. PICTOU

CAMPION, JOHN, 22, M, SEAMAN, 12/30/1853
1. U.S. 2. U.S. 3. MATANZAS

CAMRON, RODERICK, 25, M, CARPENTER, 07/08/1848
1. PICTOU 2. PROVIDENCE 3. PICTOU

CANADY, CATHARIN, 38, F, , 08/29/1836
1. SCOTLAND 2. NEW YORK 3. PICTOU

CARCICO, JOANAH, 18, , , 05/18/1868
1. 2. 3. BRAVA

CARGILL, G.C., 42, , MERCHANT, 03/25/1841
1. LUNKENTIEN 2. 3. TURKS ISLAND

CARLATEN, LANGDON, 18, M, , 06/14/1859
1. U.S. 2. U.S. 3. PICTOU

CARLILE, FRANCISCO, 30, M, MERCHANT, 07/19/1824
1. CUBA 2. CUBA 3. HAVANA

CARMICHAEL, ROBERT, 27, M, SHIP CARPENTER, 07/26/1848
1. BRITISH AMERICA 2. BRITISH AMERICA 3. PICTOU

CARMICHAL, HENRY, 18, M, CARPENTER, 07/30/1846
1. PICTOU 2. U.S. 3. PICTOU

CARNEY, PATRICK, 34, M, WHEELWRIGHTS, 06/16/1828
1. IRELAND 2. U.S. 3. LIVERPOOL

CARPENTER, POWELL H., 28, M, GENTLEMAN, 04/25/1840
1. U.S. 2. U.S. 3. MATANZAS

CARPENTER, WM. L., 25, M, MARINER, 02/20/1833
1. U.S. 2. U.S. 3. MATANZAS

CARR, JOHN B., 35, M, MECHANIC, 03/11/1841
1. U.S. 2. U.S. 3. HAVANA

CARREIRO, MANUEL, 20, M, FARMER, 08/28/1872
1. SAN MIQUEL 2. BOSTON 3.

CARROLL, ANNABEL, 18, , SERVANT, 09/01/1867
1. 2. 3. PICTOU

CARROLL, CATHARINE, 19, F, LABORER, 08/09/1839
1. NOVA SCOTIA 2. U.S. 3. PICTOU

CARROLL, PHILIP, 18, M, LABORER, 05/09/1859
1. NOVA SCOTIA 2. U.S. 3. PICTOU

CARSON, ISABEL, 22, F, NONE, 07/22/1856
1. GREAT BRITAIN 2. U.S. 3. PICTOU

CARTER, JOHN C., 30, M, SHOE MAKER, 09/13/1844
1. NOVA SCOTIA 2. U.S. 3. PICTOU

CARTER, JOHN W., 26, M, SHIP CARPENTER, 11/05/1834
1. NOVA SCOTIA 2. PAWTUCKET 3. PICTOU

CARTER, JOSEPH, 22, M, Tailor, 10/22/1834
1. NOVA SCOTIA 2. U.S. 3. CUMBERLAND, N.S.

CARUTHERS, ELISABETH A., 27, F, LADY, 10/08/1849
1. U.S. 2. U.S. 3. PICTOU

CARUTHERS, ROBERT, 31, M, SHIP CARPENTER, 10/08/1849
1. U.S. 2. U.S. 3. PICTOU

CARUTHERS, SARAH E., 2, F, CHILD, 10/08/1849
1. U.S. 2. U.S. 3. PICTOU

CARWELL, JANE, 18, F, LABORER, 09/09/1847
1. IRELAND 2. CANADA 3. PICTOU

CASADA, MARTHA, 18, F, SERVANT, 06/22/1863
1. PICTOU 2. U.S. 3. PICTOU

CASADA, MITCHELL, 30, M, CARPENTER, 06/22/1863
1. PICTOU 2. U.S. 3. PICTOU

CASEY, JAMES, 32, M, LABORER, 09/18/1823
1. IRELAND 2. U.S. 3. HONDURAS

CASHEIR, EDMUND, 19, M, LABORER, 06/24/1856
1. NOVA SCOTIA 2. U.S. 3. PICTOU

CASHEN, MARY, 18, F, NONE, 10/08/1856
1. NOVA SCOTIA 2. U.S. 3. PICTOU

CASSIDAY, MARGARET, 19, F, NONE, 08/20/1857
1. NOVA SCOTIA 2. U.S. 3. PICTOU

CASSIDY, MARTHA, 17, F, NONE, 07/31/1857
1. NOVA SCOTIA 2. U.S. 3. PICTOU

CASSIDY, MARTHA, 24, F, SERVANT, 07/05/1864
1. NOVA SCOTIA 2. U.S. 3. PICTOU

CASTLEHOUSE, GEORGE, 39, M, GROCER, 05/19/1837
1. U.S. 2. U.S. 3. HAVANA

CATORINA, ANA, 26, F, SEAMSTRESS, 08/28/1872
1. FLORES 2. PROVIDENCE 3.

CATTON, JOHN, 1, M, CHILD, 09/12/1848
   1. BRITISH AMERICA 2. U.S. 3. PICTOU

CATTON, PHEBE, 22, F, LADY, 09/12/1848
   1. BRITISH AMERICA 2. U.S. 3. PICTOU

CAVANAH, JOHN, 14, , , 11/04/1869
   1. U.S. 2. 3. SINGAN

CAVEN, JAMES, 45, M, FARMER, 08/08/1837
   1. NOVA SCOTIA 2. U.S. 3. PICTOU

CAVEN, JR., JAMES, 16, M, FARMER, 08/08/1837
   1. NOVA SCOTIA 2. U.S. 3. PICTOU

CEELEY, SAMUEL, 25, M, FARMER, 04/07/1845
   1. ENGLAND 2. ENGLAND 3. NEW ZEALAND

CERONON, JOHN, 30, , LABORER, 05/09/1837
   1. IRELAND 2. NEW YORK 3. LIVERPOOL

CHACE, JOHN, 22, M, CARPENTER, 06/23/1834
   1. U.S. 2. U.S. 3. HAVANA

CHAMBERS, CHARLES, 28, M, LABORER, 07/24/1849
   1. IRELAND 2. U.S. 3. SYDNEY

CHAMBERS, WM, 19, M, LABORER, 07/24/1849
   1. IRELAND 2. U.S. 3. SYDNEY

CHAMPELL, WILLIAM, 20, M, TAILOR, 10/04/1848
   1. BRITISH AMERICA 2. U.S. 3. PICTOU

CHAMPNEY, JONATHAN, 22, M, JEWELER, 04/29/1828
   1. U.S. 2. U.S. 3. HAVANA

CHANEY, JOHN, 32, M, LABORER, 08/20/1844
   1. NOVA SCOTIA 2. U.S. 3. PICTOU

CHANEY, MARY, 25, F, LABORER, 08/20/1844
   1. NOVA SCOTIA 2. U.S. 3. PICTOU

CHAPATIN, LEON, 40, M, MERCHANT, 07/20/1848
   1. U.S. 2. U.S. 3. MATANZAS

CHARTER, MARY ANN, 20, F, SERVANT GIRL, 09/02/1845
   1. NOVA SCOTIA 2. U.S. 3. PICTOU

CHARTERS, JOHN, 13, M, , 08/06/1849
   1. BRITISH AMERICA 2. U.S. 3. PICTOU

CHARTERS, MARY, 52, F, LADY, 08/06/1849
   1. BRITISH AMERICA 2. U.S. 3. PICTOU

CHEEVER, LEVI T., 40, M, MERCHANT, 05/18/1840
1. U.S. 2. AMERICA 3. MATANZAS

CHENEY, ARTHUR B., 2, , , 10/24/1855
1. U.S. 2. U.S. 3. ZANZIBAR, MOZAMBIQUE

CHENEY, CRAWFORD G., 7 MONTHS, , , 10/24/1855
1. U.S. 2. U.S. 3. ZANZIBAR, MOZAMBIQUE

CHENEY, GEO. A., 28, , MERCHANT, 10/24/1855
1. U.S. 2. U.S. 3. ZANZIBAR, MOZAMBIQUE

CHENEY, SARAH B., 25, , , 10/24/1855
1. U.S. 2. U.S. 3. ZANZIBAR, MOZAMBIQUE

CHISEM, JOHN, 23, M, TAILOR, 09/19/1850
1. BRITISH AMERICA 2. U.S. 3. PICTOU

CHISHOLM, DONALD, 21, M, FARMER, 06/22/1863
1. PICTOU 2. U.S. 3. PICTOU

CHISHOLM, RODERICK B., 25, M, MERCHANT, 10/23/1823
1. U.S. 2. U.S. 3. HONDURAS

CHISLOM, ANGUS, 21, M, , 08/17/1850
1. PICTOU 2. U.S. 3. PICTOU

CHISOLM, JOHN, 18, M, FARMER, 06/22/1863
1. PICTOU 2. U.S. 3. PICTOU

CHISOM, ALEXANDER, 40, M, FARMER, 07/29/1846
1. NOVA SCOTIA 2. BRITISH AMERICA 3. PICTOU

CHITICHIN, JOSEPH, 15, M, CARPENTER, 09/13/1844
1. NOVA SCOTIA 2. U.S. 3. PICTOU

CHRISHOLM, AESINE, 47, M, MASON, 07/20/1857
1. NOVA SCOTIA 2. U.S. 3. PICTOU

CHRISTA, ELIZA J., 20, F, SERVANT, 09/06/1855
1. NOVA SCOTIA 2. NOVA SCOTIA 3. PICTOU

CHRISTIE, MARY, 20, F, DOMESTIC, 09/21/1859
1. NOVA SCOTIA 2. U.S. 3. PICTOU

CHRISTY, JAMES, 37, M, MECHANIC, 03/11/1841
1. U.S. 2. U.S. 3. HAVANA

CHRISTY, MRS. JAMES, 52, F, , 03/11/1841
1. U.S. 2. U.S. 3. HAVANA

CHRYSTIE, THOMS W., 21, M, STUDENT AT LAW, 06/25/1832
1. U.S. 2. U.S. 3. ST. CROIX

CHURCH, CHARLES, 35, M, CARPENTER, 07/17/1835
1. U.S. 2. U.S. 3. HAVANA

CHURCH, F.S., 30, M, MERCHANT, 03/22/1837
1. U.S. 2. U.S. 3. HAVANA

CHURCH, GEORGE, 12, M, LAD, 07/03/1845
1. BRITISH AMERICA 2. U.S. 3. PICTOU

CHURCH, JOHN, 16, M, LAD, 07/03/1845
1. BRITISH AMERICA 2. U.S. 3. PICTOU

CHURCH, MARY ANN, 18, F, SERVANT, 07/03/1845
1. BRITISH AMERICA 2. U.S. 3. PICTOU

CHURCH, ROBERT, 23, M, LABORER, 07/03/1845
1. BRITISH AMERICA 2. U.S. 3. PICTOU

CHURCH, SARAH ANN, 44, F, LABORER, 07/03/1845
1. BRITISH AMERICA 2. U.S. 3. PICTOU

CISTOMUO, JOSE, 30, M, FARMER, 08/28/1872
1. FLORES 2. PROVIDENCE 3.

CLANCY, BIDDY, 24, , SERVANT, 05/09/1837
1. IRELAND 2. U.S. 3. LIVERPOOL

CLANNEN, TIMOTHY, 20, , LABORER, 05/09/1837
1. IRELAND 2. U.S. 3. LIVERPOOL

CLAPP, BRADIM R., 22, M, ----, 09/17/1825
1. U.S. 2. U.S. 3. BUENOS AIRES

CLAPP, LYMAN, 28, M, GENTLEMAN, 07/10/1854
1. U.S. 2. U.S. 3. MOZAMBIQUE AND ST. HELENA

CLARK, BENJAMIN, 25, M, SCHOOLMASTER, 08/23/1845
1. BRITISH AMERICA 2. U.S. 3. PICTOU

CLARK, JANE, 11, F, SERVANT, 07/08/1844
1. NOVA SCOTIA 2. U.S. 3. PICTOU

CLARK, JESSIE, 19, F, SERVANT, 11/16/1863
1. PICTOU 2. U.S. 3. PICTOU

CLARK, JOHN, 22, M, FARMER, 10/04/1848
1. 2. U.S. 3. PICTOU

CLARK, MARION, 32, , HOUSEKEEPER, 10/19/1868
1. U.S. 2. U.S. 3. PICTOU

CLARK, MARTHA, 18, F, LADY, 09/27/1848
1. PICTOU 2. PROVIDENCE 3. PICTOU

CLARK, N.W., 30, M, MARINER, 06/18/1839
1. U.S. 2. U.S. 3.

CLARKE, GEORGE, 18, M, SAILOR, 09/30/1839
1. U.S. 2. U.S. 3. CAPE PALMA

CLARKE, GEORGE, 40, M, SUGAR BOILER, 05/21/1845
1. U.S. 2. U.S. 3. PICTOU

CLARKE, HARTFORD G., 21, M, MERCHANT, 06/22/1848
1. PROVIDENCE 2. PROVIDENCE 3. MATANZAS

CLARKE, IVORY, 45, M, MISSIONARY, 05/24/1848
1. U.S. 2. U.S. 3. COAST OF AFRICA

CLARKE, MRS. IVORY, 44, F, LADY, 05/24/1848
1. U.S. 2. U.S. 3. COAST OF AFRICA

CLARKE, JANET, 26, F, SERVANT, 08/05/1856
1. NOVA SCOTIA 2. NOVA SCOTIA 3. PICTOU

CLARKE, PELEG, 24, M, COOPER, 05/24/1828
1. U.S. 2. U.S. 3. HAVANA

CLARKE, WILLIAM, 3, M, CHILD, 05/24/1848
1. U.S. 2. U.S. 3. COAST OF AFRICA

CLARSON, ANN, 20, F, DOMESTIC, 09/21/1859
1. NOVA SCOTIA 2. U.S. 3. PICTOU

CLARSON, EDWARD, 24, M, LABORER, 09/21/1859
1. NOVA SCOTIA 2. U.S. 3. PICTOU

CLARSON, ELISABETH, 18, F, , 10/01/1850
1. BRITISH AMERICA 2. U.S. 3. PICTOU

CLARSON, MARY, 66, F, DOMESTIC, 09/21/1859
1. NOVA SCOTIA 2. U.S. 3. PICTOU

CLENNEN, MARTIN, 18, , LABORER, 05/09/1837
1. IRELAND 2. U.S. 3. LIVERPOOL

CLIFF, MARY, 28, F, DOMESTIC, 09/28/1859
1. NOVA SCOTIA 2. U.S. 3. PICTOU

CLIFFORD, JR., BENJ., 25, M, MERCHANT, 07/25/1826
1. U.S. 2. U.S. 3. HAVANA

COBB, ALEXANDER, 25, M, MECHANIC, 07/28/1826
1. U.S. 2. U.S. 3. CURACOA

COELHO, JOSE FRANCISO, 28, M, MARINER, 08/28/1872
1. FLORES 2. BOSTON 3.

COGAN, PETER, 25, M, WHEELWRIGHT, 07/05/1836
1. U.S. 2. U.S. 3. HAVANA

COLE, WILLIAM, 30, M, NONE, 07/19/1858
1. NOVA SCOTIA 2. NOVA SCOTIA 3. PICTOU

COLITE, JAMES, 36, M, MECHANIC, 06/17/1838
1. SCOTLAND 2. U.S. 3. HAVANA

COLLEY, A.A., 27, M, COOPER, 07/07/1846
1. MAINE 2. MAINE 3. MATANZAS

COLON, P.W., 32, M, , 05/16/1821
1. U.S. 2. 3. MATANZAS

COLQUHIN, MRSS., 30, F, HOUSE SERVANT, 07/07/1865
1. BRITISH AMERICA 2. U.S. 3. PICTOU

COLQUHOUN, ELIZABETH, 21, F, , 08/01/1859
1. NOVA SCOTIA 2. U.S. 3. PICTOU

COLT, GEORGE D.W., 4, M, , 04/28/1842
1. U.S. 2. U.S. 3. MATANZAS

COLT, THEODORA, 23, F, LADY, 04/28/1842
1. U.S. 2. U.S. 3. MATANZAS

COLT, JR., CHRISTOPHER, 29, M, GENTLEMAN, 04/28/1842
1. U.S. 2. U.S. 3. MATANZAS

COLWELL, ALFRED, 23, M, MECHANIC, 08/03/1855
1. GREAT BRITAIN 2. U.S. 3. LIVERPOOL

COMEAUX, AMBROSE, 15, M, SEAMAN, 05/16/1853
1. NOVA SCOTIA 2. NOVA SCOTIA 3. ARDROSSAN

COMEAUX, AUGUSTUS, 22, M, SEAMAN, 05/16/1853
1. NOVA SCOTIA 2. NOVA SCOTIA 3. ARDROSSAN

COMINGS, JESSEY, 18, F, LADY, 10/02/1839
1. NOVA SCOTIA 2. U.S. 3. PICTOU

COMINGS, JOSEPH, 35, M, ENGINEER, 07/30/1855
1. SPAIN 2. CUBA 3. MATANZAS

CONDON, MARY, 18, F, SERVANT, 08/20/1844
1. NOVA SCOTIA 2. U.S. 3. PICTOU

CONER, PATRICK, 29, M, SHIP CAPTAIN, 09/11/1837
1. IRELAND 2. UTICA 3. PICTOU

CONGDON, DANIEL, 48, M, CARPENTER, 07/22/1847
1. U.S. 2. U.S. 3. MATANZAS

CONGDON, JOEL, 12, M, MARINER, 05/27/1823
1. U.S. 2. U.S. 3. L. BARTS

CONLY, HANNAH, 14, F, SERVANT, 09/20/1851
1. BRITISH AMERICA 2. U.S. 3. PICTOU

CONLY, MARGARET, 18, F, SERVANT, 09/20/1851
1. BRITISH AMERICA 2. U.S. 3. PICTOU

CONNOLY, EDWARD, 25, M, MERCHANT, 08/17/1831
1. NEW YORK 2. U.S. 3. SURINAM

CONNOR, BIDDY, 18, , SPINSTER, 05/09/1837
1. IRELAND 2. U.S. 3. LIVERPOOL

CONNOY, BRIDGETT, 29, F, WIFE OF JOHN, 1836
1. GALWAY 2. NEW YORK 3. PICTOU

CONNOY, JOHN, 33, M, LABOUR MARRIED, 1836
1. GALWAY 2. NEW YORK 3. PICTOU

CONNOY, JOHN, 1, , CHILD OF JOHN, 1836
1. GALWAY 2. NEW YORK 3. PICTOU

CONNOY, MARY, 3, , CHILD OF JOHN, 1836
1. GALWAY 2. NEW YORK 3. PICTOU

CONNOY, MICHAEL, 7, , CHILD OF JOHN, 1836
1. GALWAY 2. NEW YORK 3. PICTOU

CONNOY, PARCHUA, 10, , CHILD OF JOHN, 1836
1. GALWAY 2. NEW YORK 3. PICTOU

CONWAY, JOHN, 50, M, MERCHANT, 08/14/1823
1. U.S. 2. U.S. 3. BUENOS AIRES

COOK, JANE, 29, F, TAILORESS, 06/23/1857
1. PICTOU 2. BOSTON 3. PICTOU

COOLON, FRANCIS, 23, M, LABORER, 06/16/1828
1. IRELAND 2. U.S. 3. LIVERPOOL

COOPER, JAH, 27, M, TRADESMAN, 03/22/1826
1. ENGLAND 2. MASSACHUSETTS 3. LIVERPOOL

COOPER, ROBERT, 28, M, COOPER, 07/03/1839
1. U.S. 2. U.S. 3. MATANZAS

COPELAND, KATE, 24, F, SERVANT, 06/20/1863
1. NOVA SCOTIA 2. U.S. 3. PICTOU

COPELAND, NANCY, 20, F, SERVANT, 06/20/1863
1. NOVA SCOTIA 2. U.S. 3. PICTOU

COPELAND, NANCY, 26, F, SERVANT, 06/20/1863
1. NOVA SCOTIA 2. U.S. 3. PICTOU

COPELAND, SMITH, 23, M, GENTLEMAN, 07/29/1862
1. NOVA SCOTIA 2. NOVA SCOTIA 3. PICTOU

COREY, CALEB, 22, M, COOPER, 05/27/1823
1. U.S. 2. U.S. 3. HAVANA

COREY, DANIEL, 21, M, COOPER, 06/14/1821
1. U.S. 2. 3. HAVANA

COREY, DANIEL W., 25, M, COOPER, 05/12/1820
1. U.S. 2. U.S. 3. HAVANA

COREY, W., 47, M, MERCHANT, 08/02/1827
1. VIRGINIA 2. VIRGINIA 3. MATANZAS

CORLIS, JAMES, 21, M, SADDLER, 07/08/1844
1. NOVA SCOTIA 2. U.S. 3. PICTOU

CORNELL, CHARLES E., 30, M, DRUGGIST, 08/03/1835
1. U.S. 2. U.S. 3. HAVANA

CORNELL, JOHN P., 27, M, CARPENTER, 06/26/1835
1. U.S. 2. U.S. 3. HAVANA

COROBA, MANUEL J., 57, M, GENTLEMAN, 04/24/1854
1. SPAIN 2. SPAIN 3. MARIEL

CORRAL, MARGARET, 23, F, SERVANT, 09/08/1837
1. NOVA SCOTIA 2. NEW YORK 3. PICTOU

CORWIN, ANNIE, 24, F, , 05/30/1860
1. PRINCE EDWARD ISLAND 2. MASSACHUSETTS 3. PRINCE EDWARD ISLAND

CORWIN, ELIZABETH, 3, F, , 05/30/1860
1. PRINCE EDWARD ISLAND 2. MASSACHUSETTS 3. PRINCE EDWARD ISLAND

CORWIN, JOHN, 1, M, , 05/30/1860
1. PRINCE EDWARD ISLAND 2. MASSACHUSETTS 3. PRINCE EDWARD ISLAND

CORY, THOMAS M., 32, M, GENTLEMAN, 04/25/1840
1. U.S. 2. U.S. 3. MATANZAS

COSTLEY, CHARLES, 1, M, CHILD, 10/29/1850
1. U.S. 2. U.S. 3. PICTOU

COSTLEY, MARGARET, 25, F, , 10/29/1850
1. U.S. 2. U.S. 3. PICTOU

COTTLEY, BRIDGETT, 49, , MARRIED, 1836
1. GALWAY 2. NEW YORK 3. PICTOU

COTTREL, RUSSEL, 25, M, CARPENTER, 07/05/1837
1. U.S. 2. 3. HAVANA

COTY, E., 12, M, , 06/29/1829
1. U.S. 2. U.S. 3. HAVANA

COTY, ELIZA, 22, F, LADY, 06/29/1829
1. U.S. 2. U.S. 3. HAVANA

COTY, PETER, 24, M, GENTLEMAN, 06/29/1829
1. U.S. 2. U.S. 3. HAVANA

COVENTRY, ANNA, 28, F, DRESS MAKER, 09/01/1865
1. U.S. 2. U.S. 3. PICTOU

COWAN, CHARLES, 14, M, , 06/09/1834
1. CUBA 2. U.S. 3. MATANZAS

CRAIG, JANE, 55, , , 08/27/1835
1. GLASGOW 2. 3. PICTOU

CRAIG, MAY, 18, , , 08/27/1835
1. GLASGOW 2. 3. PICTOU

CRAY, DAVID, 34, M, ENGINEER, 06/11/1840
1. U.S. 2. U.S. 3. MATANZAS

CREAD, MARGARET, 20, F, SERVANT, 10/18/1836
1. PRINCE EDWARD ISLAND 2. PROVIDENCE 3. PICTOU

CREIGHTON, ELISABETH, 44, , , 08/25/1866
1. BRITISH AMERICA 2. BRITISH AMERICA 3. PICTOU

CREIGHTON, ELISABETH, 12, , , 08/25/1866
1. BRITISH AMERICA 2. BRITISH AMERICA 3. PICTOU

CREIGHTON, PETER, 45, , MERCHANT, 08/25/1866
1. BRITISH AMERICA 2. BRITISH AMERICA 3. PICTOU

CREIGHTON, WILLIAM, 23, M, LABORER, 09/14/1858
1. NOVA SCOTIA 2. U.S. 3. PICTOU

CROCKET, JANE, 24, F, SERVANT, 09/29/1852
1. BRITISH AMERICA 2. U.S. 3. PICTOU

CRONK, E.A., 18, F, , 01/21/1834
1. U.S. 2. U.S. 3. MATANZAS

CROOKSHANK, JOHN, 8, M, , 11/03/1835
1. 2. FALL RIVER 3. PICTOU

CULLEN, WILLIAM, 38, M, MASTER MARINER, 01/16/1849
1. U.S. 2. U.S. 3. NASSAU

CULTON, ANNA, 44, F, DOMESTIC, 09/21/1859
1. NOVA SCOTIA 2. U.S. 3. PICTOU

CULTON, CATHARINE, 19, F, DOMESTIC, 09/21/1859
1. NOVA SCOTIA 2. U.S. 3. PICTOU

CULTON, ELISABETH MARY, 18, F, SERVANT, 07/03/1851
1. BRITISH AMERICA 2. U.S. 3. PICTOU

CULTREN, SOPHIA, 18, F, , 08/01/1859
1. NOVA SCOTIA 2. U.S. 3. PICTOU

CUMMINGS, BETSEY, 16, F, SERVICE, 08/10/1838
1. PICTOU 2. 3. PICTOU

CUMMINGS, BRENA, 60, F, BLACKS FROM US RETURNED, 10/06/1828
1. PHILADELPHIA 2. PHILADELPHIA 3. PUERTA PLATA

CUMMINGS, JOHN, 12, M, LABORER, 10/20/1845
1. NOVA SCOTIA 2. U.S. 3. PICTOU

CUMMINGS, MARGARET, 12, F, MISS, 08/29/1845
1. BRITISH AMERICA 2. U.S. 3. PICTOU

CUMMINGS, REBECAAH, 19, F, SERVICE, 08/10/1838
1. PICTOU 2. U.S. 3. PICTOU

CUMMINGS, REBECCA, 40, F, HOUSEKEEPER, 08/29/1845
1. BRITISH AMERICA 2. U.S. 3. PICTOU

CUMMINGS, RICHARD, 14, M, BLACKS FROM US RETURNED, 10/06/1828
1. PHILADELPHIA 2. PHILADELPHIA 3. PUERTA PLATA

CUMMINGS, WILLIAM, 70, M, LABORER, 10/20/1845
1. IRELAND 2. U.S. 3. PICTOU

CUMMINGS, WILLIAM, 18, M, SEAMAN, 07/30/1846
1. PICTOU 2. U.S. 3. PICTOU

CUNNINGHAM, JAMES, 23, M, MERCHANT, 08/16/1822
1. U.S. 2. U.S. 3. HONDURAS

CURLAY, BARNARD, 70, M, LABORER, 09/18/1845
1. NOVA SCOTIA 2. U.S. 3. PICTOU

CURRAN, LAVINA, 24, , HOUSEKEEPER, 08/02/1869
1. U.S. 2. U.S. 3. WALLACE

CURRIE, CAROLINE, 22, F, , 04/15/1824
1. U.S. 2. U.S. 3. HAVANA

CUTHBURT, CHARLES, 5, M, BLACKS FROM US RETURNED, 10/06/1828
1. PHILADELPHIA 2. PHILADELPHIA 3. PUERTA PLATA

CUTHBURT, RICHARD, 4, M, BLACKS FROM US RETURNED, 10/06/1828
1. PHILADELPHIA 2. PHILADELPHIA 3. PUERTA PLATA

D'WOLF, ALLEN, 23, M, MARINER, 05/13/1831
1. WEST INDIES 2. WEST INDIES 3. HAVANA

D'WOLF, CHARLES, 55, M, MERCHANT, 07/02/1832
1. U.S. 2. U.S. 3. HAVANA

D'WOLF, MRS. GEO. B., 24, F, , 05/12/1834
1. U.S. 2. U.S. 3. MATANZAS

D'WOLF, JIEDARA, 3, F, , 05/12/1834
1. U.S. 2. U.S. 3. MATANZAS

D'WOLF, MARY ANN, 25, F, , 03/08/1833
1. U.S. 2. U.S. 3. HAVANA

D'WOLF, MARY ANN, 12, F, , 05/12/1834
1. U.S. 2. U.S. 3. MATANZAS

D'WOLFE, CHARLES, 28, M, MERCHANT, 05/03/1832
1. U.S. 2. U.S. 3. HAVANA

DA ENCARNACIO, ANNA DE JAREUS, 25, F, LADY, 10/17/1867
1. CAPE DE VERDE ISLANDS 2. U.S. 3. FLORES

DAGGETT, PRESTON, 27, M, CARPENTER, 05/19/1839
1. U.S. 2. U.S. 3. HAVANA

DAILEY, CATHARINE, 9, F, CHILD, 09/27/1852
1. BRITISH AMERICA 2. U.S. 3. PICTOU

DAILEY, MARGARET, 46, F, , 09/27/1852
1. BRITISH AMERICA 2. U.S. 3. PICTOU

DAILEY, RICHARD, 50, M, LABORER, 09/27/1852
1. BRITISH AMERICA 2. U.S. 3. PICTOU

DAINDERADA, ISABELLA, 19, , , 05/18/1868
1. 2. 3. BRAVA

DAINDERADA, MARGUERITA, 2, , , 05/18/1868
1. 2. 3. BRAVA

DALCOMBA, ISABELLA, 19, , , 05/18/1868
1. 2. 3. BRAVA

DALEY, BRYANT, 32, , MASON, 05/09/1837
1. IRELAND 2. U.S. 3. LIVERPOOL

DALEY, MARY, 22, , WIFE, 05/09/1837
1. IRELAND 2. U.S. 3. LIVERPOOL

DAMOTA, ANTONIO JOU, 29, M, FARMER, 1872
1. SAN MIGUEL 2. PROVIDENCE 3.

DAMOTHA, ANTONIO, 29, M, FARMER, 08/28/1872
1. SAN MIQUEL 2. PROVIDENCE 3.

DANSON, ROBERT, 47, M, GENTLEMAN, 10/02/1839
1. NOVA SCOTIA 2. U.S. 3. PICTOU

DAPONTE, MANUEL, 17, M, FARMER, 08/28/1872
1. SAN MIQUEL 2. BOSTON 3.

DARLARO, CAROLINE, 26, , , 05/18/1868
1. 2. 3. BRAVA

DARLASA, JOSEPH, 14, , , 05/18/1868
1. 2. 3. BRAVA

DARLASA, JOSEPHINE, 23, , , 05/18/1868
1. 2. 3. BRAVA

DARLING, WM., 28, M, CARPENTER, 05/23/1831
1. U.S. 2. U.S. 3. HAVANA

DARTHY, CATHARINE, 24, F, SERVANT, 08/11/1834
1. NOVA SCOTIA 2. U.S. 3. PICTOU

DARUDA, JOSE, 29, M, FARMER, 08/28/1872
1. SAN MIQUEL 2. BOSTON 3.

DATRINIDADE, ANNA, 40, F, SEAMSTRESS, 08/28/1872
1. FLORES 2. BOSTON 3.

DAVIDSON, ALFRED, 21, M, HOUSE CARPENTER, 09/12/1835
1. NOVA SCOTIA 2. NEW ORLEANS 3. ST. JOHN

DAVIDSON, BETSEY, 30, F, SPINSTER, 09/18/1845
1. NOVA SCOTIA 2. U.S. 3. PICTOU

DAVIDSON, EMILINE, 20, F, DOMESTIC, 09/21/1859
1. NOVA SCOTIA 2. U.S. 3. PICTOU

DAVIDSON, GEORGE, 63, M, SHIP CARPENTER, 10/21/1853
1. U.S. 2. U.S. 3. PICTOU

DAVIDSON, PETER, 21, M, , 08/01/1859
1. NOVA SCOTIA 2. U.S. 3. PICTOU

DAVIES, GEOR. R., 24, M, GENTLEMAN, 07/29/1862
1. NOVA SCOTIA 2. NOVA SCOTIA 3. PICTOU

DAVIS, ELLEN, 60, F, NONE, 10/08/1856
1. SCOTLAND 2. U.S. 3. PICTOU

DAVIS, GEORGE, 57, M, SHIP CARPENTER, 10/08/1856
1. SCOTLAND 2. U.S. 3. PICTOU

DAVIS, JANE, 25, F, LADY, 07/20/1844
1. NOVA SCOTIA 2. U.S. 3. PICTOU

DAVIS, JANE, 22, F, TAILORESS, 10/02/1850
1. ST. JOHN 2. U.S. 3. PICTOU

DAVIS, JOHN, 27, M, CARPENTER, 07/20/1844
1. NOVA SCOTIA 2. U.S. 3. PICTOU

DAVIS, LAWRENCE A., 40, M, GENTLEMEN, 10/04/1827
1. FRANCE 2. U.S. 3. PUERTA PLATA

DAVIS, MORGAN, 50, M, HANNER, 06/16/1828
1. ENGLAND 2. U.S. 3. LIVERPOOL

DAVIS, THOMAS, 40, M, CARPENTER, 07/28/1831
1. U.S. 2. U.S. 3. HAVANA

DAVIS, WILLIAM, 23, M, TAILOR, 10/02/1850
1. ST. JOHN 2. U.S. 3. PICTOU

DAY, JOSEPH, 32, M, MERCHANT, 07/07/1841
1. MATANZAS 2. MATANZAS 3. MATANZAS

DAY, SUSAN, 26, F, SERVANT, 09/24/1866
1. BRITISH AMERICA 2. NOVA SCOTIA 3. SINGAN

DE COSSE, JEAN BAPTISTE, , , , 12/14/1823
1. NEW YORK 2. MARTINIQUE 3. PROVIDENCE

DE COSSE, MRS., , , , 12/14/1823
1. NEW YORK 2. MARTINIQUE 3. PROVIDENCE

DE HAART, GYSBERTHUS M., , , , 12/30/1823
1. BOSTON 2. DEMERARA 3. PROVIDENCE

DE SILVA, JOSEPHINE, 16, F, LADY, 10/17/1867
1. CAPE DE VERDE IS. 2. U.S. 3. FLORES

DEANS, EDWARD, 25, M, TAILOR, 10/24/1842
1. ENGLAND 2. U.S. 3. LIVERPOOL

DEANS, JANE, 37, F, , 10/24/1842
1. 2. 3. LIVERPOOL

DEANS, JANE, 2, F, , 10/24/1842
1. 2. 3. LIVERPOOL

DEASEY, MARTHA, 21, F, SERVANT, 07/20/1844
1. NOVA SCOTIA 2. U.S. 3. PICTOU

DEBARROS, LOUIS J., 34, M, TAILOR, 08/28/1872
1. SAN MIQUEL 2. BOSTON 3.

DECLUSAR, JACOB M., 19, M, MERCHANT CLERK, 04/14/1828
1. HOLLAND 2. HOLLAND 3. OMOA

DEFRIETOS, JOSE, 30, M, FARMER, 08/28/1872
1. FLORES 2. BOSTON 3.

DEJESUS, ANNA, 20, F, SEAMSTRESS, 08/28/1872
1. FLORES 2. BOSTON 3.

DEJESUS, EMILA, 14, F, SEAMSTRESS, 08/28/1872
1. FLORES 2. BOSTON 3.

DEJESUS, MARIA, 19, F, SEAMSTRESS, 08/28/1872
1. FLORES 2. PROVIDENCE 3.

DEJESUS, MARIANA, 25, F, SEAMSTRESS, 08/28/1872
1. FLORES 2. PROVIDENCE 3.

DEJESUS, MARIANA, 20, F, SEAMSTRESS, 08/28/1872
1. FLORES 2. BOSTON 3.

DEJESUS, POHUINA, 22, F, SEAMSTRESS, 08/28/1872
1. FLORES 2. PROVIDENCE 3.

DEKOVEN, WILLIAM, 20, M, MIDSHIPMAN, U.S.N., 06/09/1847
1. U.S. 2. U.S. 3. MONROVIA

DELA NATCH, JOHN RODRIGARY, 19, M, GENTLEMAN, 05/19/1833
1. CUBA 2. U.S. 3. MATANZAS

DELANA, ANNA, 17, F, SERVANT, 08/20/1844
1. NOVA SCOTIA 2. U.S. 3. PICTOU

DELANA, ELISABETH, 19, F, SERVANT, 08/20/1844
1. NOVA SCOTIA 2. U.S. 3. PICTOU

DELANCY, THOMAS, 30, M, MINER, 06/23/1846
1. IRELAND 2. U.S. 3. PICTOU

DELANEY, MARGREA, 20, F, SERVANT GIRL, 09/02/1845
1. NOVA SCOTIA 2. U.S. 3. PICTOU

DELANEY, MARY ELIZABETH, 22, F, IN PURSUIT OF EMPLOY, 08/04/1841
1. BRITISH AMERICA 2. U.S. 3. PICTOU

DELANY, JOHN, 27, M, LABORER, 09/09/1857
1. U.S. 2. U.S. 3. WINSOR

DELAROCHE, CHARLES, , , CHILD OF MADAME DELAROCHE, 12/14/1823
1. NEW YORK 2. MARTINIQUE 3. PROVIDENCE

DELAROCHE, HIPPOLITE, , , CHILD OF MADAME DELAROCHE, 12/14/1823
1. NEW YORK 2. MARTINIQUE 3. PROVIDENCE

DELAROCHE, MADAME, , , , 12/14/1823
1. NEW YORK 2. MARTINIQUE 3. PROVIDENCE

DELENIER, ANN, 30, F, LADY, 09/20/1847
1. NOVA SCOTIA 2. U.S. 3. PICTOU

DELGADA, EMEBRA, 20, , , 05/18/1868
1. 2. 3. BRAVA

DELORIA, MRS. LOUISE, 19, , HOUSEKEEPER, 11/04/1869
1. U.S. 2. U.S. 3. SINGAN

DENISON, THOMAS, 22, , CLERK, 05/09/1837
1. IRELAND 2. NEW YORK 3. LIVERPOOL

DERBERRY, WILLIAM, 20, M, SEAMAN, 07/05/1836
1. U.S. 2. U.S. 3. HAVANA

DEROSOISO, MARIA, 20, F, SEAMSTRESS, 08/28/1872
1. FLORES 2. PROVIDENCE 3.

DESOUSA, JOSE, 35, M, MARINER, 08/28/1872
1. FLORES 2. PROVIDENCE 3.

DEVIOUS, EDWIN, 23, M, EQUESTRIAN, 05/08/1833
1. U.S. 2. U.S. 3. HAVANA

DEVITA, JOSE COELHO, 26, M, MARINER, 08/28/1872
1. FLORES 2. BOSTON 3.

DEWAR, MARGARET, 25, F, SERVANT, 07/11/1867
1. BRITISH AMERICA. 2. U.S. 3.

DEWAR, MARY, 20, F, SERVANT, 07/11/1867
1. BRITISH AMERICA 2. U.S. 3.

DEWER, NATHANIEL, 32, M, MECHANIC, 03/11/1841
1. U.S. 2. U.S. 3. HAVANA

DEWINT, JAMES D., 50, M, MERCHANT, 07/28/1826
1. DENMARK 2. DENMARK 3. CURACOA

DICKENSON, CHARLES, 23, M, SHOE MAKER, 06/14/1841
1. CORTLAND CO., NY 2. CORTLAND CO., NY 3. PICTOU,

DICKS, AMELIA, 17, F, , 07/08/1867
1. BRITISH AMERICA 2. U.S. 3. PICTOU

DICKS, AMELIA, 14, F, , 05/25/1861
1. PICTOU 2. U.S. 3. PICTOU

DICKS, ANN, 19, F, , 07/09/1860
1. NOVA SCOTIA 2. U.S. 3. PICTOU

DICKS, CHARLOTTE, 18, F, , 05/25/1861
1. PICTOU 2. U.S. 3. PICTOU

DICKS, CHRICHTON, 8, M, , 07/08/1867
1. BRITISH AMERICA 2. U.S. 3. PICTOU

DICKS, ELVINA, 44, F, , 05/25/1861
1. PICTOU 2. U.S. 3. PICTOU

DICKS, H.R., 12, M, , 05/25/1861
1. PICTOU 2. U.S. 3. PICTOU

DICKS, J. E., 3, M, , 05/25/1861
1. PICTOU 2. U.S. 3. PICTOU

DICKS, MRS. WILLIAM, 50, F, HOUSEKEEPER, 07/08/1867
1. BRITISH AMERICA 2. U.S. 3. PICTOU

DICKS, WILLIAM, 16, M, , 05/25/1861
1. PICTOU 2. U.S. 3. PICTOU

DIGOMES, ANTONIO, 30, M, MARINER, 1872
1. FLORES 2. BOSTON 3.

DIKEMANS, JR., JOHN, 27, M, MERCHANT, 08/14/1823
1. U.S. 2. U.S. 3. BUENOS AIRES

DILLABEN, JAMES, 18, M, ENGINEER, 06/04/1835
1. U.S. 2. U.S. 3. MATANZAS

DIMON, JOHN, 60, M, COOPER, 07/24/1848
1. U.S. 2. U.S. 3. MATANZAS

DINWON, JANE, 25, F, SERVANT, 09/09/1836
1. NOVA SCOTIA 2. U.S. 3. PICTOU

DITMORE, E.L., 23, M, MERCHANT, 09/11/1825
1. HAMBURG 2. HAMBURG 3. HONDURAS

DIVINE, CATHERINE, 20, , SERVANT, 05/09/1837
1. IRELAND 2. NEW YORK 3. LIVERPOOL

DIVINE, NOVEH, 26, , LABORER, 05/09/1837
1. IRELAND 2. NEW YORK 3. LIVERPOOL

DIX, ROPER, 11, M, , 08/13/1867
1. U.S. 2. U.S. 3. PICTOU

DIX, WILLIAM, 16, M, , 08/13/1867
1. U.S. 2. U.S. 3. PICTOU

DOBSEN, ALENA, 18, F, SERVANT, 09/18/1856
1. NOVA SCOTIA 2. U.S. 3. PICTOU

DODGE, MARY ANN, 24, F, LADY, 06/28/1849
1. U.S. 2. U.S. 3. PICTOU

DODGE, MARY JANE, 1, F, CHILD, 06/28/1849
1. U.S. 2. U.S. 3. PICTOU

DOGLORIO, MARIA, 19, F, SEAMSTRESS, 08/28/1872
1. FLORES 2. BOSTON 3.

DOLFIN, MARY, 22, , LABORER, 05/09/1837
1. IRELAND 2. U.S. 3. LIVERPOOL

DOLTON, MARIA, 6, F, CHILD, 09/23/1846
1. U.S. 2. U.S. 3. PICTOU

DOLTON, MARY, 33, F, LADY, 09/23/1846
1. U.S 2. U.S. 3. PICTOU

DOMATIOS, CHARLES, 28, M, MECHANIC, 05/16/1842
1. NORWAY 2. NORWAY 3. HAVANA

DONALDSON, HUGH, 21, M, SHOEMAKER, 09/09/1844
1. NOVA SCOTIA 2. U.S. 3. PICTOU

DOREGO, JOSE, 28, M, FARMER, 08/28/1872
1. SAN MIQUEL 2. PROVIDENCE 3.

DORONEN, HENRY O., 30, M, MERCHANT, 06/19/1844
1. U.S. 2. U.S. 3. LAGUIEVU, MEXICO, MEXICO

DORR, EDWARD, 35, M, MERCHANT, 10/18/1831
1. U.S. 2. U.S. 3. GOTENBURG

DORR, SAMUEL A., 48, M, MERCHANT, 07/12/1824
1. MASSACHUSETTS 2. MASSACHUSETTS 3. CANTON

DOTY, BENJAMIN, 44, M, COOPER, 04/08/1854
1. U.S. 2. U.S. 3.

DOTY, BENJAMIN F., 38, M, MECHANIC, 05/10/1842
1. U.S. 2. U.S. 3. MATANZAS

DOTY, GEORGE, 40, M, MECHANIC, 05/10/1842
1. U.S. 2. U.S. 3. MATANZAS

DOTY, GEORGE, 38, M, COOPER, 05/21/1838
1. N.A. 2. N.A. 3. MATANZAS

68   *RHODE ISLAND PASSENGER LISTS*

DOUGLAS, ADELAIDE, 19, F, , 08/23/1852
  1. BRITISH AMERICA 2. BRITISH AMERICA 3. PICTOU

DOUGLAS, DANL, 18, M, HOUSE CARPENTER, 06/03/1857
  1. NOVA SCOTIA 2. U.S. 3. PICTOU

DOUGLAS, JOHN, 18, M, BLACKSMITH, 06/28/1855
  1. NOVA SCOTIA 2. U.S. 3. PICTOU

DOUGLAS, JOHN, 19, M, NONE, 07/31/1857
  1. NOVA SCOTIA 2. NOVA SCOTIA 3. PICTOU

DOUGLAS, SARAH, 25, F, SERVANT, 05/29/1848
  1. BRITISH AMERICA 2. U.S. 3. PICTOU

DOULL, ALEXANDER, 56, M, FARMER, 10/03/1854
  1. NOVA SCOTIA 2. U.S. 3. PICTOU

DOULL, CATHARINE, 50, F, HOUSEWIFE, 10/03/1854
  1. NOVA SCOTIA 2. U.S. 3. PICTOU

DOULL, ELIZABETH, 24, F, NONE, 10/03/1854
  1. NOVA SCOTIA 2. U.S. 3. PICTOU

DOULL, JOUNAH G., 7, F, NONE, 10/03/1854
  1. NOVA SCOTIA 2. U.S. 3. PICTOU

DOULL, LEWIS, 17, M, NONE, 10/03/1854
  1. NOVA SCOTIA 2. U.S. 3. PICTOU

DOULL, MARGARET A., 11, F, NONE, 10/03/1854
  1. NOVA SCOTIA 2. U.S. 3. PICTOU

DOULL, ROBERT, 20, M, NONE, 10/03/1854
  1. NOVA SCOTIA 2. U.S. 3. PICTOU

DOULL, WILLIAM, 14, M, NONE, 10/03/1854
  1. NOVA SCOTIA 2. U.S. 3. PICTOU

DOUMARD, CHARLOTTE, 20, F, MILLINER, 10/10/1853
  1. GREAT BRITAIN 2. U.S. 3. PICTOU

DOWLS, CATHARINE, 20, F, SERVANT, 08/23/1850
  1. PICTOU 2. PROVIDENCE 3. PICTOU

DOWRY, JOHN, 60, M, NONE, 06/02/1856
  1. U.S. 2. U.S. 3. PICTOU

DOYLE, CATHARINE, 23, F, SERVANT, 09/16/1858
  1. NOVA SCOTIA 2. U.S. 3. PICTOU

DRAPER, GEORGE R., 27, M, MERCHANT, 06/18/1839
  1. U.S. 2. U.S. 3.

DRESCOTT, KINNE, 25, M, MECHANIC, 03/11/1841
1. U.S. 2. U.S. 3. HAVANA

DRISCOLL, SANDY, 21, M, LABORER, 07/08/1853
1. IRELAND 2. U.S. 3. NEWPORT, ENGLAND

DRIVER, GEORGE H., 17, M, , 04/03/1861
1. U.S. 2. 3. ZANZIBAR

DRUAULT, LOUIS, , , , 12/14/1823
1. PHILADELPHIA 2. ST. MARTINS 3. PROVIDENCE

DUARTES, JUAN PABLO, 16, M, CLERK, 07/02/1829
1. ST. DOMINGO, HAITI 2. HAVRE DE GRACE 3. ST. DOMINGO, HAITI

DUFFIE, ANN, 16, F, LABORER, 09/09/1847
1. IRELAND 2. CANADA 3. PICTOU

DUGAN, JOHN, 3, M, CHILD, 09/29/1848
1. BRITISH AMERICA 2. U.S. 3. PICTOU

DUGAN, MARY ANN, 24, F, LADY, 09/29/1848
1. BRITISH AMERICA 2. U.S. 3. PICTOU

DUNBAR, ELISABETH, 21, F, SERVANT, 07/20/1844
1. NOVA SCOTIA 2. U.S. 3. PICTOU

DUNCAN, ELISABETH, 20, F, , 07/11/1850
1. BRITISH AMERICA 2. U.S. 3. PICTOU

DUNHAM, CHARLES C., 38, , ENGINEER, 01/27/1842
1. U.S. 2. U.S. 3. MATANZAS

DUNHAM, JANE, 26, F, SERVANT, 08/20/1845
1. BRITISH AMERICA 2. U.S. 3. PICTOU

DUNN, MRS. EDWARD, 30, F, LADY, 09/19/1842
1. U.S. 2. U.S. 3. PICTOU

DUNNAHOE, THOS., 24, , LABORER, 05/09/1837
1. IRELAND 2. NEW YORK 3. LIVERPOOL

DUPYN, P., 27, M, MERCHANT, 08/25/1828
1. CURACOA 2. U.S. 3. CURACOA

DURFEY, PATRICK, 21, M, MECHANIC, 12/10/1851
1. BRITISH AMERICA 2. U.S. 3. PICTOU

DWYER, G. RYAN, 25, M, AMERICAN CONSUL, 07/08/1853
1. U.S. 2. U.S. 3. MOZAMBIQUE

DYER, ELLEN, 26, F, , 10/18/1837
1. U.S. 2. U.S. 3. PICTOU

DYER, MATHEW, 28, M, TANNER, 10/18/1837
1. U.S. 2. U.S. 3. PICTOU

EAMES, CUTLER, 21, M, MERCHANT, 03/23/1826
1. U.S. 2. U.S. 3. ST. JOHN

EARLEY, MARY, 60, F, LABORER, 09/18/1845
1. NOVA SCOTIA 2. U.S. 3. PICTOU

EASHERAN, ROWLAND, 28, M, BLACKSMITH, 09/15/1856
1. GREAT BRITAIN 2. U.S. 3. PICTOU

EASTERBROOKS, JOHN C., 40, M, MARINER, 07/08/1853
1. U.S. 2. U.S. 3. ZANZIBAR

EATHFORTH, SAM.L C., 35, M, COOPER, 06/04/1835
1. U.S. 2. U.S. 3. MATANZAS

ELDRIDGE, HERBERT R., 23, M, CARPENTER, 05/30/1860
1. MASSACHUSETTS 2. MASSACHUSETTS 3. PRINCE EDWARD ISLAND

ELLIOT, MRS. MARY, 60, F, , 05/22/1857
1. GREAT BRITAIN 2. U.S. 3. PICTOU

ELLIS, OREN, 30, M, CARPENTER, 04/25/1840
1. AMERICA 2. AMERICA 3. HAVANA

ELLISON, JONATHAN, 23, M, FARMER, 06/14/1841
1. HERKIMER CO., NY 2. HERKIMER CO., NY 3. PICTOU

ELTEZ, ANN, 42, F, , 06/30/1831
1. U.S. 2. U.S. 3. HAVANA

ELTEZ, PHILLIP, 42, M, TAILOR, 06/30/1831
1. U.S. 2. U.S. 3. HAVANA

ELTEZ, SUSAN, 7, F, , 06/30/1831
1. U.S. 2. U.S. 3. HAVANA

ELWELL, WILLIAM, 47, M, MARINER, 04/26/1834
1. U.S. 2. U.S. 3. HAVANA

EMANUEL, JOSEPH, 35, M, COOPER, 07/01/1822
1. HAVANA 2. U.S. 3. HAVANA

ENDICOTT, TIMOTHY, 36, M, MARINER, 04/16/1821
1. U.S. 2. U.S. 3. LISBON

ENGLISH, ANN, 22, F, , 06/05/1860
1. NOVA SCOTIA 2. U.S. 3. PICTOU

ENGLISH, MARGARET, 20, F, , 06/05/1860
1. NOVA SCOTIA 2. U.S. 3. PICTOU

ENGLISH, MICHAEL, 23, M, BLACK MAKER, 08/07/1855
1. NOVA SCOTIA 2. U.S. 3. PICTOU

ERDALL, JAMES, 26, M, MARINER, 12/11/1822
1. U.S. 2. U.S. 3. GIBRALTAR

ETHFORTH, SAML., 45, M, COOPER, 07/03/1839
1. U.S. 2. U.S. 3. MATANZAS

ETTOZ, PHILLIP, 32, M, TAILOR, 05/19/1839
1. U.S. 2. U.S. 3. HAVANA

EVANS, FRANCIS L., 34, M, MERCHANT, 10/16/1824
1. IRELAND 2. U.S. 3. SURINAM

EVANS, HUGH M., 30, M, MASTER MARINER, 07/19/1858
1. U.S. 2. U.S. 3. PICTOU

FAIN, MARY, 21, F, SERVANT, 09/09/1844
1. NOVA SCOTIA 2. U.S. 3. PICTOU

FALCONER, JAMES W., 19, M, JOINER, 11/02/1850
1. BRITISH AMERICA 2. U.S. 3. PICTOU

FALES, BARNABAS, 30, M, MERCHANT, 07/11/1827
1. U.S. 2. U.S. 3. HAVANA

FALES, LEWIS F., 28, M, MERCHANT, 06/13/1836
1. U.S. 2. U.S. 3. HAVANA

FALES, MRS. ANNE G., 26, F, LADY, 04/28/1842
1. U.S. 2. U.S. 3. MATANZAS

FANON, ROBERT, 20, M, MILLER, 07/20/1844
1. NOVA SCOTIA 2. U.S. 3. PICTOU

FARA, PETER, 13, M, SERVANT, 07/24/1848
1. CUBA 2. CUBA 3. MATANZAS

FARREL, JOHN, 34, , LABORER, 05/09/1837
1. IRELAND 2. NEW YORK 3. LIVERPOOL

FARREL, JOHN, 13, , CHILD, 05/09/1837
1. IRELAND 2. NEW YORK 3. LIVERPOOL

FARWELL, JOHN N., 40, M, MARINER, 08/06/1836
1. U.S. 2. 3. HAVANA

FATKIN, WILLIAM, 25, M, MINER, 06/23/1846
1. SCOTLAND 2. U.S. 3. PICTOU

FATKINS, JANE, 2, F, CHILDREN, 06/23/1846
1. SCOTLAND 2. U.S. 3. PICTOU

FATKINS, JOHN, 6, M, CHILDREN, 06/23/1846
1. SCOTLAND 2. U.S. 3. PICTOU

FATKINS, MARGARET, 27, F, LADY, 06/23/1846
1. SCOTLAND 2. U.S. 3. PICTOU

FELIPIPE, MANUEL, 40, M, MARINER, 08/28/1872
1. FLORES 2. BOSTON 3.

FELIX, AMELIA, 6, F, , 03/08/1833
1. U.S. 2. U.S. 3. HAVANA

FELIX, HENRY, 33, M, PLANTER, 03/08/1833
1. SPAIN 2. U.S. 3. HAVANNA

FELIX, JOAN, 18, F, , 03/08/1833
1. U.S. 2. U.S. 3. HAVANA

FELIX, JOHN, 3, M, , 03/08/1833
1. U.S. 2. U.S. 3. HAVANA

FELIX, NANCY, 30, F, , 03/08/1833
1. U.S. 2. U.S. 3. HAVANA

FELIX, SERVIS, 6 MONTHS, M, , 03/08/1833
1. U.S. 2. U.S. 3. HAVANA

FELLEN, CATHERINE, 24, , LABORER, 05/09/1837
1. IRELAND 2. NEW YORK 3. LIVERPOOL

FELT, JOHNSON, 21, M, MARINER, 04/16/1821
1. U.S. 2. U.S. 3. LISBON

FENCIN, BRIDGETT, 21, F, , 08/17/1850
1. PICTOU 2. U.S. 3. PICTOU

FENESEY, MARGARET, 26, F, HOUSE MAID, 09/17/1860
1. NOVA SCOTIA 2. U.S. 3. PICTOU

FENNER, MISS, 18, F, , 06/07/1841
1. U.S. 2. 3. HAVANA

FENNESY, ANN, 26, F, SERVANTS OR ASSISTANTS, 10/01/1853
1. NOVA SCOTIA 2. U.S. 3. PICTOU

FERAND, GEORGE, 25, M, MERCHANT, 05/28/1823
1. FRANCE 2. U.S. 3. RIO DE JANEIRO

FERNANDES, ANTONIO, 28, M, FARMER, 08/28/1872
1. FLORES 2. BOSTON 3.

FERNANDEZ, EDWARD, 21, M, GENTLEMAN, 07/22/1822
1. CUBA 2. CUBA 3. HAVANA

FERNANDEZ, RICHD CORNELIUS, 11, M, MINOR, 11/02/1830
1. SPAIN 2. U.S. IN SCHOOL 3. HAVANA

FERNANDEZ, SUSAN, 27, , , 05/18/1868
1. 2. 3. BRAVA

FILOMINA, MARIA, 20, F, SEAMSTRESS, 08/28/1872
1. FLORES 2. PROVIDENCE 3.

FINNAY, EDWARD, 25, M, LABORER, 05/30/1837
1. NOVESCATAY 2. U.S. 3. PICTOU

FINTON, CATHERINE, 26, , WIFE, 05/09/1837
1. IRELAND 2. NEW YORK 3. LIVERPOOL

FINTON, JAMES, 7, , CHILD, 05/09/1837
1. IRELAND 2. NEW YORK 3. LIVERPOOL

FINTON, STEPHEN, 13, , CHILD, 05/09/1837
1. IRELAND 2. NEW YORK 3. LIVERPOOL

FINTON, THOMAS, 37, M, LABORER, 05/09/1837
1. IRELAND 2. NEW YORK 3. LIVERPOOL

FINTON, THOMAS, 5, , CHILD, 05/09/1837
1. IRELAND 2. NEW YORK 3. LIVERPOOL

FINTON, TIMOTHY, 11, , CHILD, 05/09/1837
1. IRELAND 2. NEW YORK 3. LIVERPOOL

FISHER, J. ARCH, 19, M, NONE, 10/07/1857
1. NOVA SCOTIA 2. U.S. 3. PICTOU

FITZCALD, MORRA, 18, F, , 09/27/1837
1. 2. 3. PICTOU

FITZPATRICK, CATHARINE, 18, F, LADY, 06/28/1849
1. BRITISH AMERICA 2. U.S. 3. PICTOU

FITZPATRICK, JANE, 19, F, , 07/09/1860
1. NOVA SCOTIA 2. U.S. 3. PICTOU

FLEMING, ANDREW, 26, M, SEAMAN, 11/20/1854
1. GREAT BRITAIN 2. GREAT BRITAIN 3. TURKS ISLAND

FLEMING, MARY J., 22, F, SERVANT, 11/07/1870
1. ARICHAT 2. U.S. 3. ARICHAT

FLETCHER, NATHAN P., 43, M, ATTORNEY, 09/04/1828
1. U.S. 2. U.S. 3. LIVERPOOL

FLIN, DANL., 35, , LABORER, 05/09/1837
1. IRELAND 2. NEW YORK 3. LIVERPOOL

FLIN, ELLEN, 14, , CHILD, 05/09/1837
 1. IRELAND 2. NEW YORK 3. LIVERPOOL

FLIN, MARGARET, 10, , CHILD, 05/09/1837
 1. IRELAND 2. NEW YORK 3. LIVERPOOL

FLIN, MICHEAL, 19, , CLERK, 05/09/1837
 1. IRELAND 2. NEW YORK 3. LIVERPOOL

FLINN, WILLIAM, 24, M, LABORER, 08/05/1858
 1. NOVA SCOTIA 2. U.S. 3. PICTOU

FOLEY, CATHARINE, 21, F, SERVANT, 09/27/1852
 1. BRITISH AMERICA 2. U.S. 3. PICTOU

FOLEY, ELISABETH, 25, F, SERVANT, 07/03/1851
 1. BRITISH AMERICA 2. U.S. 3. PICTOU

FOLEY, MARTIN, 31, M, MINER, 08/03/1857
 1. NOVA SCOTIA 2. NOVA SCOTIA 3. PICTOU

FOLLEY, ROSY, 26, , SERVANT, 05/09/1837
 1. IRELAND 2. U.S. 3. LIVERPOOL

FONTANA, EUGENIA, 35, F, LADY, 10/17/1867
 1. CAPE DE VERDE IS. 2. U.S. 3. FLORES

FORBES, ANNA, 22, F, LADY, 06/28/1849
 1. U.S. 2. U.S. 3. PICTOU

FORBES, ANNE, 20, F, SERVANT GIRL, 09/02/1845
 1. NOVA SCOTIA 2. U.S. 3. PICTOU

FORBES, C.G., 20, F, TRAV---, 08/31/1872
 1. NOVA SCOTIA 2. U.S. 3.

FORBES, C.J., 25, F, HOUSEKEEPER, 08/31/1872
 1. NOVA SCOTIA 2. U.S. 3.

FORBES, CHRISTINA, 20, , SERVANT, 09/01/1867
 1. 2. 3. PICTOU

FORBES, DANIEL, 21, M, MILLER, 08/05/1856
 1. NOVA SCOTIA 2. U.S. 3. PICTOU

FORBES, JOHN, 22, M, SHOE MAKER, 05/30/1860
 1. PRINCE EDWARD ISLAND 2. OREGON 3. PRINCE EDWARD ISLAND

FORBES, JOHN W., 26, M, HOUSE CARPENTER, 08/27/1860
 1. NOVA SCOTIA 2. U.S. 3. PICTOU

FORBES, JULIET, 20, F, HOUSE SERVANT, 07/07/1865
 1. BRITISH AMERICA 2. U.S. 3. PICTOU

FORBES, KENNETH D., 24, M, HOUSE CARPENTER, 08/27/1860
1. NOVA SCOTIA 2. U.S. 3. PICTOU

FORBES, MARY ANN, 25, , SERVANT, 09/01/1867
1. NOVA SCOTIA 2. U.S. 3. PICTOU

FORBES, RUTH, 21, F, SERVANT, 06/24/1856
1. NOVA SCOTIA 2. U.S. 3. PICTOU

FORBIS, MARGARET, 18, F, SERVANT, 09/09/1844
1. NOVA SCOTIA 2. U.S. 3. PICTOU

FORTADO, FRANCISCO, 30, M, MARINER, 08/28/1872
1. FLORES 2. CALIFORNIA 3.

FOSTER, (INFANT), 1, F, CHILD, 07/03/1845
1. BRITISH AMERICA 2. U.S. 3. PICTOU

FOSTER, ANN, 21, F, SERVANT, 09/09/1844
1. NOVA SCOTIA 2. U.S. 3. PICTOU

FOSTER, CATHARINE, 17, F, LADY, 07/03/1845
1. BRITISH AMERICA 2. U.S. 3. PICTOU

FOSTER, CATHARINE, 19, F, SERVANT, 08/20/1857
1. NOVA SCOTIA 2. NOVA SCOTIA 3. PICTOU

FOSTER, CATHARINE, 22, F, HOUSE MAID, 09/17/1860
1. NOVA SCOTIA 2.'U.S. 3. PICTOU

FOSTER, CHARLES, 12, M, LAD, 07/03/1845
1. BRITISH AMERICA 2. U.S. 3. PICTOU

FOSTER, DANIEL, 19, M, SHIP WRIGHT, 09/09/1844
1. NOVA SCOTIA 2. U.S. 3. PICTOU

FOSTER, DANIEL, 21, M, SHIP CARPENTER, 06/23/1846
1. BRITISH AMERICA 2. U.S. 3. PICTOU

FOSTER, DAVID, 22, M, , 08/17/1850
1. PICTOU 2. U.S. 3. PICTOU

FOSTER, GEORGE, 48, M, CARPENTER, 07/20/1844
1. NOVA SCOTIA 2. U.S. 3. PICTOU

FOSTER, GEORGE, 15, M, LAD, 07/03/1845
1. BRITISH AMERICA 2. U.S. 3. PICTOU

FOSTER, HENRY, 30, M, SHIP WRIGHT, 11/11/1844
1. NOVA SCOTIA 2. U.S. 3. PICTOU

FOSTER, HENRY, 10, M, LAD, 07/03/1845
1. BRITISH AMERICA 2. U.S 3. PICTOU

FOSTER, JANE, 18, F, SERVANT, 09/09/1844
 1. NOVA SCOTIA 2. U.S. 3. PICTOU

FOSTER, JOHN, 22, M, CARPENTER, 07/20/1844
 1. NOVA SCOTIA 2. U.S. 3. PICTOU

FOSTER, MARGARET, 37, F, LADY, 07/03/1845
 1. BRITISH AMERICA 2. U.S. 3. PICTOU

FOSTER, MARY, 4, F, CHILD, 07/03/1845
 1. BRITISH AMERICA 2. U.S. 3. PICTOU

FOSTER, MARY ANN, 25, F, DRESS MAKER, 08/13/1855
 1. NOVA SCOTIA 2. U.S. 3. PICTOU

FOSTER, THOMAS, 26, M, , 08/17/1850
 1. PICTOU 2. U.S. 3. PICTOU

FOSTER, WALTER, 11, M, LAD, 07/03/1845
 1. BRITISH AMERICA 2. U.S. 3. PICTOU

FOSTER, WILLIAM, 25, M, SHIP CARPENTER, 06/03/1844
 1. NOVA SCOTIA 2. U.S. 3. PICTOU

FOSTER, WILLIAM, 50, M, SHIP WRIGHT, 11/11/1844
 1. NOVA SCOTIA 2. U.S. 3. PICTOU

FOSTER, WILLIAM, 25, M, CARPENTER, 07/02/1845
 1. NOVA SCOTIA 2. UNKNOWN 3. PICTOU

FOSTER, WILLIAM, 25, M, CARPENTER, 08/05/1847
 1. BRITISH AMERICA 2. U.S. 3. PICTOU

FOSTER, WILLIAM, 24, M, CARPENTER, 08/05/1847
 1. BRITISH AMERICA 2. U.S. 3. PICTOU

FOWLER, JANE, , , , 12/14/1823
 1. NEW HAVEN 2. BARBADOS/DEMERARA 3. PROVIDENCE

FOX, PAT., 23, , LABORER, 05/09/1837
 1. IRELAND 2. U.S. 3. LIVERPOOL

FRADING, JOHN P., 20, M, MERCHANT, 08/17/1820
 1. SWEDEN 2. U.S. 3. GOTENBURG

FRAIGNEAU, ALEXANDER, 32, M, MERCHANT, 04/16/1827
 1. FRANCE 2. FRANCE 3. MATANZAS

FRANCHAL, CHARLES, 24, M, GENTLEMAN, 10/27/1834
 1. U.S. 2. 3. PICTOU

FRANCIS, ROSANNA, 26, F, , 04/15/1824
 1. U.S. 2. U.S. 3. HAVANA

FRANCISCO, MANUEL, 21, M, FARMER, 08/28/1872
1. FLORES 2. BOSTON 3.

FRANCOIS AMCILL, JEAN BAPTISTE, , , , 12/14/1823
1. NEW YORK 2. MARTINIQUE 3. PROVIDENCE

FRANK, CHARLES, 34, M, ENGINEER, 07/07/1846
1. NEW YORK 2. NEW YORK 3. MATANZAS

FRASER, ALEXANDER, 28, M, CARPENTER, 07/20/1844
1. NOVA SCOTIA 2. U.S. 3. PICTOU

FRASER, AMELIA, 25, F, NONE, 08/27/1846
1. NOVA SCOTIA 2. U.S. 3. PICTOU

FRASER, ANN, 22, F, , 09/19/1851
1. U.S. 2. U.S. 3. PICTOU

FRASER, ANN B., 15, F, DRESS MAKER, 09/05/1846
1. PICTOU 2. U.S. 3. PICTOU

FRASER, ANNIE, 38, F, HOUSE MAID, 09/17/1860
1. NOVA SCOTIA 2. U.S. 3. PICTOU

FRASER, CATHARINE, 23, F, , 08/17/1850
1. PICTOU 2. U.S. 3. PICTOU

FRASER, CATHERINE, 43, F, LADY, 07/02/1844
1. NOVA SCOTIA 2. NOVA SCOTIA 3. PICTOU

FRASER, CHARLES, 35, M, FARMER, 08/16/1859
1. NOVA SCOTIA 2. NOVA SCOTIA 3. PICTOU

FRASER, CHRISTIANNA, 36, F, LADY, 06/16/1845
1. BRITISH AMERICA 2. U.S. 3. PICTOU

FRASER, CHRISTINA, 23, , SERVANT, 08/31/1869
1. BRITISH AMERICA 2. U.S. 3. PICTOU

FRASER, EDWARD, 19, M, CARPENTER, 10/12/1846
1. 2. 3. PICTOU

FRASER, ELEZABETH, 2, F, , 06/23/1857
1. PICTOU 2. BOSTON 3. PICTOU

FRASER, ELISABETH ANN, 23, F, LADY, 06/16/1845
1. BRITISH AMERICA 2. U.S. 3. PICTOU

FRASER, ELIZABETH, 20, F, , 07/29/1846
1. 2. RHODE ISLAND 3. PICTOU

FRASER, ISABELLA, 20, F, SERVANT, 07/20/1844
1. NOVA SCOTIA 2. U.S. 3. PICTOU

FRASER, ISABELLA, 22, F, SERVANT, 05/29/1848
1. BRITISH AMERICA 2. U.S. 3. PICTOU

FRASER, ISABELLA, 26, F, HOUSE MAID, 09/17/1860
1. NOVA SCOTIA 2. U.S. 3. PICTOU

FRASER, JAMES, 21, M, TAILOR, 10/14/1846
1. NOVA SCOTIA 2. U.S. 3. PICTOU

FRASER, JAMES, 39, M, LABOUR, 05/22/1857
1. GREAT BRITAIN 2. U.S. 3. PICTOU

FRASER, JAMES D.B., 38, M, CHEMIST, 06/16/1845
1. BRITISH AMERICA 2. U.S. 3. PICTOU

FRASER, JANE, 28, F, LADY, 07/20/1844
1. NOVA SCOTIA 2. U.S. 3. PICTOU

FRASER, JANE, 30, F, HOUSE MAID, 09/17/1860
1. NOVA SCOTIA 2. U.S. 3. PICTOU

FRASER, JESSE, 33, F, SEAMAN, 10/03/1853
1. PICTOU 2. U.S. 3. PICTOU

FRASER, JESSE, 16, F, SERVANT, 07/12/1864
1. BRITISH AMERICA 2. U.S. 3. PICTOU

FRASER, JESSIE, 25, F, TAILORESS, 08/17/1850
1. PICTOU 2. U.S. 3. PICTOU

FRASER, JESSY, 25, F, SERVANT, 07/03/1845
1. BRITISH AMERICA 2. U.S. 3. PICTOU

FRASER, JOHN, 18, M, CARPENTER, 07/20/1844
1. NOVA SCOTIA 2. U.S. 3. PICTOU

FRASER, JOHN, 20, M, BLACKSMITH, 07/31/1857
1. NOVA SCOTIA 2. NOVA SCOTIA 3. PICTOU

FRASER, JOHN R.P., 20, M, GENTLEMAN, 06/16/1845
1. BRITISH AMERICA 2. U.S. 3. PICTOU

FRASER, MARGARET, 41, F, LADY, 07/02/1844
1. NOVA SCOTIA 2. NOVA SCOTIA 3. PICTOU

FRASER, MARGARET, 24, F, , 06/23/1857
1. PICTOU 2. PROVIDENCE 3. PICTOU

FRASER, MARY, 30, F, SERVANT, 05/29/1848
1. BRITISH AMERICA 2. U.S. 3. PICTOU

FRASER, MARY, 25, F, , 05/22/1857
1. GREAT BRITAIN 2. U.S. 3. PICTOU

FRASER, MARY ANN, 2, F, , 06/23/1857
1. PICTOU 2. BOSTON 3. PICTOU

FRASER, MARY ANN, 4, F, , 06/05/1860
1. NOVA SCOTIA 2. U.S. 3. PICTOU

FRASER, MARY C, 21, F, HOUSSE MAID, 09/17/1860
1. NOVA SCOTIA 2. U.S. 3. PICTOU

FRASER, SARAH, 15, F, HOUSE MAID, 09/17/1860
1. NOVA SCOTIA 2. U.S. 3. PICTOU

FRASER, WILLIAM, 29, M, FARMER, 06/16/1845
1. BRITISH AMERICA 2. U.S. 3. PICTOU

FRASER, WM., 24, M, SHIP CARPENTER, 11/05/1834
1. NOVA SCOTIA 2. PAWTUCKET, MASS 3. PICTOU

FRASHER, WM., 29, M, FARMER, 11/03/1835
1. HALIFAX 2. FALL RIVER 3. PICTOU

FRAZER, ANN, 22, F, SERVANT, 07/26/1855
1. NOVA SCOTIA 2. U.S. 3. PICTOU

FRAZER, ANN, 19, F, HOUSE SERVANT, 06/02/1856
1. NOVA SCOTIA 2. NOVA SCOTIA 3. PICTOU

FRAZER, ANNIE, 16, F, , 08/14/1860
1. NOVA SCOTIA 2. U.S. 3. PICTOU

FRAZER, CATHARINE, 35, F, SERVANT, 09/20/1851
1. BRITISH AMERICA 2. U.S. 3. PICTOU

FRAZER, DAVID, 45, M, CARPENTER, 07/07/1851
1. NOVA SCOTIA 2. U.S. 3. PICTOU

FRAZER, ELISABETH, 37, F, LADY, 07/07/1851
1. NOVA SCOTIA 2. U.S. 3. PICTOU

FRAZER, ELIZABETH, 32, F, , 06/05/1860
1. NOVA SCOTIA 2. U.S. 3. PICTOU

FRAZER, HENRY, 19, M, DRUGGIST, 04/28/1860
1. NOVA SCOTIA 2. U.S. 3. PICTOU

FRAZER, HUGH, 60, M, MARINER, 11/04/1851
1. BRITISH AMERICA 2. U.S. 3. PICTOU

FRAZER, JANE, 24, F, SERVANT GIRL, 10/03/1853
1. PICTOU 2. U.S. 3. PICTOU

FRAZER, JOHN, 32, M, SHIP CARPENTER, 07/01/1858
1. GREAT BRITAIN 2. U.S. 3. PICTOU

FRAZER, MARGARET, 39, F, , 09/20/1851
1. U.S. 2. U.S. 3. PICTOU

FRAZER, MARGARET, 20, F, SERVANT, 07/03/1851
1. BRITISH AMERICA 2. U.S. 3. PICTOU

FRAZER, MARGARET, 19, F, , 06/05/1860
1. NOVA SCOTIA 2. U.S. 3. PICTOU

FRAZER, MARTHA A., 18, F, LADY, 08/18/1849
1. BRITISH AMERICA 2. U.S. 3. PICTOU

FRAZER, MARY, 5, F, NONE, 09/15/1854
1. NOVA SCOTIA 2. U.S. 3. PICTOU

FRAZER, SARAH C, 19, F, CHAMBER MAID, 09/20/1851
1. U.S. 2. U.S. 3. PICTOU

FRAZIER, ALEXA, 20, M, NONE, 06/11/1847
1. PICTOU 2. U.S. 3. PICTOU

FRAZIER, CHRISTY, 28, F, LADY, 06/28/1849
1. BRITISH AMERICA 2. U.S. 3. PICTOU

FRAZIER, JANE, 32, F, SERVANT, 08/30/1855
1. NOVA SCOTIA 2. U.S. 3. PICTOU

FRAZIER, ROBERT, 17, M, NONE, 06/11/1847
1. PICTOU 2. U.S. 3. PICTOU

FREEBORN, JAMES G., 27, , CARPENTER, 04/20/1841
1. BRISTOL, RI 2. 3. MATANZAS

FREEMAN, ASA, 34, M, MACHINIST, 06/04/1858
1. U.S. 2. U.S. 3. MATANZAS

FREITAS, JOSE F., 32, M, MARINER, 08/28/1872
1. FLORES 2. PROVIDENCE 3.

FREITAS, JOSE F., 30, M, MARINER, 08/28/1872
1. FLORES 2. BOSTON 3.

FREITAS, MANUEL C., 31, M, MARINER, 08/28/1872
1. FLORES 2. BOSTON 3.

FREITAS, MANUEL M., 30, M, MARINER, 08/28/1872
1. FLORES 2. BOSTON 3.

FRENCH, G. W., 21, M, PHYSICIAN, 07/05/1825
1. ANTIQUA 2. ENGLAND 3. ANTIQUA

FRETAS, ANTONIO, 20, M, MARINER, 08/28/1872
1. FLORES 2. PROVIDENCE 3.

FREY, SAMUEL, 45, M, COOPER, 05/08/1838
1. U.S. 2. U.S. 3. HAVANA

FRODING, JOHN PETER, 22, M, MERCHANT, 05/07/1822
1. SWEDEN 2. U.S. 3. GOTENBURG

FROST, JOHN, 25, M, CARPENTER, 04/14/1825
1. U.S. 2. U.S. 3. HAVANA

FROST, JOSHUA, 39, M, MACHINE MAKER, 06/13/1827
1. U.S. 2. U.S. 3. HAVANA

FROTH, GEORGE A., 24, M, CARPENTER, 08/13/1829
1. U.S. 2. U.S. 3. MATANZAS

FULENTON, JOHN, 16, M, , 05/22/1857
1. GREAT BRITAIN 2. U.S. 3. PICTOU

FULLERTON, JESSIE, 18, F, SERVANT, 09/08/1862
1. PICTOU 2. PROVIDENCE 3. PICTOU

FULLERTON, MARY JANE, 23, , SERVANT, 08/31/1869
1. BRITISH AMERICA 2. U.S. 3. PICTOU

FURLING, ALFRED, 7, M, SERVICE, 08/10/1838
1. 2. 3. PICTOU

FURLING, JAMES, 40, M, SHIP CARPENTER, 08/10/1838
1. 2. 3. PICTOU

FURLING, JAMES, 3, M, , 08/10/1838
1. 2. 3. PICTOU

FURLING, MARTHA, 9, F, SERVICE, 08/10/1838
1. 2. 3. PICTOU

FURLING, MAY, 36, F, SERVICE, 08/10/1838
1. 2. 3. PICTOU

GAISFORD, ANN, 39, F, HOUSEWIFE, 08/03/1855
1. GREAT BRITAIN 2. U.S. 3. LIVERPOOL

GAISFORD, ANN, 6, F, NONE, 08/03/1855
1. GREAT BRITAIN 2. U.S. 3. LIVERPOOL

GAISFORD, ANN, , F, INFANT, 08/03/1855
1. GREAT BRITAIN 2. U.S. 3. LIVERPOOL

GAISFORD, DORCAS, 2, F, NONE, 08/03/1855
1. GREAT BRITAIN 2. U.S. 3. LIVERPOOL

GAISFORD, EMMA, 16, F, SERVANT, 08/03/1855
1. GREAT BRITAIN 2. U.S. 3. LIVERPOOL

GAISFORD, JAMES, 7, M, NONE, 08/03/1855
1. GREAT BRITAIN 2. U.S. 3. LIVERPOOL

GAISFORD, MARTHA, , F, INFANT, 08/03/1855
1. GREAT BRITAIN 2. U.S. 3. LIVERPOOL

GAISFORD, SARAH, 35, F, HOUSEWIFE, 08/03/1855
1. GREAT BRITAIN 2. U.S. 3. LIVERPOOL

GAISFORD, WILLIAM, 5, M, NONE, 08/03/1855
1. GREAT BRITAIN 2. U.S. 3. LIVERPOOL

GALE, O.M., 28, M, MERCHANT, 04/02/1827
1. BOSTON 2. 3. HAVANA

GALLAY, GEORGE, 36, M, MINER, 08/08/1837
1. IRELAND 2. U.S. 3. HAVANA

GALVAO, MARIA G., 34, F, SEAMSTRESS, 08/28/1872
1. SAN MIQUEL 2. BOSTON 3.

GAMBOA, CONSTANCIA PREI, 22, F, LADY, 10/17/1867
1. CAPE DE VERDE IS. 2. U.S. 3. FLORES

GAMBOA, JURURA PREIRA, 40, F, LADY, 10/17/1867
1. CAPE DE VERDE IS. 2. U.S. 3. FLORES

GARCIA, J.C., 34, M, MERCHANT, 05/23/1831
1. SPAIN 2. U.S. 3. HAVANA

GARCIA, JOSE, 20, M, FARMER, 08/28/1872
1. FLORES 2. BOSTON 3.

GARCIA, JOSE M., 30, M, MERCHANT, 04/01/1839
1. HAVANA 2. ON A VISIT 3. HAVANA

GARCIA, MANUEL, 32, M, PHYSICIAN, 11/11/1828
1. SPAIN 2. SPAIN 3. HAVANA

GARSIDE, AMICASSA, 11, M, BOY, 10/04/1827
1. ST. DOMINGO 2. ST. DOMINGO 3. PUERTA PLATA

GARVEY, ALEXANDER, 10, M, , 10/10/1853
1. GREAT BRITAIN 2. GREAT BRITAIN 3. PICTOU

GARVEY, ANDREW, 3, M, , 10/10/1853
1. GREAT BRITAIN 2. GREAT BRITAIN 3. PICTOU

GARVEY, ARCHIBALD, 12, M, , 10/10/1853
1. GREAT BRITAIN 2. GREAT BRTIAIN 3. PICTOU

GARVEY, DAVID, 8, M, , 10/10/1853
1. GREAT BRITAIN 2. GREAT BRITAIN 3. PICTOU

GASKELL, GEOG. L., 21, M, CLERK, 08/21/1861
1. U.S. 2. U.S. 3. ZANZIBAR

GASPAR, JOSE, 18, M, FARMER, 08/28/1872
1. FLORES 2. PROVIDENCE 3.

GASS, MARY M., 25, F, , 06/27/1849
1. 2. 3. PICTOU

GAY, JAMES, 3, , CHILD, 05/09/1837
1. IRELAND 2. NEW YORK 3. LIVERPOOL

GAY, JUDITH, 25, , WIFE, 05/09/1837
1. IRELAND 2. NEW YORK 3. LIVERPOOL

GAY, PETER, 26, , GROOM, 05/09/1837
1. IRELAND 2. NEW YORK 3. LIVERPOOL

GELDANE, CARNIE, 20, F, VISITOR, 08/24/1870
1. PICTOU 2. U.S. 3. PICTOU

GERARD, NANCY, 16, F, LADY, 09/20/1847
1. NOVA SCOTIA 2. U.S. 3. PICTOU

GERREGAR, ANDROS, 14, M, GENTLEMAN, 07/18/1839
1. CUBA 2. RHODE ISLAND 3. HAVANA

GERREGAR, HOSA, 17, M, GENTLEMAN, 07/18/1839
1. CUBA 2. RHODE ISLAND 3. HAVANA

GERRISH, ANDREW D., 22, M, MECHANIC, 05/22/1837
1. PORTSMOUTH 2. U.S. 3. MATANZAS

GEYER, RODOLPE C., 24, M, MERCHANT, 08/14/1823
1. U.S. 2. U.S. 3. BUENOS AIRES

GIBSON, MR., 31, M, MECHANIC, 03/22/1837
1. U.S. 2. U.S. 3. HAVANA

GIDDINGS, ANNA, 15, F, LADY, 06/28/1849
1. BRITISH AMERICA 2. U.S. 3. PICTOU

GIDDINGS, EDWIN, 9, M, FARMER, 06/28/1849
1. BRITISH AMERICA 2. U.S. 3. PICTOU

GIDDINGS, ISAAC, 9, M, FARMER, 06/28/1849
1. BRITISH AMERICA 2. U.S. 3. PICTOU

GIDDINGS, JACOB, 1, M, CHILD, 06/28/1849
1. BRITISH AMERICA 2. U.S. 3. PICTOU

GIDDINGS, JOHN, 7, M, CHILD, 06/28/1849
1. BRITISH AMERICA 2. U.S. 3. PICTOU

GIDDINGS, JOSEPH, 50, M, GUNSMITH, 08/23/1845
1. BRITISH AMERICA 2. U.S. 3. PICTOU

GIDDINGS, RACHAEL, 5, F, CHILD, 06/28/1849
1. BRITISH AMERICA 2. U.S. 3. PICTOU

GIDDINGS, RACHAL, 32, F, LADY, 06/28/1849
1. BRITISH AMERICA 2. U.S. 3. PICTOU

GIDDINGS, SILVIA, 20, F, LADY, 08/23/1845
1. BRITISH AMERICA 2. U.S. 3. PICTOU

GIDDINGS, THOMAS, 37, M, BLACKSMITH, 06/28/1849
1. BRITISH AMERICA 2. U.S. 3. PICTOU

GIDDINGS, THOMAS, 13, M, FARMER, 06/28/1849
1. BRITISH AMERICA 2. U.S. 3. PICTOU

GIDDINGS, WILLIAM, 3, M, CHILD, 06/28/1849
1. BRITISH AMERICA 2. U.S. 3. PICTOU

GIFFORD, FREDERICK, 28, M, ENGINEER, 05/13/1839
1. U.S. 2. U.S. 3. MATANZAS

GIFFORD, SYLVANUS, 29, M, SEAMAN, 10/31/1854
1. U.S. 2. U.S. 3. BOMBAY, ADEN AND ZANZIBAR

GILDERMASTER, CHARLES A., 41, M, MERCHANT, 07/14/1829
1. BREMEN 2. UNCERTAIN 3. HAVANA

GILFILLIN, BETSEY, 20, F, LADY, 07/27/1845
1. BRITISH AMERICA 2. U.S. 3. PICTOU

GILFILLIN, JAMES, 53, M, FARMER, 07/27/1845
1. BRITISH AMERICA 2. U.S. 3. PICTOU

GILFILLIN, JANE, 10, F, CHILD, 07/27/1845
1. BRITISH AMERICA 2. U.S. 3. PICTOU

GILFILLIN, JANET, 63, F, LADY, 07/27/1845
1. BRITISH AMERICA 2. U.S. 3. PICTOU

GILFILLIN, WILLIAM, 26, M, FARMER, 07/27/1845
1. BRITISH AMERICA 2. U.S. 3. PICTOU

GILL, THOMAS, 29, M, MERCHANT, 08/14/1860
1. NOVA SCOTIA 2. U.S. 3. PICTOU

GILLESPIE, JOHN, 28, M, WHEELWRIGHT, 07/19/1824
1. U.S. 2. U.S. 3. HAVANA

GILLETT, PHILANDER, 23, M, EXHIBITOR OF WILD ANIMALS, 06/29/1826
1. U.S. 2. U.S. 3. HAVANA

GILLIGAN, BRIDGET, 32, , WIFE, 05/09/1837
1. IRELAND 2. U.S. 3. LIVERPOOL

GILLIGAN, MARY, 8, , CHILD, 05/09/1837
1. IRELAND 2. U.S. 3. LIVERPOOL

GILLIGAN, MICHEL, 32, , LABORER, 05/09/1837
1. IRELAND 2. U.S. 3. LIVERPOOL

GILMETT, MARY, 22, , , 05/18/1868
1. 2. 3. BRAVA

GILVAUGHN, JOHN, 14, , , 07/18/1864
1. U.S. 2. 3. PICTOU

GIVEN, ROBERT, 47, M, SEA FARING, SHIP MASTER, 04/09/1828
1. U.S. 2. U.S. 3. PUERTA PLATA

GLADDING, SAMUEL, 23, M, COOPER, 07/11/1827
1. U.S. 2. U.S. 3. HAVANA

GLADDING, SAMUEL, 43, M, COOPER, 07/22/1847
1. U.S. 2. U.S. 3. MATANZAS

GLENN, JEFFERSON, 24, M, ATTORNEY, 06/16/1827
1. U.S. 2. U.S. 3. SANTOS BANE

GLINDER, DANIEL, 45, M, SHOE MAKER, 07/25/1832
1. NOVA SCOTIA 2. U.S. 3. HALIFAX

GLINDER, MRS., 37, F, WIFE OF DANIEL, 07/25/1832
1. NOVA SCOTIA 2. U.S. 3. HALIFAX

GLOVER, ANDREW, 8, M, , 07/31/1857
1. NOVA SCOTIA 2. U.S. 3. PICTOU

GLOVER, ANNA, 16, F, NONE, 09/15/1854
1. NOVA SCOTIA 2. U.S. 3. PICTOU

GLOVER, CATHERAN H., 24, F, DRESS MAKER, 07/31/1857
1. NOVA SCOTIA 2. U.S. 3. PICTOU

GLOVER, DAVID, 14, M, , 07/31/1857
1. NOVA SCOTIA 2. U.S. 3. PICTOU

GLOVER, EDWARD, 23, M, SEAMAN, 08/03/1855
1. U.S. 2. U.S. 3. LIVERPOOL

GLOVER, ISABEL, 10, F, NONE, 09/15/1854
1. NOVA SCOTIA 2. U.S. 3. PICTOU

GLOVER, ISABELLA, 10, F, , 07/31/1857
1. NOVA SCOTIA 2. U.S. 3. PICTOU

GLOVER, JAMES, 40, M, CARPENTER, 09/15/1854
1. NOVA SCOTIA 2. U.S. 3. PICTOU

GLOVER, JAMES, 6, M, NONE, 09/15/1854
1. NOVA SCOTIA 2. U.S. 3. PICTOU

GLOVER, JOHN, 39, M, SHOE MAKER, 07/31/1857
1. NOVA SCOTIA 2. U.S. 3. PICTOU

GLOVER, JOHN, 12, M, , 07/31/1857
1. NOVA SCOTIA 2. U.S. 3. PICTOU

GLOVER, MARY, 36, F, HOUSEWIFE, 09/15/1854
1. NOVA SCOTIA 2. U.S. 3. PICTOU

GLOVER, MARY, 4, F, NONE, 09/15/1854
1. NOVA SCOTIA 2. U.S. 3. PICTOU

GLOVER, PHEBY, 2, F, , 07/31/1857
1. NOVA SCOTIA 2. U.S. 3. PICTOU

GLOVER, RACHEL, 37, F, HOUSEWIFE, 07/31/1857
1. NOVA SCOTIA 2. U.S. 3. PICTOU

GLOVER, SARAH, 8, F, NONE, 09/15/1854
1. NOVA SCOTIA 2. U.S. 3. PICTOU

GLOVER, THOMAS, 14, M, NONE, 09/15/1854
1. NOVA SCOTIA 2. U.S. 3. PICTOU

GLOVER, THOMAS, 5, M, , 07/31/1857
1. NOVA SCOTIA 2. U.S. 3. PICTOU

GLUER, JOHN N., 43, M, MERCHANT, 07/14/1829
1. HAMBURG 2. UNCERTAIN 3. HAVANA

GODDAT, JOSEPH, 23, M, SEAMAN, 05/16/1853
1. NOVA SCOTIA 2. NOVA SCOTIA 3. ARDROSSAN

GODFREY, SARAH, 18, , TAILORESS, 08/13/1866
1. BRITISH AMERICA 2. U.S. 3. HILLSBOROUGH

GOLDING, DANIEL, 24, M, CONTRACTOR, 08/08/1837
1. IRELAND 2. U.S. 3. HAVANA

GOMES, FRANCISCO, 25, M, MARINER, 08/28/1872
1. FLORES 2. BOSTON 3.

GOMES, JOAO M., 24, M, MARINER, 08/28/1872
1. FLORES 2. PROVIDENCE 3.

GOMES, JOAO F., 23, M, FARMER, 08/28/1872
1. FLORES 2. PROVIDENCE 3.

GOMES, JOAO F., 28, M, MARINER, 08/28/1872
1. FLORES 2. BOSTON 3.

GOMES, JOSEPH, 14, M, , 10/17/1867
1. CAPE DE VERDE IS 2. U.S. 3. FLORES

GOMES, JOSEPHINE, 45, F, LADY, 10/17/1867
1. CAPE DE VERDE IS. 2. U.S. 3. FLORES

GOMES, MANUEL, 10, M, , 10/17/1867
1. CAPE DE VERDE IS. 2. U.S. 3. FLORES

GOMES, MARIA, 30, F, LADY, 10/17/1867
1. CAPE DE VERDE IS. 2. U.S. 3. FLORES

GOMES, MARIANNA, 18, F, LADY, 10/17/1867
1. CAPE DE VERDE IS. 2. U.S. 3. FLORES

GOMEZ, GEORGE F., 1, M, , 06/09/1834
1. CUBA 2. U.S. 3. MATANZAS

GOMEZ, IGNATIUS, 13, M, SCHOOLBOY, 09/11/1825
1. GUATEMALA 2. GUATEMALA 3. HONDURAS

GOMEZ, SARAH, 6, F, , 06/09/1834
1. CUBA 2. U.S. 3. MATANZAS

GOMEZ, STEPHEN, 4, M, , 06/09/1834
1. CUBA 2. U.S. 3. MATANZAS

GOMEZ, STEPHEN H., 39, M, MERCHANT, 06/09/1834
1. CUBA 2. U.S. 3. MATANZAS

GOMEZ, WILLIAM, 12, M, , 06/09/1834
1. U.S. 2. U.S. 3. MATANZAS

GOMEZ, WM., 35, F, , 06/09/1834
1. U.S. 2. U.S. 3. MATANZAS

GONCALVES, JOAO FORTADO, 30, M, FARMER, 08/28/1872
1. FLORES 2. PROVIDENCE 3.

GONCALVES, JOSE F., 33, M, MARINER, 08/28/1872
1. FLORES 2. PROVIDENCE 3.

GONCALVES, JOSE F., 35, M, MARINER, 08/28/1872
1. FLORES 2. BOSTON 3.

GOODFELLOW, GEORGE, 48, M, ENGINEER, 05/19/1839
1. U.S. 2. U.S. 3. HAVANA

GOODKIN, JOHN, 22, M, TANNER AND CURRIER, 07/08/1844
1. NOVA SCOTIA 2. U.S. 3. PICTOU

GOODRICH, GEORGE O., 1 MONTH, M, , 06/29/1833
1. U.S. 2. U.S. 3. MATANZAS

GOODRICH, MARY ANN, 4, F, , 06/29/1833
1. U.S. 2. U.S. 3. MATANZAS

GOODRICH, SARAH JANE, 28, F, NONE, 06/29/1833
1. U.S. 2. U.S. 3. MATANZAS

GOODRIDGE, SAMUEL W., 24, M, COOPER, 09/26/1831
1. BOSTON 2. U.S. 3. HAVANA

GOODWIN, DANIEL, 50, M, MARINER, 05/07/1827
1. U.S. 2. U.S. 3. HAVANA

GOODWIN, JOHN, 41, M, FARMER, 11/08/1827
1. ENGLAND 2. U.S. 3. LIVERPOOL

GOODWIN, THOMAS, 23, M, HOUSE CARPENTER, 09/12/1835
1. NOVA SCOTIA 2. NEW ORLEANS 3. ST. JOHN

GORDON, ANN, 28, F, SERVANT, 09/09/1844
1. NOVA SCOTIA 2. U.S. 3. PICTOU

GORDON, BARBARY, 17, F, SERVANT, 07/31/1852
1. BRITISH AMERICA 2. U.S. 3. PICTOU

GORDON, GEORGE, 23, M, DYER, 06/16/1828
1. ENGLAND 2. U.S. 3. LIVERPOOL

GORE, STANLEY, 27, M, MECHANIC, 03/11/1841
1. U.S. 2. U.S. 3. HAVANA

GOREMLEY, MORY, 26, , LABORER, 05/09/1837
1. IRELAND 2. NEW YORK 3. LIVERPOOL

GORRIN, CAPT. CYPRIAN, 28, M, MERCHANT, 06/29/1829
1. SPAIN 2. U.S. 3. HAVANA

GORTON, F.S., 22, M, MARINER, 02/13/1838
1. U.S. 2. U.S. 3. HAVANA

GOSS, ORRE, 29, M, GROCER, 05/19/1837
1. U.S. 2. U.S. 3. HAVANA

GOSS, SAMUEL R., 23, M, MERCHANT, 06/27/1825
1. BARBADOS 2. U.S. 3. BARBADOS

GOVERN, BARBARA, 22, F, HOUSEWIFE, 07/20/1857
1. NOVA SCOTIA 2. U.S. 3. PICTOU

GOVERN, RICHARD, 2, M, NONE, 07/20/1857
1. NOVA SCOTIA 2. U.S. 3. PICTOU

GOWDEY, JAMES, 28, M, GROCER, 07/08/1844
1. NOVA SCOTIA 2. U.S. 3. PICTOU

GOWDEY, JAMES W.H., 6 MONTHS, M, INFANT, 07/08/1844
1. NOVA SCOTIA 2. U.S. 3. PICTOU

GOWDEY, MARGARET, 28, F, LADY, 07/08/1844
1. NOVA SCOTIA 2. U.S. 3. PICTOU

GOWDEY, MARGARET A., 2, F, CHILD, 07/08/1844
1. NOVA SCOTIA 2. U.S. 3. PICTOU

GOXEY, BARNEY, 30, M, LABORER, 09/09/1847
1. IRELAND 2. CANADA 3. PICTOU

GRAHAM, ANNA, 20, F, LADY, 06/27/1849
1. 2. 3. PICTOU

GRAHAM, ELISABETH, 20, , SERVANT, 05/09/1837
1. IRELAND 2. NEW YORK 3. LIVERPOOL

GRAHAM, GEO., 13, M, SCHOOL BOY, 09/25/1833
1. NOVA SCOTIA 2. 3. PICTOU

GRAHAM, GEORGE G., 26, M, FARMER, 11/08/1827
1. ENGLAND 2. U.S. 3. LIVERPOOL

GRAHAM, HANNAH, 18, F, HOUSE SERVANT, 08/05/1858
1. NOVA SCOTIA 2. U.S. 3. PICTOU

GRAHAM, JESSIE, 16, F, DRESS MAKER, 08/21/1852
1. BRITISH AMERICA 2. U.S. 3. PICTOU

GRAHAM, JESSIE, 21, F, SERVANT, 09/04/1856
1. PICTOU 2. U.S. 3. PICTOU

GRAHAM, MARGARET, 18, F, SERVANT OR ASSISTANT, 10/01/1853
1. NOVA SCOTIA 2. U.S. 3. PICTOU

GRAHAM, MARY ANN, 19, F, , 08/01/1859
1. NOVA SCOTIA 2. U.S. 3. PICTOU

GRAHAM, ROBERT, 30, , TAILOR, 05/09/1837
1. IRELAND 2. NEW YORK 3. LIVERPOOL

GRAIN, ANN, 18, F, SERVANT, 09/09/1844
1. NOVA SCOTIA 2. U.S. 3. PICTOU

GRAMMONT, C., 36, M, MERCHANT, 05/20/1839
1. FRANCE 2. MEXICO 3. HAVANA

GRANDY, WM., 25, M, LABORER, 08/08/1837
1. NOVA SCOTIA 2. NEW YORK 3. PICTOU

GRANGER, B., 51, M, MERCHANT, 07/06/1835
1. PROVIDENCE 2. 3. MATANZAS

GRANGER, BENJAMIN, 45, M, MARINER, 07/20/1826
1. PROVIDENCE 2. PROVIDENCE 3. MATANZAS

GRANGER, BENJAMIN, 50, M, MERCHANT, 06/23/1830
1. PROVIDENCE 2. PROVIDENCE 3. MATANZAS

GRANGER, BENJAMIN, 52, M, MARINER, 07/28/1831
1. U.S. 2. U.S. 3. MATANZAS

GRANGER, BENJAMIN, 50, M, MERCHANT, 06/29/1833
1. U.S. 2. U.S. 3. MATANZAS

GRANGER, BENJAMIN, 55, M, MERCHANT, 06/17/1842
1. U.S. 2. U.S. 3. MATANZAS

GRANITZ, BRIDGET, 24, , LABORER, 05/09/1837
1. IRELAND 2. NEW YORK 3. LIVERPOOL

GRANT, DANIEL, 18, M, NONE, 07/28/1857
1. NOVA SCOTIA 2. U.S. 3. PICTOU

GRANT, ISABELLA, 19, F, SERVANT, 08/24/1840
1. PICTOU 2. PROVIDENCE 3. PICTOU

GRANT, ISABELLA, 18, F, SERVANT, 08/21/1852
1. BRITISH AMERICA 2. U.S. 3. PICTOU

GRANT, ISEBELL, 15, F, SERVANT, 05/30/1837
1. NOVESCATAY 2. U.S. 3. PICTOU

GRANT, JANE, 26, F, LADY, 07/20/1844
1. NOVA SCOTIA 2. U.S. 3. PICTOU

GRANT, JOHANNA, 26, F, LADY, 11/03/1849
1. BRITISH AMERICA 2. U.S. 3. PICTOU

GRANT, JOHN, 29, M, BLACKSMITH, 11/03/1849
1. BRITISH AMERICA 2. U.S. 3. PICTOU

GRANT, WALTER, 1, M, NONE, 09/26/1859
1. NOVA SCOTIA 2. U.S. 3. PICTOU

GRAY, ANN, 33, F, NONE, 10/08/1856
1. NOVA SCOTIA 2. U.S. 3. PICTOU

GRAY, BENAJAMIN, 25, M, WHEELWRIGHT, 07/05/1836
1. U.S. 2. U.S. 3. HAVANA

GRAY, DANIEL, 2, M, CHILD, 11/02/1847
1. BRITISH AMERICA 2. U.S. 3. PICTOU

GRAY, DANIEL, 11, M, NONE, 10/08/1856
1. U.S. 2. U.S. 3. PICTOU

GRAY, EBENEZER, 6, M, NONE, 10/08/1856
1. U.S. 2. U.S. 3. PICTOU

GRAY, FRANCIS, 23, M, MANUFACTURER, 04/13/1857
1. U.S. 2. U.S. 3. MATANZAS

GRAY, HANDY, 9, M, NONE, 10/08/1856
1. U.S. 2. U.S. 3. PICTOU

GRAY, ISABELLA, 25, F, SEAMSTRESS, 09/19/1835
1. PICTOU 2. U.S. 3. PICTOU

GRAY, JOHN, 27, M, , 11/02/1847
1. BRITISH AMERICA 2. U.S. 3. PICTOU

GRAY, MARY, 17, F, , 09/21/1868
1. 2. U.S. 3. PICTOU

GRAY, MRS., 24, F, LADY, 07/22/1822
1. CUBA 2. CUBA 3. HAVANA

GRAY, MRS. JOHN, 24, F, LADY, 11/02/1847
1. BRITISH AMERICA 2. U.S. 3. PICTOU

GRAY, ROBERT, 2, M, NONE, 10/08/1856
1. U.S. 2. U.S. 3. PICTOU

GRAY, VINCENT, 6, M, BOY, 07/22/1822
1. CUBA 2. CUBA 3. HAVANA

GREEN, THOMAS T., 25, M, MERCHANT, 01/19/1824
1. U.S. 2. U.S. 3. GIBRALTER

GREENE, JOHN, 30, M, FARMER, 11/08/1822
1. U.S. 2. U.S. 3. CAPE HAYTIAN

GREENE, JOSEPH, 27, M, CARPENTER, 06/26/1835
1. U.S. 2. U.S. 3. HAVANA

GREENE, NATHANIEL, 45, M, MARINER, 05/19/1839
1. U.S. 2. U.S. 3. HAVANA

GREENE, ROBERT W., 48, M, MARINER, 01/13/1827
1. U.S. 2. U.S. 3. OMOA

GREENE, SARAH H., 40, F, LADY, 07/24/1858
1. LIVERPOOL 2. YARMOUTH 3. ARDROSSAN

GREENE, WELCOME A., 24, M, MERCHANT, 04/25/1820
1. PROVIDENCE 2. U.S. 3. HAVANA

GRENET, JAMES, 50, M, LABORER, 09/02/1845
1. FRANCE 2. U.S. 3. PICTOU

GRENET, LOUISE, 50, F, LABORER, 09/02/1845
1. 2. U.S. 3. PICTOU

GRENET, LOUISE, 12, F, MISS, 09/02/1845
1. 2. U.S. 3. PICTOU

GRIFFITHS, MARTHA J., 18, F, LADY, 09/21/1846
1. NOVA SCOTIA 2. BRITISH AMERICA 3. PICTOU

GRISWOLD, ALEX. H., 29, M, PLANTER, 07/15/1834
1. BRISTOL, RI 2. CUBA 3. MATANZAS

GUINTEN, LOUIS, 21, M, MARINER, 11/05/1823
1. FRANCE 2. U.S. 3. HAVRE DE GRACE

GUITERA, ANTONIO, 20, M, GENTLEMAN, 08/01/1839
1. SPAIN 2. 3. MATANZAS

GUNN, LIBBIE, 18, F, VISITOR, 08/24/1870
1. PICTOU 2. U.S. 3. PICTOU

H---RAN, JOHN, 26, M, LABOR SINGLE, 1836
1. KERRY 2. PROVIDENCE 3. PICTOU

HAFFNER, CHRISTIAN M., 40, M, MERCHANT, 08/17/1831
1. AMSTERDAM 2. HOLLAND 3. SURINAM

HALE, ENOCH, 32, M, MERCHANT, 08/16/1851
1. BRITISH AMERICA 2. BRITISH AMERICA 3. PICTOU

HALE, PAUL, 22, M, COACHMAN, 07/25/1832
1. NOVA SCOTIA 2. U.S. 3. HALIFAX

HALL, ANN, 36, F, , 08/31/1866
1. U.S. 2. U.S. 3. PICTOU

HALSTEAD, CHARLES, 36, M, , 09/30/1868
1. 2. 3. ARDROSSAN

HALSTEAD, MRS., 32, F, , 09/30/1868
1. 2. 3. ARDROSSAN

HALSTEAD, ROBERT, 29, M, WHEELWRIGHT, 06/16/1828
1. ENGLAND 2. U.S. 3. LIVERPOOL

HAMILTON, DAVID, 25, M, MARINER, 09/27/1855
1. U.S. 2. U.S. 3. TURKS ISLAND

HAMMOND, JAMES F., 30, M, SEAMAN, 05/10/1853
1. U.S. 2. U.S. 3. HONOLULU

HAMMOND, MRS. JAMES F., 24, F, HOUSEWIFE, 05/10/1853
1. U.S. 2. U.S. 3. HONOLULU

HANNUM, JOSIAH, , , DISTRESSED SEAMEN, 01/16/1849
1. 2. 3. NASSAU

HARADEN, OLE, 28, M, MARINER, 07/19/1850
1. DENMARK 2. DENMARK 3. EAST CAICOS, TURKS ISLAND

HARNEY, PATRICK, 33, M, LABORER, 09/13/1841
1. IRELAND 2. U.S. 3. PICTOU

HARPER, MONTGOMERY, 19, M, ENGINEER, 08/12/1846
1. PICTOU 2. BOSTON, MA 3. PICTOU

HARPER, SAMUEL, 46, M, CARPENTER, 02/21/1820
1. U.S. 2. U.S. 3. HONDURAS

HARPER, SAMUEL, 47, M, HOUSE CARPENTER, 07/02/1821
1. CUMBERLAND 2. U.S 3. HONDURAS

HARRIETT, BENJA., 2, M, CHILD OF ELIZABETH, 06/30/1830
1. U.S. 2. U.S. 3. HAVANA

HARRIETT, ELIZABETH, , F, , 06/30/1830
1. U.S. 2. U.S. 3. HAVANA

HARRIS, CATHERINE, 20, F, DOMESTIC, 09/26/1859
1. NOVA SCOTIA 2. U.S. 3. PICTOU

HARRIS, CHARLES, 28, M, MILLER, 09/19/1831
1. ENGLAND 2. U.S. 3. SYDNEY

HARRIS, EDWARD, 17, M, LABORER, 06/19/1860
1. NOVA SCOTIA 2. U.S. 3. PICTOU

HARRIS, ELIZABETH, 36, F, FARMER, 09/19/1831
1. ENGLAND 2. U.S. 3. SYDNEY

HARRIS, ELIZABETH, 21, F, SERVANT, 07/05/1864
1. NOVA SCOTIA 2. U.S. 3. PICTOU

HARRIS, GEORGE, 15, , , 06/29/1833
1. U.S. 2. U.S. 3. MATANZAS

HARRIS, GEORGE, 19, M, SAILMAKER, 05/22/1857
1. GREAT BRITAIN 2. U.S. 3. PICTOU

HARRIS, HERB S., 27, M, TOBACCONIST, 02/29/1840
1. U.S. 2. U.S. 3. MATANZAS

HARRIS, JAMES, 27, M, LABORER, 05/07/1824
1. U.S. 2. U.S. 3. HAITI

HARRIS, JANE, 23, F, SERVANT, 09/09/1844
1. NOVA SCOTIA 2. U.S. 3. PICTOU

HARRIS, JANE B., 22, F, SERVANT, 07/05/1864
1. NOVA SCOTIA 2. U.S. 3. PICTOU

HARRIS, MARIA L., 23, F, WEAVER, 09/19/1860
1. NOVA SCOTIA 2. U.S. 3. PICTOU

HARRIS, MARY ANN, 22, F, , 08/02/1850
1. BRITISH AMERICA 2. U.S. 3. PICTOU

HARRIS, SAMUEL, 45, M, MARINER, 01/02/1826
1. NOVA SCOTIA 2. NOVA SCOTIA 3. HAVANA

HARRIS, THOMAS, 24, M, PRINTER, 08/28/1872
1. NOVA SCOTIA 2. U.S. 3. PICTOU

HARRIS, WILLIAM, 37, M, FARMER, 09/19/1831
1. ENGLAND 2. U.S. 3. SYDNEY

HARROCKS, ELISABETH, 38, F, LADY, 11/11/1844
1. ENGLAND 2. U.S. 3. PICTOU

HART, MARY, 20, F, , 08/14/1860
1. NOVA SCOTIA 2. U.S. 3. PICTOU

HARTZ, MICAL, 24, M, SEAMAN, 10/27/1834
1. U.S. 2. BOSTON 3. PICTOU

HASKELL, LUCY M., 24, F, WIFE OF W.R., 10/25/1853
1. U.S. 2. U.S. 3. ZANZIBAR

HASKELL, MARK H., 26, , MERCHANT, 10/24/1855
1. U.S. 2. U.S. 3. ZANZIBAR, MOZAMBIQUE

HASKELL, W.R., 26, M, MERCHANT, 10/25/1853
1. U.S. 2. U.S. 3. ZANZIBAR

HASKILL, GEORGE, 16, M, MARINER, 09/07/1838
1. U.S. 2. U.S. 3. PICTOU

HASSEL, EDWARD, 25, M, LABORER, 09/13/1841
1. IRELAND 2. U.S. 3. PICTOU

HASWELL, DOROTHY, , , , 12/30/1823
1. BOSTON 2. BARBADOS 3. PROVIDENCE

HAWKINS, DAVID, 52, M, FARMER, 02/29/1840
1. U.S. 2. U.S. 3. MATANZAS

HAWKINS, G.W., 35, M, MECHANIC, 06/11/1840
1. U.S. 2. U.S. 3. MATANZAS

HAWKINS, WM. F., 30, M, GENTLEMAN, 04/25/1840
1. U.S. 2. U.S. 3. MATANZAS

HAYES, ELIZA A., 32, F, HOUSEWIFE, 07/03/1854
1. U.S. 2. U.S. 3. CARDENAS

HAYES, JOSEPH W., 36, M, MECHANIC, 07/03/1854
1. U.S. 2. U.S. 3. CARDENAS

HAYWOOD, D.A., 29, M, MECHANIC, 03/22/1837
1. U.S. 2. U.S. 3. HAVANA

HEAD, JANE, 24, F, HOUSEWIFE, 07/15/1867
1. NOVA SCOTIA 2. U.S. 3. PICTOU

HEAD, JESSIE, 24, M, SERVANT, 06/03/1862
1. NOVA SCOTIA 2. U.S. 3. PICTOU

HEAD, JESSIE, 19, F, NONE, 08/20/1857
1. NOVA SCOTIA 2. U.S. 3. PICTOU

HEAD, JESSIE, 19, F, NONE, 08/20/1857
1. NOVA SCOTIA 2. U.S. 3. PICTOU

HEADLY, MARY, 2, F, NONE, 07/01/1862
1. NOVA SCOTIA 2. U.S. 3. PICTOU

HEADLY, MRS. MARY, 30, F, NONE, 07/01/1862
1. NOVA SCOTIA 2. U.S. 3. PICTOU

HEADLY, ROBERT, 3, M, NONE, 07/01/1862
1. NOVA SCOTIA 2. U.S. 3. PICTOU

HEART, BENJAMIN, 6, M, , 07/08/1867
1. 2. 3. PICTOU

HEART, JANE, 39, F, HOUSEWIFE, 07/08/1867
1. NOVA SCOTIA 2. U.S. 3. PICTOU

HEART, JOHN D., 11, M, , 07/08/1867
1. NOVA SCOTIA 2. U.S. 3. PICTOU

HEART, MARGARET JANE, 1, F, , 07/08/1867
1. 2. 3. PICTOU

HEART, MARY E., 4, F, , 07/08/1867
1. 2. 3. PICTOU

HEART, ROBERT, 9, M, , 07/08/1867
1. 2. 3. PICTOU

HEART, SARAH ANN, 13, F, , 07/08/1867
1. 2. 3. PICTOU

HEART, WILLIAM J., 44, M, LABORER, 07/08/1867
1. NOVA SCOTIA 2. U.S. 3. PICTOU

HEATLEY, ROBERT, 21, M, GENTLEMAN, 04/28/1843
1. ENGLAND 2. ENGLAND 3. LIVERPOOL

HEBERT, AMELIA ANN, 16, F, SERVANT, 1872
1. NOVA SCOTIA 2. 3.

HELENY, JANE, 17, F, , 10/18/1837
1. NOVA SCOTIA 2. U.S. 3. PICTOU

HELLEN, ANNA, 24, , SPINSTER, 05/09/1837
1. IRELAND 2. U.S. 3. LIVERPOOL

HENDERSEN, SARAH J., 18, F, , 08/14/1860
1. NOVA SCOTIA 2. U.S. 3. PICTOU

HENDERSON, ALONZO, 20, , CARPENTER, 05/28/1869
1. NOVA SCOTIA 2. NOVA SCOTIA 3. PICTOU

HENDERSON, C., 21, F, , 09/25/1863
1. BRITISH AMERICA 2. U.S. 3. PICTOU

HENDERSON, ISABELLA, 18, F, LADY, 11/02/1847
1. BRITISH AMERICA 2. U.S. 3. PICTOU

HENDERSON, J.W., 18, M, LABORER, 07/07/1865
1. BRITISH AMERICA 2. U.S. 3. PICTOU

HENDERSON, MARGARET, 12, F, SPINSTER, 09/18/1845
1. NOVA SCOTIA 2. U.S. 3. PICTOU

HENDERSON, MARGARET, 52, F, NONE, 10/08/1856
1. NOVA SCOTIA 2. U.S. 3. PICTOU

HENDERSON, PRISCILLA, 21, , HOUSEWIFE, 08/21/1866
1. U.S. 2. U.S. 3. PICTOU

HENDERSON, ROBERT, 28, M, MECHANIC, 10/21/1837
1. U.S. 2. U.S. 3. PICTOU

HENDERSON, SARAH JANE, 16, F, NONE, 10/08/1856
1. NOVA SCOTIA 2. U.S. 3. PICTOU

HENDERSON, SUSANNA, 19, F, NONE, 10/08/1856
1. NOVA SCOTIA 2. U.S. 3. PICTOU

HENDERSON, WILLIAM, 49, M, TEACHER, 08/14/1860
1. NOVA SCOTIA 2. U.S. 3. PICTOU

HENDERSON, WILSON, 15, , LABORER, 07/08/1865
1. BRITISH AMERICA 2. U.S. 3. PICTOU

HENDY, HENRY, 37, M, MILITARY OFFICER, 08/08/1826
1. GREAT BRITAIN 2. GREAT BRITAIN 3. HONDURAS

HENRY, JAMES FITZ, 22, M, MANUFACTURER, 06/08/1829
1. U.S. 2. U.S. 3. HAVANA

HERDMEN, ANDREW, 15, , , 05/28/1869
1. NOVA SCOTIA 2. NOVA SCOTIA 3. PICTOU

HERNDON, J---TH, 40, M, MACHINIST, 06/29/1840
1. U.S. 2. MASSACHUSETTS 3. MATANZAS

HEWE, HANNAH, 30, F, TAILORESS, 09/08/1843
1. U.S. 2. U.S. 3. PICTOU

HEWE, MARY, 5, F, , 09/08/1843
1. U.S. 2. U.S. 3. PICTOU

HEWES, SUMNER J., , , , SEAMAN SENT HOME BY CONSUL, 01/16/1849
1. 2. 3. SANDWICH ISLANDS

HEWINS, AMASA, 37, M, ARTIST, 08/13/1833
1. BOSTON 2. BOSTON 3. LIVERPOOL

HEYSICK, AUGUSTUS, 35, M, CABINET MAKER, 07/01/1850
1. HOLLAND 2. U.S. 3. SAGUA LE GRANDE

HIBBARD, WILLIAM, 24, M, MECHANIC, 06/07/1841
1. U.S. 2. 3. HAVANA

HICKEY, BARTHOLOMEW, 9, M, CHILD OF JOHN AND MARY, 09/25/1848
1. BRITISH AMERICA 2. BRITISH AMERICA 3. PICTOU

HICKEY, CATHARINE, 15, F, CHILD OF JOHN AND MARY, 09/25/1848
1. BRITISH AMERICA 2. BRITISH AMERICA 3. PICTOU

HICKEY, ELLEANOR, 6, F, CHILD OF JOHN AND MARY, 09/25/1848
1. BRITISH AMERICA 2. BRITISH AMERICA 3. PICTOU

HICKEY, HONORA, 1, F, CHILD OF JOHN AND MARY, 09/25/1848
1. BRITISH AMERICA 2. BRITISH AMERICA 3. PICTOU

HICKEY, JOHN, 41, M, SHIP CAULKER, 09/25/1848
1. BRITISH AMERICA 2. BRITISH AMERICA 3. PICTOU

HICKEY, MARGARET, 4, F, CHILD OF JOHN AND MARY, 09/25/1848
1. BRITISH AMERICA 2. BRITISH AMERICA 3. PICTOU

HICKEY, MARY ANN, 36, F, LADY, 09/25/1848
1. BRITISH AMERICA 2. BRITISH AMERICA 3. PICTOU

HIEKLING, WM. A., 34, M, SHIP MASTER, 05/26/1838
1. BOSTON 2. U.S. 3. ST. THOMAS, AFRICA

HIGGINS, MARGARET, 25, F, HOUSEWIFE, 10/13/1846
1. BRITISH AMERICA 2. U.S. 3. PICTOU

HIGGINS, WM., 1, M, CHILD, 10/13/1846
1. BRITISH AMERICA 2. U.S. 3. PICTOU

HILL, CATHARINE, 20, F, SERVANT, 11/16/1863
1. PICTOU 2. U.S. 3. PICTOU

HINDS, ELEN, 25, F, MILLINER, 10/27/1834
1. NOVA SCOTIA 2. BOSTON 3. PICTOU

HINDS, GEORGE, 27, M, SEAMAN, 10/27/1834
1. NOVA SCOTIA 2. BOSTON 3. PICTOU

HINDS, MARY, 2, F, , 10/27/1834
1. NOVA SCOTIA 2. BOSTON 3. PICTOU

HINES, WILLIAM, 33, M, MERCHANT, 08/15/1860
1. U.S. 2. AFRICA 3. ZANZIBAR

HINES, WILLIAM E., 40, M, MERCHANT, 05/05/1862
1. U.S. 2. U.S. 3. ZANZIBAR

HINKLEY, BENJ L., 26, M, MARINER, 06/18/1839
1. U.S. 2. U.S. 3.

HOALT, GEORGE, 25, M, TRADESMAN, 03/22/1826
1. ENGLAND 2. MASSACHUSETTS 3. LIVERPOOL

HOBBS, JONATHAN, 30, M, CARPENTER, 07/28/1831
1. U.S. 2. U.S. 3. HAVANA

HODGES, WM., 22, , CARPENTER, 04/20/1841
1. NORTON 2. 3. MATANZAS

HODGSON, MATHEW, 22, M, TRADESMAN, 03/22/1826
1. ENGLAND 2. MASSACHUSETTS 3. LIVERPOOL

HOGAN, ELISABETH, 24, F, LADY, 09/25/1848
1. BRITISH AMERICA 2. U.S. 3. PICTOU

HOGAN, JOHN, 35, M, BRICKLAYER, 09/25/1848
1. BRITISH AMERICA 2. U.S. 3. PICTOU

HOGAN, P. J., 25, M, MERCHANT, 05/13/1831
1. WEST INDIES 2. WEST INDIES 3. HAVANA

HOLBROOK, SYLVANNUS, 26, M, CARPENTER, 06/23/1834
1. U.S. 2. U.S. 3. HAVANA

HOLDEN, HELLIN, 18, F, SERVANT, 09/08/1862
1. PICTOU 2. PROVIDENCE 3. PICTOU

HOLDEN, MARGARET, 19, F, SERVANT, 07/31/1863
1. PICTOU 2. PROVIDENCE 3. PICTOU

HOLLADDRENE, MILADY, 36, F, , 03/20/1835
1. 2. FRANCE 3. MARTINIQUE

HOLLIDAY, MISS, 24, F, HOUSEWIFE, 06/02/1856
1. U.S. 2. U.S. 3. PICTOU

HOLMES, HECTOR, 22, M, LABORER, 09/13/1844
1. SCOTLAND 2. U.S. 3. PICTOU

HOLMES, MARGARET, 20, F, HOUSE SERVANT, 07/07/1865
1. BRITISH AMERICA 2. U.S. 3. PICTOU

HOLMES, JR., SAMUEL, 25, M, SHIP MASTER, 06/13/1828
1. U.S. 2. U.S. 3. HAVANA

HOM, PETER, 23, M, EXHIBITOR OF WILD ANIMALS, 06/29/1826
1. U.S. 2. U.S. 3. HAVANA

HONESTED, MRS. MARY, 40, F, LADY, 06/22/1863
1. PICTOU 2. U.S. 3. PICTOU

HONEY, CALVIN, 26, M, MECHANIC, 06/08/1838
1. U.S. 2. PROVIDENCE 3. HAVANA

HOOD, AGNES, 40, , , 08/27/1835
1. GRUNOCK 2. 3. PICTOU

HOOD, AGNES, 7, , , 08/27/1835
1. PICTOU 2. 3. PICTOU

HOOD, JANE, 19, F, LADY, 11/03/1849
1. BRITISH AMERICA 2. U.S. 3. PICTOU

HOOD, JOHN, 12, , , 08/27/1835
1. PICTOU 2. 3. PICTOU

HOOD, MARGARET, 5, , , 08/27/1835
1. PICTOU 2. 3. PICTOU

HOOD, SARAH, 2, , , 08/27/1835
1. PICTOU 2. 3. PICTOU

HOOD, WM., 10, , , 08/27/1835
1. PICTOU 2. 3. PICTOU

HOOPER, (CHILD), 6, , CHILD OF EPHRAIM, 08/23/1845
1. BRITISH AMERICA 2. U.S. 3. PICTOU

HOOPER, (CHILD), 4, , CHILD OF EPHRAIM, 08/23/1845
1. BRITISH AMERICA 2. U.S. 3. PICTOU

HOOPER, (CHILD), 2, , CHILD OF EPHRAIM, 08/23/1845
1. BRITISH AMERICA 2. U.S. 3. PICTOU

HOOPER, DEBORAH, 16, F, NONE, 07/28/1857
1. NOVA SCOTIA 2. U.S. 3. PICTOU

HOOPER, EPHRAIM, 35, M, CARPENTER, 08/23/1845
1. BRITISH AMERICA 2. U.S. 3. PICTOU

HOOPER, EPHRAIM, 38, M, MINER, 07/28/1857
1. NOVA SCOTIA 2. U.S. 3. PICTOU

HOOPER, ISABELLA, 34, F, HOUSEWIFE, 07/28/1857
1. NOVA SCOTIA 2. U.S. 3. PICTOU

HOOPER, JOSEPH, 18, M, NONE, 07/28/1857
1. NOVA SCOTIA 2. U.S. 3. PICTOU

HOOPER, LEVI, 4, M, NONE, 07/28/1857
1. NOVA SCOTIA 2. U.S. 3. PICTOU

HOOPER, MARIA, 20, F, NONE, 07/28/1857
1. NOVA SCOTIA 2. U.S. 3. PICTOU

HOOPER, MRS., 30, F, LADY, 08/23/1845
1. BRITISH AMERICA 2. U.S. 3. PICTOU

HOOPER, ROBERT C., 25, M, MERCHANT, 06/17/1829
1. U.S. 2. U.S. 3. HAVANA

HOOPER, SARAH, 1, F, NONE, 07/28/1857
1. NOVA SCOTIA 2. U.S. 3. PICTOU

HOOPER, SILVEY, 14, F, NONE, 07/28/1857
1. NOVA SCOTIA 2. U.S. 3. PICTOU

HOOPER, WASHINGTON, 7, M, NONE, 07/28/1857
1. NOVA SCOTIA 2. U.S. 3. PICTOU

HORN, MICHEL, 23, , LABORER, 05/09/1837
1. IRELAND 2. U.S. 3. LIVERPOOL

HORNEY, CATHARINE, 15, F, SERVANT, 07/22/1856
1. GREAT BRITAIN 2. U.S. 3. PICTOU

HOULES, THOMAS, 31, M, ENGINEER, 06/05/1843
1. U.S. 2. U.S. 3. MATANZAS

HOWARD, BENJAMIN, 27, M, COOPER, 05/24/1828
1. U.S. 2. U.S. 3. HAVANA

HOWARD, JOHN, 27, M, MECHANIC, 08/08/1826
1. HONDURAS 2. HONDURAS 3. HONDURAS

HOWARD, MARY, 18, F, SERVANT, 09/09/1844
1. NOVA SCOTIA 2. U.S. 3. PICTOU

HOWARD, PHILIP, 25, M, SERVANT, 08/15/1825
1. U.S. 2. BOSTON 3. HAVANA

HOWARD, SAMUEL, 27, M, CARPENTER, 06/26/1835
1. U.S. 2. U.S. 3. HAVANA

HOWE, GEORGE, 43, M, MERCHANT, 05/19/1833
1. U.S. 2. U.S. 3. MATANZAS

HOWE, HAMMOND, 23, M, CARPENTER, 04/14/1828
1. U.S. 2. U.S. 3. OMOA

HOWLS, THOMAS, 37, M, ENGINEER, 06/11/1845
1. U.S. 2. U.S. 3. CARDENAS

HUBBARD, CHARLES T., 21, M, MERCHANT, 06/08/1838
1. U.S. 2. BOSTON 3. HAVANA

HUBBARD, JAMES C., 17, M, CARPENTER, 04/21/1820
1. U.S. 2. U.S. 3. MATANZAS

HUGHES, HENRY, 18, M, MERCHANT, 10/17/1834
1. BOSTON 2. BOSTON 3. PICTOU

HUGHES, MARGARET S., 20, F, LADY, 08/18/1849
1. BRITISH AMERICA 2. U.S. 3. PICTOU

HUGHS, ANN, 9, F, , 07/28/1834
1. NOVA SCOTIA 2. U.S. 3. PICTOU

HUGHS, CATHERINE, 3, F, , 07/28/1834
1. NOVA SCOTIA 2. U.S. 3. PICTOU

HUGHS, EDWARD, 7, M, , 07/28/1834
1. NOVA SCOTIA 2. U.S. 3. PICTOU

HUGHS, JOHN, 5 MONTHS, M, , 07/28/1834
1. NOVA SCOTIA 2. U.S. 3. PICTOU

HUGHS, MARY, 40, F, , 07/28/1834
1. NOVA SCOTIA 2. U.S. 3. PICTOU

HUGHS, PATRICK, 8, M, , 07/28/1834
1. NOVA SCOTIA 2. U.S. 3. PICTOU

HUGHS, WILLIAM, 2, M, , 07/28/1834
1. NOVA SCOTIA 2. U.S. 3. PICTOU

HUMPHREY, ASAHEL J., 34, M, SOAP BOILER, 05/28/1835
1. U.S. 2. U.S. 3. HAVANA

HUNTER, ELIZABETH, 6, F, , 08/08/1837
1. 2. 3. HAVANA

HUNTER, ELLEN, 30, F, DRESS MAKER, 08/08/1837
1. AMERICAN 2. U.S. 3. HAVANA

HUNTER, ROBERT, 50, M, FARMER, 09/15/1856
1. GREAT BRITAIN 2. GREAT BRITAIN 3. PICTOU

HUREL, MADAME, , , , 12/14/1823
1. PHILADELPHIA 2. GUADELOUPE 3. PROVIDENCE

HUTCHINSON, ROBERT, 40, , MINER, 08/27/1835
1. GRUNOCK 2. 3. PICTOU

HUTTON, ELENA, 6, F, LADY, 06/08/1843
1. AFRICA CAPE COAST 2. CAPE COAST AFRICA 3. AFRICA

IDE, W., 23, M, , 05/16/1821
1. U.S. 2. 3. MATANZAS

IMAEKAY, GEORGE, 20, M, DRUGGIST, 09/27/1848
1. PICTOU 2. PROVIDENCE 3. PICTOU

INGRAHAM, JOHN, 45, M, COOPER, 07/24/1848
1. U.S. 2. U.S. 3. MATANZAS

INGRAHAM, MARGARET, 30, F, MILLINER, 10/28/1836
1. ENGLAND 2. PROVIDENCE 3. PICTOU

IRISH, AUGUSTUS, 40, M, MECHANIC, 10/21/1837
1. U.S. 2. U.S. 3. PICTOU

IRVIN, ISABELLA, 22, F, , 07/03/1851
1. BRITISH AMERICA 2. U.S. 3. PICTOU

IRVINE, JOHN, 21, M, HOUSE CARPENTER, 05/24/1858
1. NOVA SCOTIA 2. U.S. 3. PICTOU

IRVINE, MARGARET, 18, F, SERVANT, 09/03/1853
1. PICTOU 2. U.S. 3. PICTOU

IRVINE, MRS. W., 21, F, HOUSEWIFE, 05/24/1858
1. NOVA SCOTIA 2. U.S. 3. PICTOU

IRVINE, WILLIAM, 30, M, HOUSE CARPENTER, 05/24/1858
1. NOVA SCOTIA 2. U.S. 3. PICTOU

IRVING, ANDREW, 24, M, STUDENT MEDICINE, 10/27/1845
1. CANADA 2. NEW YORK 3. PICTOU

IRVING, CHRISTIANA, 22, F, SERVANT, 09/03/1853
1. PICTOU 2. U.S. 3. PICTOU

IRVING, JANE, 24, F, HOUSE MAID, 09/19/1860
   1. NOVA SCOTIA 2. U.S. 3. PICTOU

IRWIN, ANN, 50, F, , 11/14/1853
   1. NOVA SCOTIA 2. U.S. 3. PICTOU

IRWIN, AYLETTE, 22, M, , 11/14/1853
   1. NOVA SCOTIA 2. U.S. 3. PICTOU

ISLEY, FREDERICK, 22, M, MARINER, 06/25/1856
   1. U.S. 2. U.S. 3. PICTOU

IVES, GEORGE, 22, M, MERCHANT, 07/31/1863
   1. PICTOU 2. PICTOU 3. PICTOU

JACINTO, ANTONIO, 35, M, MARINER, 08/28/1872
   1. FLORES 2. BOSTON 3.

JACINTO, EMILIA, 20, F, SEAMSTRESS, 08/28/1872
   1. FLORES 2. BOSTON 3.

JACINTO, MANUEL, 27, M, FARMER, 08/28/1872
   1. SAN MIQUEL 2. PROVIDENCE 3.

JACINTO, MARIA, 25, F, SEAMSTRESS, 08/28/1872
   1. FLORES 2. BOSTON 3.

JACK, JOHN, 27, , MASTER MARINER, 05/28/1869
   1. NOVA SCOTIA 2. NOVA SCOTIA 3. PICTOU

JACKSON, ABRAHAM, 21, , SHIP CARPENTER, 11/04/1869
   1. CAPE BRETON 2. U.S. 3. SINGAN

JACKSON, JAMES, 22, M, MERCHANT, 10/23/1823
   1. U.S. 2. PORTLAND 3. HONDURAS

JACKSON, JAMES S., 19, M, GENTLEMAN, 08/21/1822
   1. U.S. 2. U.S. 3. BELIZE

JACKSON, JAMES F., 26, M, MERCHANT, 04/04/1825
   1. U.S. 2. U.S. 3. HONDURAS

JACKSON, NATHAN W., 20, M, GENTLEMAN, 09/27/1841
   1. U.S. 2. AMERICAN 3. TURKS ISLAND

JACKSON, WALTER P., 27, M, COACH MAKER, 07/11/1827
   1. U.S. 2. U.S. 3. HAVANA

JACOBS, WILLIAM V., 26, M, COOPER, 07/07/1846
   1. MAINE 2. MAINE 3. MATANZAS

JAMES, B.V.R., 32, M, GENTLEMAN, 04/17/1845
   1. U.S. 2. U.S. 3. AFRICA

JAMES, CLARA, 2, F, CHILD, 04/17/1845
  1. U.S. 2. U.S. 3. AFRICA

JAMES, HENRY, 60, M, GARDENER, 11/08/1872
  1. U.S. 2. U.S. 3. PORT AU PRINCE

JAMES, MARGARET, 40, F, LADY, 04/17/1845
  1. U.S. 2. U.S. 3. AFRICA

JAMES, SARAH, 45, F, SERVANT, 11/08/1872
  1. U.S. 2. U.S. 3. PORT AU PRINCE

JAMISON, HENRY, , , SEAMAN SENT HOME FROM PERNAM, 01/16/1849
  1. 2. 3. SANDWICH ISLANDS

JANVRINE, MRS. ANN, 40, F, , 08/08/1860
  1. NOVA SCOTIA 2. NOVA SCOTIA 3. PICTOU

JEFFERSON, SARAH, 24, F, , 08/02/1850
  1. U.S. 2. U.S. 3. PICTOU

JEFFERSON, THOMAS, 28, M, SEAMAN, 08/02/1850
  1. U.S. 2. U.S. 3. PICTOU

JENCKES, F.C., 31, M, MERCHANT, 03/22/1837
  1. U.S. 2. U.S. 3. HAVANA

JENCKES, F.C. MRS., 20, F, , 03/22/1837
  1. CUBA 2. U.S. 3. HAVANA

JENCKS, FRANCIS C., 30, M, MERCHANT, 06/05/1834
  1. U.S. 2. U.S. 3. HAVANA

JENCKS, JOHN, 72, , GENTLEMAN (CAPT.), 01/27/1842
  1. U.S. 2. U.S. 3. MATANZAS

JENKINS, ANNA, 20, F, LADY, 08/18/1849
  1. BRITISH AMERICA 2. U.S. 3. PICTOU

JENKINS, LE BARON U., 26, M, SHIP CARPENTER, 07/28/1858
  1. U.S. 2. U.S. 3. SAINT JOHN

JENKS, FRANCIS C., 27, M, MERCHANT, 05/13/1833
  1. PROVIDENCE 2. U.S. 3. HAVANA

JENKS, ROBERT W., 28, M, ENGRAVER, 06/04/1858
  1. U.S. 2. U.S. 3. MATANZAS

JILLSON, DANL, 2, M, NONE, 07/18/1857
  1. U.S. 2. U.S. 3. PICTOU

JOAQUINA, ANNA, 25, F, SEAMSTRESS, 08/28/1872
  1. FLORES 2. BOSTON 3.

JOAQUINA, MARIA, 31, F, SEAMSTRESS, 08/28/1872
1. FLORES 2. PROVIDENCE 3.

JOHNSON, ANN, 30, F, SERVANT, 08/08/1827
1. 2. 3. GOTENBURG

JOHNSON, ANN, 51, F, , 09/22/1851
1. BRITISH AMERICA 2. BRITISH AMERICA 3. PICTOU

JOHNSON, CHARLES, 26, M, MARINER, 02/17/1823
1. U.S. 2. U.S. 3. CURACOA

JOHNSON, FRANK, 10, M, , 09/24/1866
1. BRITISH AMERICA 2. NOVA SCOTIA 3. SINGAN

JOHNSON, FREDERICK, 12, M, , 09/24/1866
1. BRITISH AMERICA 2. NOVA SCOTIA 3. SINGAN

JOHNSON, JAMES, 2, M, NONE, 07/07/1857
1. NOVA SCOTIA 2. U.S. 3. PICTOU

JOHNSON, JANE, 20, , SERVANT, 09/01/1867
1. 2. 3. PICTOU

JOHNSON, JOHANNA, 16, F, SERVANT, 07/01/1862
1. NOVA SCOTIA 2. U.S. 3. PICTOU

JOHNSON, JOHN, 6, M, NONE, 07/07/1857
1. NOVA SCOTIA 2. U.S. 3. PICTOU

JOHNSON, JOHN, 3, M, NONE, 07/07/1857
1. NOVA SCOTIA 2. U.S. 3. PICTOU

JOHNSON, JOSEPH, 24, M, BLACKSMITH, 07/20/1844
1. NOVA SCOTIA 2. U.S. 3. PICTOU

JOHNSON, MARGARET, 18, F, SERVANT, 09/09/1844
1. NOVA SCOTIA 2. U.S. 3. PICTOU

JOHNSON, MARGARET, 44, F, HOUSEKEEPER, 09/24/1866
1. BRITISH AMERICA 2. NOVA SCOTIA 3. SINGAN

JOHNSON, MARY, 1, F, NONE, 07/07/1857
1. NOVA SCOTIA 2. U.S. 3. PICTOU

JOHNSON, MARY A., 24, F, SERVANT, 08/30/1855
1. NOVA SCOTIA 2. U.S. 3. PICTOU

JOHNSON, MARY ANN, 20, F, SERVANT, 09/20/1851
1. BRITISH AMERICA 2. U.S. 3. PICTOU

JOHNSON, MATHEW, 23, M, FULLN OF CLOTH, 10/14/1872
1. GREAT BRITAIN 2. U.S. 3. ST. JOHN

JOHNSON, MRS., 35, F, , 09/20/1838
1. ENGLAND 2. RHODE ISLAND 3. PICTOU

JOHNSON, MRS. JAMES, 23, F, NONE, 07/07/1857
1. NOVA SCOTIA 2. U.S. 3. PICTOU

JOHNSON, MRS. JOHN, 29, F, NONE, 07/07/1857
1. NOVA SCOTIA 2. U.S. 3. PICTOU

JOHNSON, REV. WM.G., 35, M, MINISTER, 09/20/1838
1. ENGLAND 2. RHODE ISLAND 3. PICTOU

JOHNSON, SARAH, 23, F, SERVANT OR ASSISTANT, 10/01/1853
1. NOVA SCOTIA 2. U.S. 3. PICTOU

JOHNSON, SARAH M, 14, F, SERVANT, 09/09/1844
1. NOVA SCOTIA 2. U.S. 3. PICTOU

JOHNSON, SIDNEY L., 24, M, GENTLEMAN, 08/13/1833
1. NEW HAVEN 2. NEW HAVEN 3. LIVERPOOL

JOHNSON, THOMAS, 4, M, NONE, 07/07/1857
1. NOVA SCOTIA 2. U.S. 3. PICTOU

JOHNSON, WILLIAM, 32, , OVERSEER, 09/21/1869
1. DENMARK 2. U.S. 3. ST. MARTINS

JOHNSON, WILLIAM G., 34, M, PREACHER, 09/25/1833
1. SCOTLAND 2. U.S. 3. PICTOU

JOHNSTON, ANN, 31, F, SERVANT, 07/05/1866
1. BRITISH AMERICA 2. U.S. 3. PICTOU

JOHNSTON, ELIZA, 18, F, DOMESTIC, 09/26/1859
1. NOVA SCOTIA 2. U.S. 3. PICTOU

JOHNSTON, HANNAH, 27, F, DOMESTIC, 09/26/1859
1. NOVA SCOTIA 2. U.S. 3. PICTOU

JOICY, JOHN, 20, M, LABORER, 09/03/1847
1. PICTOU 2. U.S. 3. PICTOU

JOICY, MARY, 28, F, LABORER, 09/03/1847
1. PICTOU 2. U.S. 3. PICTOU

JONES, ISABELLA, 6, F, , 10/13/1865
1. BRITISH AMERICA 2. U.S. 3. COW BAY

JONES, JOHN, 27, M, ENGINEER, 06/11/1845
1. U.S. 2. U.S. 3. CARDENAS

JONES, JOHN, 40, , MARINER, 10/24/1855
1. U.S. 2. U.S. 3. ZANZIBAR, MOZAMBIQUE

JONES, JOHN, 54, M, MASTER MARINER, 06/14/1859
1. U.S. 2. U.S. 3. ZANZIBAR

JONES, JOHN, 35, M, MINER, 10/13/1865
1. BRITISH AMERICA 2. U.S. 3. COW BAY

JONES, MARGAREET, 28, F, HOUSEWIFE, 10/13/1865
1. BRITISH AMERICA 2. U.S. 3. COW BAY

JONES, MARY JANE, 4, F, , 10/13/1865
1. BRITISH AMERICA 2. U.S. 3. COW BAY

JONES, PELEG G., 33, M, MARINER, 03/13/1829
1. U.S. 2. U.S. 3. HAVANA

JONES, RICHARD, 22, M, HANNNER, 06/16/1828
1. ENGLAND 2. U.S. 3. LIVERPOOL

JONES, THOMAS, 26, M, WHEELWRIGHT, 06/04/1835
1. U.S. 2. U.S. 3. MATANZAS

JONES, WM., 30, M, LABORER, 08/25/1834
1. NOVA SCOTIA 2. U.S. 3. PICTOU

JONTE, ISABELE, 18, F, , 09/11/1837
1. IRELAND 2. UTICA 3. PICTOU

JOSE, COSTODIO, 56, M, FARMER, 08/28/1872
1. SAN MIQUEL 2. PROVIDENCE 3.

JOSE, FRANCISCO, 16, M, FARMER, 08/28/1872
1. SAN MIQUEL 2. BOSTON 3.

JOSE, FRANCISCO, 30, M, MARINER, 08/28/1872
1. FLORES 2. PROVIDENCE 3.

JOSE, MANUEL, 25, M, FARMER, 08/28/1872
1. FLORES 2. BOSTON 3.

JOSE, MARIA, 20, F, SEAMSTRESS, 08/28/1872
1. FLORES 2. BOSTON 3.

JOSHUON, CATHARINE, 32, F, , 07/03/1839
1. U.S. 2. U.S. 3. MATANZAS

JUBAFAN, WM., 38, M, LABORER, 08/08/1837
1. NOVA SCOTIA 2. NEW YORK 3. PICTOU

JURDSON, JOHN, 25, M, MACHINIST, 11/03/1849
1. BRITISH AMERICA 2. U.S. 3. PICTOU

JZIDARA, C., 40, M, , 06/09/1834
1. HAITI 2. U.S. 3. MATANZAS

KAVANAUGH, MARY ANN, 20, F, DOMESTIC, 08/19/1840
1. IRELAND 2. U.S. 3. SYDNEY

KEATH, ROBERT, 30, M, ENGINEER, 04/13/1857
1. U.S. 2. U.S. 3. MATANZAS

KELLEY, ANDREW, 21, M, MOULDER, 04/16/1835
1. U.S. 2. U.S. 3. HAVANA

KELLEY, MARY ANN, 17, F, SERVANT, 07/28/1862
1. NOVA SCOTIA 2. U.S. 3. PICTOU

KELLEY, PATRICK, 32, M, MASON, 04/16/1827
1. IRELAND 2. U.S. 3. MATANZAS

KELLY, , , , CHILD, 06/18/1850
1. PRINCE EDWARD ISLAND 2. U.S. 3. PICTOU

KELLY, CORNELIUS, 21, M, MERCHANT, 05/07/1824
1. IRELAND 2. U.S. 3. HAITI

KELLY, JOHN, 23, , CLERK, 05/09/1837
1. IRELAND 2. U.S. 3. LIVERPOOL

KELLY, MARY, 23, F, , 10/01/1850
1. BRITISH AMERICA 2. U.S. 3. PICTOU

KELLY, MARY, 23, F, SERVANT, 06/18/1850
1. PRINCE EDWARD ISLAND 2. U.S. 3. PICTOU

KELLY, MICHAEL, 38, M, COOPER, 06/28/1849
1. BRITISH AMERICA 2. U.S. 3. PICTOU

KELLY, THOMAS, 22, , CLERK, 05/09/1837
1. IRELAND 2. NEW YORK 3. LIVERPOOL

KELLY, WILLIAM, 26, M, LABORER, 06/03/1844
1. IRELAND 2. U.S. 3. PICTOU

KELPS, JOHN, 23, , GARDENER, 05/09/1837
1. IRELAND 2. NEW YORK 3. LIVERPOOL

KELPS, WM., 20, , WEAVER, 05/09/1837
1. IRELAND 2. NEW YORK 3. LIVERPOOL

KEMP, SIDNEY, 45, , MERCHANT, 09/01/1866
1. GREAT BRITAIN 2. GREAT BRITAIN 3. GREAT HARBOUT BAHAMA BANKS

KENEDY, MORRIS, 21, M, LABOR SINGLE, 1836
1. COUNTY TIPPERARY, IRE. 2. NEW YORK 3. PICTOU

KENNEDY, THOMAS, 39, M, BLACKSMITH, 08/20/1857
1. NOVA SCOTIA 2. NOVA SCOTIA 3. PICTOU

KENNY, B.M., 42, M, PHYSICIAN, 07/07/1846
1. NEW YORK STATE 2. NEW YORK 3. MATANZAS

KERN, FRANCIS, 26, M, MILLER, 06/03/1844
1. NOVA SCOTIA 2. NOVA SCOTIA 3. PICTOU

KERR, AGNES, 20, F, DOMESTIC, 09/21/1859
1. NOVA SCOTIA 2. U.S. 3. PICTOU

KERVAN, BRIDGET, 30, F, , 08/16/1850
1. NOVA SCOTIA 2. U.S. 3. PICTOU

KERVAN, MICHAEL, 13, M, , 08/16/1850
1. NOVA SCOTIA 2. U.S. 3. PICTOU

KEYSER, ADAM, 28, M, OF THE THEATRE, 06/26/1832
1. U.S. 2. U.S. 3. ST. BARTHOLOMEW

KEYSER, RACHAEL, 30, F, OF THE THEATRE, 06/26/1832
1. U.S. 2. U.S. 3. ST. BARTHOLOMEW

KILBERT, THOMAS, 53, M, ENGINEER, 04/16/1835
1. U.S. 2. U.S. 3. HAVANA

KILBURN, P.C., 32, M, SHIP MASTER, 02/08/1841
1. U.S. 2. U.S. 3. MATANZAS

KILLEN, MARY, 24, F, LADY, 07/20/1844
1. NOVA SCOTIA 2. U.S. 3. PICTOU

KILSER, MRS., 35, F, LADY, 07/07/1841
1. MATANZAS 2. MATANZAS 3. MATANZAS

KILSER, THOS., 54, M, ENGINEER, 07/07/1841
1. MATANZAS 2. MATANZAS 3. MATANZAS

KING, JAMES, 59, M, PRINTER, 10/24/1854
1. GREAT BRITAIN 2. U.S. 3. GLASGOW

KING, JAMES, 4, M, NONE, 10/24/1854
1. GREAT BRITAIN 2. U.S. 3. GLASGOW

KING, JOHN, 25, M, LABORER, 09/25/1833
1. IRELAND 2. U.S. 3. PICTOU

KING, JOHN, 26, M, PRINTER, 10/24/1854
1. GREAT BRITAIN 2. U.S. 3. GLASGOW

KING, MARY, 18, F, NONE, 10/24/1854
1. GREAT BRITAIN 2. U.S. 3. GLASGOW

KING, MRS. JAMES, 58, F, HOUSEWIFE, 10/24/1854
1. GREAT BRITAIN 2. U.S. 3. GLASGOW

KINGELING, JAN GERARD, 35, M, GENTLEMAN, 12/02/1828
1. SURINAM 2. U.S. 3. SURINAM

KINGSTON, CATHARINE, 13, F, LABORER, 08/09/1839
1. NOVA SCOTIA 2. U.S. 3. PICTOU

KINGSTON, REBECCA, 62, F, LABORER, 08/09/1839
1. NOVA SCOTIA 2. U.S. 3. PICTOU

KINGSTON, SAMUEL, 68, M, LABOUR, 08/09/1839
1. NOVA SCOTIA 2. U.S. 3. PICTOU

KINGSTON, WILLIAM, 27, M, LABORER, 08/09/1839
1. NOVA SCOTIA 2. U.S. 3. PICTOU

KINZLER, MARY, 20, F, NONE, 08/20/1857
1. NOVA SCOTIA 2. U.S. 3. PICTOU

KIREAN, JAMES, , M, , 10/06/1848
1. BRITISH AMERICA 2. U.S. 3. PICTOU

KIRKRE, CATHARINE, 21, F, SERVANT, 06/18/1850
1. NOVA SCOTIA 2. U.S. 3. PICTOU

KITCHEL, EZEKIEL, 63, M, CARPENTER, 08/05/1839
1. U.S. 2. U.S. 3. HAVANA

KITCHEL, MR., 38, M, ENGINEER, 08/05/1839
1. U.S. 2. U.S. 3. HAVANA

KITCHEL, MRS., 37, F, , 08/05/1839
1. U.S. 2. U.S. 3. HAVANA

KNIGHT, JOSEPH, 19, M, , 07/03/1839
1. U.S. 2. U.S. 3. MATANZAS

KONIGSLOW, W. VAN, 45, M, MERCHANT, 03/01/1832
1. HAMBURG 2. U.S. 3. SURINAM

LACHAPELLE, B.F., 25, M, MERCHANT, 10/25/1825
1. U.S. 2. U.S. 3. MARTINIQUE

LALANNE, DELOROLA, 17, F, , 07/16/1835
1. 2. 3. MATANZAS

LALANUE, ANNLU, 28, F, , 07/16/1835
1. 2. 3. MATANZAS

LALANUE, SANTIAGO, 38, M, MERCHANT, 07/16/1835
1. --- 2. 3. MATANZAS

LAMBERT, RICHARD, 24, , LABORER, 05/09/1837
1. IRELAND 2. NEW YORK 3. LIVERPOOL

LAMPHIER, WILLIAM B., 30, M, ENGINEER, 08/08/1837
1. ALEXANDRA 2. U.S. 3. HAVANA

LAMPSON, T.G., 48, M, MERCHANT, 08/25/1828
1. U.S. 2. U.S. 3. CURACOA

LANDIRGEN, ANDREAS L., 20, M, MARINER, 07/19/1850
1. DENMARK 2. DENMARK 3. EAST CAICOS, TURKS ISLAND

LANDRY, ALFRED, 10, M, , 1872
1. NOVA SCOTIA 2. 3.

LANDRY, JULIA, 48, F, HOUSE KEEPER,1872
1. NOVA SCOTIA 2. BOSTON 3.

LANDRY, SIMON, 7, M, , 1872
1. NOVA SCOTIA 2. 3.

LANDRY, THOMAS, 10, M, , 1872
1. NOVA SCOTIA 2. 3.

LANE, EDWARD G., 40, , GENTLEMAN, 01/27/1842
1. U.S. 2. U.S. 3. MATANZAS

LANGSTON, DAVID, 8, M, , 07/03/1851
1. BRITISH AMERICA 2. U.S. 3. PICTOU

LANGSTON, ELISABETH, 54, F, , 07/03/1851
1. BRITISH AMERICA 2. U.S. 3. PICTOU

LANGSTON, GEORGE, 12, M, , 07/03/1851
1. BRITISH AMERICA 2. U.S. 3. PICTOU

LANGSTON, JAMES, 10, M, , 07/03/1851
1. BRITISH AMERICA 2. U.S. 3. PICTOU

LANGSTON, MARIA, 17, F, , 07/03/1851
1. BRITISH AMERICA 2. U.S. 3. PICTOU

LANGSTON, THOMAS, 55, M, MINER, 07/03/1851
1. BRITISH AMERICA 2. U.S. 3. PICTOU

LANSTON, WILLIAM, 14, M, , 07/03/1851
1. BRITISH AMERICA 2. U.S. 3. PICTOU

LAPATES, JUAQUIER, 22, M, GENTLEMAN, 06/15/1832
1. SPAIN 2. SPAIN 3. HAVANA

LARKIN, PAT, 25, , LABORER, 05/09/1837
1. IRELAND 2. U.S. 3. LIVERPOOL

LARKIN, WM., 22, , LABORER, 05/09/1837
1. IRELAND 2. U.S. 3. LIVERPOOL

LARSON, WM. N., 28, M, SEAMAN, 11/20/1854
1. GREAT BRITAIN 2. GREAT BRITAIN 3. TURKS ISLAND

LATERI, FRANK, 30, M, CARPENTER, 05/06/1867
1. SPAIN 2. U.S. 3. ARDROSSAN

LAUGHLIN, ESABELLA R., 15, F, SERVANT, 09/13/1844
1. PICTOU 2. U.S. 3. PICTOU

LAVIN, JOHNATHAN, 46, M, MECHANIC, 03/11/1841
1. U.S. 2. U.S. 3. HAVANA

LAWLER, PATRICK, 23, , LABORER, 05/09/1837
1. IRELAND 2. NEW YORK 3. LIVERPOOL

LAWLER, THOMAS, 19, , LABORER, 05/09/1837
1. IRELAND 2. NEW YORK 3. LIVERPOOL

LAWLER, THOMAS, 6 MONTHS, , CHILD, 05/09/1837
1. IRELAND 2. NEW YORK 3. LIVERPOOL

LAYTON, HANNAH, 17, F, , 09/29/1852
1. BRITISH AMERICA 2. U.S. 3. PICTOU

LEACH, JOHN, 35, M, SEAMAN, 08/27/1860
1. U.S. 2. U.S. 3. PICTOU

LEACH, MRS.JOHN, 30, F, HOUSEWIFE, 08/27/1860
1. U.S. 2. U.S. 3. PICTOU

LEAD, BENJAMIN, 25, , LABORER, 05/09/1837
1. ENGLAND 2. U.S. 3. LIVERPOOL

LEBLANC, CELESTE, 34, F, HOUSE KEEPER, 1872
1. NOVA SCOTIA 2. 3.

LEBLANC, CLEOFAT, 12, M, , 1872
1. NOVA SCOTIA 2. 3.

LEBLANC, JANE, 5, F, , 1872
1. NOVA SCOTIA 2. 3.

LEBLANC, LOUISE, 7, F, , 1872
1. NOVA SCOTIA 2. 3.

LEBLANC, PETER, 3, M, , 1872
1. NOVA SCOTIA 2. 3.

LECT, JANE, 17, F, LADY, 08/18/1849
1. BRITISH AMERICA 2. U.S. 3. PICTOU

LEDWIEGE, ANN, 22, , SERVANT, 05/09/1837
1. IRELAND 2. U.S. 3. LIVERPOOL

LEE, FANNY, 5, F, NONE, 08/03/1855
1. GREAT BRITAIN 2. U.S. 3. LIVERPOOL

LEE, JOHN, 12, M, NONE, 08/03/1855
1. GREAT BRITAIN 2. U.S. 3. LIVERPOOL

LEE, MARY, 35, F, HOUSEWIFE, 08/03/1855
1. GREAT BRITAIN 2. U.S. 3. LIVERPOOL

LEESUM, ELIZABETH, 30, F, SERVANT, 10/18/1836
1. MADONMISHE 2. BOSTON 3. PICTOU

LELACHAN, CATHARINE, 38, , HOUSE WIFE, 07/18/1864
1. U.S. 2. U.S. 3. PICTOU

LELACHAN, JOHN, 10, , , 07/18/1864
1. 2. 3. PICTOU

LELACHAN, PAUL, 14, , , 07/18/1864
1. 2. 3. PICTOU

LELACHAN, WILLIAM, 40, , SHIP CARPENTER, 07/18/1864
1. U.S. 2. U.S. 3. PICTOU

LELACHAN, WILLIAM, 12, , , 07/18/1864
1. 2. 3. PICTOU

LELAN, D., 11, F, , 07/11/1833
1. CUBA 2. CUBA 3. MATANZAS

LELAN, LOUISA, 28, F, WIFE OF SANTIAGO, 07/11/1833
1. CUBA 2. CUBA 3. MATANZAS

LELAN, SANTIAGO, 35, M, PLANTER, 07/11/1833
1. CUBA 2. CUBA 3. MATANZAS

LELLEN, T.H. M., 30, M, SHIP CARPENTER, 07/01/1850
1. BRITISH AMERICA 2. U.S. 3. PICTOU

LEMESLE, THOMAS, , , , 12/14/1823
1. MORRISTOWN 2. GUADELOUPE 3. PROVIDENCE

LEMOIS, CATHARINE, 27, F, SERVANT, 09/16/1858
1. NOVA SCOTIA 2. U.S. 3. PICTOU

LENNON, CATHARINE, 28, F, , 06/05/1860
1. NOVA SCOTIA 2. U.S. 3. PICTOU

LENNON, MARY, 18, F, , 08/16/1850
1. NOVA SCOTIA 2. U.S. 3. PICTOU

LENNON, NANCY, 23, F, , 08/16/1850
1. NOVA SCOTIA 2. U.S. 3. PICTOU

LEONARD, MARIA, 25, F, SERVANT OR ASSISTANT, 08/09/1853
1. NOVA SCOTIA 2. U.S. 3. PICTOU

LETCHER, JAMES, 5, M, , 05/09/1859
1. NOVA SCOTIA 2. U.S. 3. PICTOU

LETCHER, JESSIE, 33, F, HOUSEWIFE, 05/09/1859
1. NOVA SCOTIA 2. U.S. 3. PICTOU

LETCHER, PAUL, 5, M, , 05/09/1859
1. NOVA SCOTIA 2. U.S. 3. PICTOU

LETCHER, WILLIAM, 39, M, SHIP CARPENTER, 05/09/1859
1. NOVA SCOTIA 2. U.S. 3. PICTOU

LETCHER, JR., WILLIAM, 3, M, , 05/09/1859
1. NOVA SCOTIA 2. U.S. 3. PICTOU

LEWELLAN, SAMUEL, 22, M, FARMER, 10/13/1846
1. BRITISH AMERICA 2. U.S. 3. PICTOU

LEWIS, JOHN, 23, M, PLACED ABOARD BY CONSUL, 09/03/1821
1. U.S. 2. U.S. 3. MADEIRA

LEWIS, MARY, 37, F, LADY, 03/17/1843
1. U.S. 2. U.S. 3. HAVANA

LIGHTBURN, ALEXANDER, 14, M, GENTLEMAN, 08/03/1835
1. TURKS ISLAND 2. GREAT BRITAIN 3. TURKS ISLAND

LIMBAUGH, CHRISTIAN, 54, M, GENTLEMAN, 06/30/1831
1. U.S. 2. U.S. 3. HAVANA

LINCOLN, RUSSELL, 35, M, MERCHANT, 04/11/1827
1. U.S. 2. U.S. 3. HAVANA

LINDSAY, ALLEN, 32, M, COOPER, 06/18/1839
1. U.S. 2. U.S. 3. MATANZAS

LINDSEY, JAMES, 28, M, BAKER, 11/05/1834
1. NOVA SCOTIA 2. PHILADELPHIA 3. PICTOU

LIPPINCOTT, JANE, 8, F, LADY, 10/02/1839
1. NOVA SCOTIA 2. U.S. 3. PICTOU

LIPPINCOTT, JOHN, 42, M, GENTLEMAN, 10/02/1839
1. NOVA SCOTIA 2. U.S. 3. PICTOU

LIPPINCOTT, MARY, 5, F, LADY, 10/02/1839
1. NOVA SCOTIA 2. U.S. 3. PICTOU

LIPPINCOTT, SARAH, 33, F, LADY, 10/02/1839
1. NOVA SCOTIA 2. U.S. 3. PICTOU

LIPPINCOTT, SARAH, 11, F, LADY, 10/02/1839
1. NOVA SCOTIA 2. U.S. 3. PICTOU

LISSETT, RICHARD, 33, M, PAINTER, 07/03/1845
1. ENGLAND 2. U.S. 3. PICTOU

LISTER, JOHN, 23, M, MECANNIC, 04/07/1831
1. U.S. 2. U.S. 3. HAVANA

LITHGOW, WM., 33, M, MARINER, 09/30/1826
1. U.S. 2. U.S. 3. HAVANA

LIVISTON, ARCHIBAL, 19, M, BLACKSMITH, 09/20/1851
1. BRITISH AMERICA 2. U.S. 3. PICTOU

LOCHEAD, DAVID, 6, M, , 06/23/1857
1. PICTOU 2. MERLAND, U.S. 3. PICTOU

LOCHEAD, ELEZABETH, 28, F, , 06/23/1857
1. PICTOU 2. MERLAND, U.S. 3. PICTOU

LOCHEAD, ELEZABETH, 4, F, , 06/23/1857
1. PICTOU 2. MERLAND, U.S. 3. PICTOU

LOCHEAD, GEORGE, 4 MONTHS, M, , 06/23/1857
1. PICTOU 2. MERLAND, U.S. 3. PICTOU

LOCHEAD, MARY, 2, F, , 06/23/1857
1. PICTOU 2. MERLAND, U.S. 3. PICTOU

LODGE, ANN, 30, F, , 06/20/1837
1. PRINCE EDWARD ISLAND 2. INDIANA 3. PICTOU

LODGE, CHARLOTT, 9, F, , 06/20/1837
1. PRINCE EDWARD ISLAND 2. INDIANA 3. PICTOU

LODGE, ELIZABETH, 50, F, , 06/20/1837
1. PRINCE EDWARD ISLAND 2. INDIANA 3. PICTOU

LODGE, ELIZABETH, 1, F, , 06/20/1837
1. PRINCE EDWARD ISLAND 2. INDIANA 3. PICTOU

LODGE, ELMAN, 30, M, YEOMAN, 06/20/1837
1. PRINCE EDWARD ISLAND 2. INDIANA 3. PICTOU

LODGE, HARIAT, 20, F, , 06/20/1837
1. PRINCE EDWARD ISLAND 2. INDIANA 3. PICTOU

LODGE, HARIAT, 12, F, , 06/20/1837
1. PRINCE EDWARD ISLAND 2. INDIANA 3. PICTOU

LODGE, HENAREY, 3, M, , 06/20/1837
   1. PRINCE EDWARD ISLAND 2. INDIANA 3. PICTOU

LODGE, NATHAN, 25, M, YEOMAN, 06/20/1837
   1. PRINCE EDWARD ISLAND 2. INDIANA 3. PICTOU

LODGE, NATHAN, 5, M, , 06/20/1837
   1. PRINCE EDWARD ISLAND 2. INDIANA 3. PICTOU

LODGE, WM., 4, M, , 06/20/1837
   1. PRINCE EDWARD ISLAND 2. INDIANA 3. PICTOU

LOGAN, ALEXANDER, 24, M, SHIP WRIGHT, 09/09/1844
   1. NOVA SCOTIA 2. U.S. 3. PICTOU

LOGAN, CATHARINE, 18, F, SERVANT, 09/09/1844
   1. NOVA SCOTIA 2. U.S. 3. PICTOU

LOGAN, ISABELLA, 21, F, SERVANT, 09/09/1844
   1. NOVA SCOTIA 2. U.S. 3. PICTOU

LOMBA, JURRINO DE, 15, M, MARINER, 10/17/1867
   1. CAPE DE VERDE IS. 2. U.S. 3. FLORES

LOONEY, ELLEN, 25, F, SERVANT, 09/25/1843
   1. IRELAND 2. U.S. 3. PICTOU

LOPES, MANUEL, 18, , , 05/18/1868
   1. 2. 3. BRAVA

LOPES, NARCIO, 55, M, MERCHANT, 07/24/1848
   1. CUBA 2. CUBA 3. MATANZAS

LORENCO, MANUEL, 32, M, MARINER, 08/28/1872
   1. FLORES 2. PROVIDENCE 3.

LOTZ, GEO., 40, M, MECHANIC, 06/22/1840
   1. U.S. 2. U.S. 3. MATANZAS

LOUGHLAN, CYBELLE, 3, F, , 08/13/1833
   1. CORK 2. MEDWAY, MASS. 3. LIVERPOOL

LOUGHLAN, CYBELLE W., 30, F, , 08/13/1833
   1. MEDWAY, MASS. 2. MEDWAY, MASS. 3. LIVERPOOL

LOUGHLAN, DAVID, 5, M, , 08/13/1833
   1. PROVIDENCE 2. MEDWAY, MASS. 3. LIVERPOOL

LOUGHLAN, EDMUND, 6 MONTHS, M, , 08/13/1833
   1. CORK 2. MEDWAY, MASS. 3. LIVERPOOL

LOUGHLAN, MARY, 7, F, , 08/13/1833
   1. MEDWAY, MASS. 2. MEDWAY, MASS. 3. LIVERPOOL

LOUGHLAN, NICOLAS, 40, M, MANUFACTURER, 08/13/1833
1. CORK/MEDWAY, MASS. 2. MEDWAY, MASS. 3. LIVERPOOL

LOVE, AGNES, 19, F, SERVANT, 08/22/1850
1. BRITISH AMERICA 2. U.S. 3. PICTOU

LOVE, CHARLES, 30, M, MECHANIC, 06/08/1838
1. U.S. 2. PROVIDENCE 3. HAVANA

LOVE, JAMES, 31, M, MINER, 08/20/1857
1. U.S. 2. U.S. 3. PICTOU

LOVITT, JOHN W., 30, M, CARPENTER, 07/16/1823
1. U.S. 2. U.S. 3. HAVANA

LOYD, JOHN, 38, M, LABORER, 08/23/1832
1. NOVA SCOTIA 2. U.S. 3. PICTOU

LUMSDEN, JAMES, 25, M, MASON, 07/05/1823
1. SCOTLAND 2. U.S. 3. HONDURAS

LUNDGREN, JOHAN, 16, M, BOY, 06/27/1827
1. SWEDEN 2. 3. GOTENBURG

LURCAS, JOAQUINA, 30, F, ---, 08/28/1872
1. FLORES 2. BOSTON 3.

LUTHER, GEORGE, 25, M, , 07/22/1834
1. U.S. 2. U.S. 3. HAVANA

LUTHER, JEREMIAH, 32, M, MECHANIC, 05/10/1842
1. U.S. 2. U.S. 3. MATANZAS

LUTHER, JEREMIAH, 38, M, COOPER, 07/22/1847
1. U.S. 2. U.S. 3. MATANZAS

LUTHER, JEREMIAH, 40, M, COOPER, 08/03/1855
1. U.S. 2. U.S. 3. MATANZAS

LYNCH, ABRAHAM, 10, M, , 09/25/1843
1. IRELAND 2. U.S. 3. PICTOU

LYNCH, BETSEY, 17, F, SERVANT, 09/25/1843
1. IRELAND 2. U.S. 3. PICTOU

LYNCH, ELLEN, 50, F, SERVANT, 09/25/1843
1. IRELAND 2. U.S. 3. PICTOU

LYNCH, MARY ANN, 15, F, SERVANT, 09/25/1843
1. IRELAND 2. U.S. 3. PICTOU

LYNCH, SAML, 16, M, LABOUR, 09/25/1843
1. IRELAND 2. U.S. 3. PICTOU

LYNCH, WILLIAM, 12, M, , 09/25/1843
1. IRELAND 2. U.S. 3. PICTOU

LYON, WILLIAM E., 27, M, GENTLEMEN, 05/26/1826
1. U.S. 2. U.S. 3. ANTIQUA

M---, JOSE JACINTO, 25, M, FARMER, 08/28/1872
1. S. MIQUEL 2. PROVIDENCE 3.

MACCLOUD, JOHN, 26, M, HOUSE JOINER, 09/26/1837
1. PICTOU 2. ALABAMA 3. PICTOU

MACHADO, ANTONIO, 27, M, MARINER, 08/28/1872
1. FLORES 2. BOSTON 3.

MACKLIN, MARY, 20, , SPINSTER, 05/09/1837
1. IRELAND 2. U.S. 3. LIVERPOOL

MACY, JOHN W., 25, M, MERCHANT, 08/14/1820
1. U.S. 2. U.S. 3. SANTIAGO

MADDEN, EVALINA, 20, F, LADY, 05/16/1842
1. CUBA 2. CUBA 3. HAVANA

MADEN, ESTHER, 17, F, SERVANT, 08/21/1852
1. BRITISH AMERICA 2. U.S. 3. PICTOU

MADEN, MARTIN, 18, , CLERK, 05/09/1837
1. IRELAND 2. NEW YORK 3. LIVERPOOL

MAGOW, PHILLIP, 40, M, MARINER, 05/27/1823
1. U.S. 2. U.S. 3. L. BARTS

MAH, JOHN, 25, M, LABORER, 09/27/1841
1. U.S. 2. U.S. 3. PICTOU

MAHANAGAN, JOHN, 19, M, LABORER, 09/18/1823
1. IRELAND 2. U.S. 3. HONDURAS

MAHANEY, MARGARET, 17, F, HOUSE MAID, 09/25/1860
1. NOVA SCOTIA 2. U.S. 3. PICTOU

MAHONY, BRIDGET, 25, F, , 10/01/1850
1. BRITISH AMERICA 2. U.S. 3. PICTOU

MAHONY, JOHN, 23, , LABORER, 05/09/1837
1. IRELAND 2. NEW YORK 3. LIVERPOOL

MALCOM, REV. HOWARD, 40, M, MISSONARY AGENT, 03/28/1838
1. U.S. 2. U.S. 3. CANTON

MALCOLM, JAMES, 26, M, MILLER, 05/23/1844
1. SCOTLAND 2. U.S. 3. PICTOU

MALDAS, JOAQUIM, 25, M, MARINER, 08/28/1872
1. FLORES 2. BOSTON 3.

MALFATHER, WM., 20, , LABORER, 05/09/1837
1. IRELAND 2. U.S. 3. LIVERPOOL

MANCHESTER, ALBERT, 42, M, COOPER, 04/08/1854
1. U.S. 2. U.S. 3.

MANCHESTER, LUTHER, 26, M, COOPER, 06/01/1843
1. U.S. 2. U.S. 3. MATANZAS

MANDEUL, JOHN, 41, M, MERCHANT, 08/06/1836
1. U.S. 2. 3. HAVANA

MANNY, JAMES, 32, M, CARPENTER, 05/05/1829
1. U.S. 2. U.S. 3. MATANZAS

MANTON, JOSEPH B., 19, M, GENTLEMAN, 09/28/1842
1. U.S. 2. U.S. 3. ST. PETERSBURG

MANUA-Z, MISS, 23, F, SERVANT, 03/22/1837
1. CUBA 2. U.S. 3. HAVANA

MANUBO, JOSE B., 34, M, MARINER, 08/28/1872
1. FLORES 2. BOSTON 3.

MARCIAL, JOHN, 35, M, CARPENTER, 07/08/1848
1. PICTOU 2. PROVIDENCE 3. PICTOU

MARDEN, A.L., 30, M, CARPENTER, 06/18/1839
1. U.S. 2. U.S. 3. MATANZAS

MARKS, MARK, 21, M, GRADY MAN, 09/09/1836
1. ENGLAND 2. NEW YORK 3. LIVERPOOL

MARNILD LACY, ANNE SATRIGE, 49, F, , 07/29/1846
1. PROVIDENCE 2. PROVIDENCE 3. PICTOU

MARRIOW, JAMES, 19, , LABORER, 05/09/1837
1. IRELAND 2. NEW YORK 3. LIVERPOOL

MARSHALL, ANNIE, 22, F, SERVANT, 07/12/1864
1. BRITISH AMERICA 2. U.S. 3. PICTOU

MARSHALL, BENJAMIN, 22, M, COOPER, 05/27/1823
1. U.S. 2. U.S. 3. HAVANA

MARSHALL, BENJAMIN, 25, M, COOPER, 07/07/1825
1. U.S. 2. U.S. 3. HAVANA

MARSHALL, SAMUEL, 21, M, ENGINEER, 05/30/1842
1. U.S. 2. U.S. 3. MATANZAS

MARSTON, SAMUEL, 40, M, CARPENTER, 06/29/1829
1. U.S. 2. U.S. 3. HAVANA

MARTIN, ANN, 22, , SPINSTER, 05/09/1837
1. IRELAND 2. U.S. 3. LIVERPOOL

MARTIN, JOHN HENRY, 20, M, MERCHANT, 05/24/1831
1. U.S. 2. U.S. 3. MATANZAS

MARTIN, MICHAEL, 16, , , 05/18/1868
1. 2. 3. BRAVA

MARTIN, ROSA MARIA, 34, , , 05/18/1868
1. 2. 3. BRAVA

MARTIN, THOMAS, 32, , LABORER, 05/09/1837
1. IRELAND 2. NEW YORK 3. LIVERPOOL

MARTINEZ, PEDRO J., 21, M, GENTLEMAN, 10/25/1853
1. CHILE 2. CHILE 3. TALCAHUANO

MARTINS, JOSE, 23, M, MARINER, 08/28/1872
1. FLORES 2. PROVIDENCE 3.

MASON, ALSEVIN, 21, M, MERCHANT, 08/18/1843
1. U.S. 2. U.S. 3. PICTOU

MASON, JOHN P., 21, M, CARPENTER, 06/29/1829
1. U.S. 2. U.S. 3. HAVANA

MASON, MARY, 20, F, DRESSMAKER, 09/21/1868
1. NEW BRUNSWICK 2. U.S. 3. NEWCASTLE

MASS, ROSA LA, 19, , SERVANT, 10/24/1855
1. ST. HELENA 2. U.S. 3. ZANZIBAR, MOZAMBIQUE

MASSCALINA, LUCIA, 18, F, SEAMSTRESS, 08/28/1872
1. FLORES 2. PROVIDENCE 3.

MASZ, ALL, 22, M, SERVANT, 10/25/1853
1. AFRICA 2. U.S. 3. ZANZIBAR

MATHESON, JESSIE, 23, F, LADY, 07/31/1845
1. NOVA SCOTIA 2. NOVA SCOTIA 3. PICTOU

MATHESON, ROBERT, 25, M, LABORER, 11/11/1844
1. SCOTLAND 2. U.S. 3. PICTOU

MATHEWS, GIDEON, 28, M, MARINA, 05/06/1867
1. U.S. 2. U.S. 3. ARDROSSAN

MATHEWS, JOSEPH C., 17, M, HOUSE CARPENTER, 05/22/1857
1. ST.BARTHOLOMEW, SWEDEN 2. U.S. 3. ST. BARTHOLOMEW, N.S.

MATHEWSON, ALEXANDER, 27, M, MASON, 09/09/1836
1. SCOTLAND 2. U.S. 3. PICTOU

MATHEWSON, C., 21, F, BOARDING HOUSE, 08/31/1853
1. U.S. 2. U.S. 3. ARICHAT

MATHEWSON, HANNAH, 24, F, LADY, 09/04/1841
1. U.S. 2. U.S. 3. PICTOU

MATHEWSON, ISAAC, 27, M, MERCHANT, 09/04/1841
1. U.S. 2. U.S. 3. PICTOU

MATHEWSON, JANE, 22, F, , 09/09/1836
1. NOVA SCOTIA 2. U.S. 3. PICTOU

MATHEWSON, M., 26, M, MERCHANT,CLOTHING DEALER, 08/31/1853
1. U.S. 2. U.S. 3. ARICHAT

MAURAN, BORDEN, 15, , , 05/28/1838
1. 2. 3. MATANZAS

MAURAN, JOSEPH, 41, M, DOCTOR, 05/28/1838
1. U.S. 2. 3. MATANZAS

MAURAN JR., JOHN, 29, , GENTLEMAN, 01/27/1842
1. U.S. 2. U.S. 3. MATANZAS

MAWNEY, ROBERT G., 24, M, MECHANIC, 03/11/1841
1. U.S. 2. U.S. 3. HAVANA

MAXION, JAMES, 24, , LABORER, 05/09/1837
1. IRELAND 2. NEW YORK 3. LIVERPOOL

MAXWELL, ANNIE, 8, F, , 08/31/1866
1. U.S. 2. U.S. 3. PICTOU

MAXWELL, ANNIE, 30, F, HOUSE MAID, 09/17/1860
1. NOVA SCOTIA 2. U.S. 3. PICTOU

MAXWELL, BARBARA, 35, F, LADY, 07/08/1848
1. PICTOU 2. BOSTON 3. PICTOU

MAXWELL, JAMES, 25, M, MINER, 08/03/1857
1. NOVA SCOTIA 2. NOVA SCOTIA 3. PICTOU

MAXWELL, MARY, 17, F, SPINSTER, 09/18/1845
1. NOVA SCOTIA 2. U.S. 3. PICTOU

MAXWELL, MRS. A., 34, F, HOUSE WIFE, 09/25/1863
1. BRITISH AMERICA 2. U.S. 3. PICTOU

MAXWORTH, ANN, 11, , SERVANT, 09/01/1867
1. 2. 3. PICTOU

MAYNE, JOHN, 21, M, LABORER, 09/02/1845
    1. ENGLAND 2. U.S. 3. PICTOU

MAYO, DORCAS, 50, F, , 06/23/1830
    1. U.S. 2. U.S. 3. MATANZAS

MCARTHUR, CHRISTY, 22, M, SERVANT, 08/30/1855
    1. NOVA SCOTIA 2. U.S. 3. PICTOU

MCARTHUR, JESSIE, 27, F, SERVANT, 07/05/1864
    1. NOVA SCOTIA 2. U.S. 3. PICTOU

MCAULAY, CHRISTIE, 19, F, HOUSE MAID, 09/19/1860
    1. NOVA SCOTIA 2. U.S. 3. PICTOU

MCBAIN, MARGARET, 23, F, SERVANT, 07/12/1864
    1. BRITISH AMERICA 2. U.S. 3. PICTOU

MCBATH, RODERICK, 24, M, FARMER, 07/11/1850
    1. BRITISH AMERICA 2. CANADA 3. PICTOU

MCBEATH, DOUMALA, 21, N, , 11/14/1853
    1. NOVA SCOTIA 2. U.S. 3. PICTOU

MCBETH, JOHN, 34, , LABORER, 09/16/1869
    1. BRITISH AMERICA 2. U.S. 3. LUIZAN

MCCABE, GEORGE, 20, M, SHIP CARPENTER, 07/26/1848
    1. BRITISH AMERICA 2. BRITISH AMERICA 3. PICTOU

MCCABE, JAMES, 13, M, NONE, 07/12/1855
    1. U.S. 2. U.S. 3. PICTOU

MCCALE, ANTHONY, 10, M, LAD, 07/03/1845
    1. BRITISH AMERICA 2. U.S. 3. PICTOU

MCCALE, JOHN HENRY, 12, M, LAD, 07/03/1845
    1. BRITISH AMERICA 2. U.S. 3. PICTOU

MCCALE, MARGARET, 17, F, SERVANT, 07/03/1845
    1. BRITISH AMERICA 2. U.S. 3. PICTOU

MCCALE, SARAH, 33, F, SERVANT, 07/03/1845
    1. BRITISH AMERICA 2. U.S. 3. PICTOU

MCCALVY, FRANCIS, 30, , MINER, 08/27/1835
    1. GRUNOCK 2. 3. PICTOU

MCCAN, JOHN, 25, M, LABORER, 08/08/1844
    1. NOVA SCOTIA 2. U.S. 3. PICTOU

MCCARBESE, KEATY, 21, F, SERVANT, 09/09/1836
    1. NOVA SCOTIA 2. U.S. 3. PICTOU

MCCARKIN, CATHARINE, 13, F, LADY, 08/05/1847
1. BRITISH AMERICA 2. U.S. 3. PICTOU

MCCARKIN, DONALD, 6, M, CHILD, 08/05/1847
1. BRITISH AMERICA 2. U.S. 3. PICTOU

MCCARKIN, JOHN, 6, M, CHILD, 08/05/1847
1. BRITISH AMERICA 2. U.S. 3. PICTOU

MCCARKIN, MARY, 38, F, LADY, 08/05/1847
1. BRITISH AMERICA 2. U.S. 3. PICTOU

MCCARKIN, NANCY, 15, F, LADY, 08/05/1847
1. BRITISH AMERICA 2. U.S. 3. PICTOU

MCCARKIN, PETER, 55, M, FARMER, 08/05/1847
1. BRITISH AMERICA 2. U.S. 3. PICTOU

MCCARKIN, PETER, 6, M, CHILD, 08/05/1847
1. BRITISH AMERICA 2. U.S. 3. PICTOU

MCCARKIN, WILSON, 7, M, CHILD, 08/05/1847
1. BRITISH AMERICA 2. U.S. 3. PICTOU

MCCARTA, EUPHEMIA, 22, F, SERVANT, 07/12/1864
1. BRITISH AMERICA 2. U.S. 3. PICTOU

MCCARTY, SAMUEL, 29, M, LABORER, 09/07/1838
1. GREAT BRITAIN 2. U.S. 3. PICTOU

MCCAULEY, HUGH, 21, , TANNER AND CURRIER, 08/09/1869
1. BRITISH AMERICA 2. U.S. 3. PICTOU

MCCLEAN, MARGARET, 19, F, , 09/05/1860
1. NOVA SCOTIA 2. U.S. 3. PICTOU

MCCLELLAN, ELISABETH, 20, F, LADY, 07/08/1848
1. PICTOU 2. PROVIDENCE 3. PICTOU

MCCLELLAN, PETER, 18, M, LABORER, 09/14/1858
1. NOVA SCOTIA 2. U.S. 3. PICTOU

MCCLELLAND, CATHARINE, 21, F, SERVANT, 08/20/1857
1. NOVA SCOTIA 2. U.S. 3. PICTOU

MCCLENNAN, DUNCAN, 25, M, CARPENTER, 05/23/1844
1. SCOTLAND 2. U.S. 3. PICTOU

MCCLOUD, DAVID, 18, M, CABINET MAKER, 09/05/1839
1. PICTOU 2. MOBILE 3. PICTOU

MCCLOUD, DAVID, 24, M, FARMER, 08/16/1850
1. NOVA SCOTIA 2. U.S. 3. PICTOU

MCCLOUD, DONAL, 22, M, SHIP CARPENTER, 11/05/1834
1. NOVA SCOTIA 2. PAWTUCKET 3. PICTOU

MCCLOUD, ELLEN, 19, F, SERVANT, 08/23/1850
1. PICTOU 2. PROVIDENCE 3. PICTOU

MCCLOUD, FENEL, 18, F, , 09/19/1835
1. PICTOU 2. 3. PICTOU

MCCLOUD, ISABELLA, 23, F, SERVANT, 10/29/1850
1. BRITISH AMERICA 2. U.S. 3. PICTOU

MCCLOUD, JANETTE, 23, F, SERVANT, 09/09/1844
1. NOVA SCOTIA 2. U.S. 3. PICTOU

MCCLOUD, LYDIA, 13, F, SERVANT, 09/09/1844
1. NOVA SCOTIA 2. U.S. 3. PICTOU

MCCLOUD, MARGARET, 50, F, DOMESTIC, 10/17/1862
1. PICTOU 2. PROVIDENCE 3. PICTOU

MCCLOUD, MARY C., 21, F, SERVANT, 09/06/1855
1. NOVA SCOTIA 2. NOVA SCOTIA 3. PICTOU

MCCLOUD, NANCY, 22, F, SERVANT, 08/23/1850
1. PICTOU 2. PROVIDENCE 3. PICTOU

MCCLOUD, SARAH, 18, F, DOMESTIC, 10/10/1853
1. GREAT BRITAIN 2. GREAT BRITAIN 3. PICTOU

MCCLOUD, WILLIAM, 20, M, , 09/19/1835
1. PICTOU 2. 3. PICTOU

MCCOMB, JANE, 30, F, , 05/22/1857
1. U.S. 2. U.S. 3. PICTOU

MCCOMB, MARY, 5, F, , 05/22/1857
1. U.S. 2. U.S. 3. PICTOU

MCCOMB, ROSEANNA, 2, F, , 05/22/1857
1. U.S. 2. U.S. 3. PICTOU

MCCOMB, WILLIAM, 7, M, , 05/22/1857
1. U.S. 2. U.S. 3. PICTOU

MCCONNELL, ROBERT, 35, M, MERCHANT, 03/11/1828
1. U.S. 2. U.S. 3. PERNAMBUES

MCCOOL, ANN, 18, F, SERVANT, 07/20/1844
1. NOVA SCOTIA 2. U.S. 3. PICTOU

MCCOOL, JESSE, 21, F, SERVANT, 07/20/1844
1. NOVA SCOTIA 2. U.S. 3. PICTOU

MCCORMICK, WM., 20, , LABORER, 05/09/1837
1. IRELAND 2. NEW YORK 3. LIVERPOOL

MCCOUL, MARGARET, 16, F, LADY, 09/20/1847
1. NOVA SCOTIA 2. U.S. 3. PICTOU

MCCOULE, ANNE, 20, F, SERVANT, 07/30/1846
1. PICTOU 2. U.S. 3. PICTOU

MCCOULE, MARGARET, 15, F, SERVANT, 07/30/1846
1. PICTOU 2. U.S. 3. PICTOU

MCCOWL, JESSIE, 22, F, NONE, 09/12/1848
1. AMERICAN 2. AMERICA 3. PICTOU

MCCOY, BURTON, 18, M, CARPENTER, 08/25/1848
1. BRITISH AMERICA 2. U.S. 3. PICTOU

MCCOY, SARAH, 28, F, , 08/17/1850
1. PICTOU 2. U.S. 3. PICTOU

MCCUMINS, THOS., 22, , LABORER, 05/09/1837
1. IRELAND 2. NEW YORK 3. LIVERPOOL

MCDONALD, ALEX, 26, M, HOUSE CARPENTER, 06/25/1856
1. GREAT BRITAIN 2. GREAT BRITAIN 3. PICTOU

MCDONALD, ALEXANDER, 2, M, CHILD, 07/16/1846
1. NOVA SCOTIA 2. U.S. 3. PICTOU

MCDONALD, ALEXANDER, 18, M, FARMER, 07/07/1851
1. NOVA SCOTIA 2. U.S. 3. PICTOU

MCDONALD, ANGUS, 60, M, FARMER, 07/06/1846
1. NOVA SCOTIA 2. U.S. 3. PICTOU

MCDONALD, ANN, 16, , SERVANT, 09/01/1867
1. 2. 3. PICTOU

MCDONALD, ANN, 20, F, SPINSTER, 09/18/1845
1. NOVA SCOTIA 2. U.S. 3. PICTOU

MCDONALD, ARCHIBALD, 24, M, CARPENTER, 05/07/1859
1. NOVA SCOTIA 2. NOVA SCOTIA 3. PICTOU

MCDONALD, CATHARINE, 25, F, SERVANT, 07/20/1844
1. NOVA SCOTIA 2. U.S. 3. PICTOU

MCDONALD, CATHARINE, 18, F, HOUSE SERVANT, 08/05/1858
1. NOVA SCOTIA 2. U.S. 3. PICTOU

MCDONALD, CATHARINE, 23, F, SERVANT, 08/27/1846
1. NOVA SCOTIA 2. U.S. 3. PICTOU

MCDONALD, CATHARINE, 21, F, LADY, 07/07/1851
1. NOVA SCOTIA 2. U.S. 3. PICTOU

MCDONALD, CATHARINE, 19, F, DRESS MAKER, 09/25/1854
1. PICTOU 2. U.S. 3. PICTOU

MCDONALD, CATHARINE, 26, , HOUSE SERVANT, 09/22/1864
1. NOVA SCOTIA 2. U.S. 3. PICTOU

MCDONALD, DANIEL, 30, M, MINER, 08/19/1840
1. IRELAND 2. U.S. 3. SYDNEY

MCDONALD, DONALD, 26, M, CARPENTER, 05/07/1859
1. NOVA SCOTIA 2. NOVA SCOTIA 3. PICTOU

MCDONALD, DUNCAN, 35, M, FARMER, 07/06/1846
1. NOVA SCOTIA 2. U.S. 3. PICTOU

MCDONALD, ELISABETH, 26, F, DRESS MAKER, 09/08/1865
1. U.S. 2. U.S. 3. PICTOU

MCDONALD, ELIZABETH, 24, F, TAILORESS, 06/11/1856
1. NOVA SCOTIA 2. NOVA SCOTIA 3. PICTOU

MCDONALD, ELIZABETH, 20, F, NONE, 08/08/1857
1. NOVA SCOTIA 2. U.S. 3. PICTOU

MCDONALD, ISABELLA, 17, F, SERVANT, 07/20/1844
1. NOVA SCOTIA 2. U.S. 3. PICTOU

MCDONALD, ISABELLA, 19, F, , 09/13/1859
1. NOVA SCOTIA 2. U.S. 3. PICTOU

MCDONALD, JAMES, 25, M, SHOEMAKER, 09/18/1845
1. NOVA SCOTIA 2. U.S. 3. PICTOU

MCDONALD, JANE, 20, F, , 08/16/1850
1. NOVA SCOTIA 2. U.S. 3. PICTOU

MCDONALD, JOHN, 23, M, BRICKLAYER, 09/01/1869
1. BRITISH AMERICA 2. U.S. 3. PICTOU

MCDONALD, JOHN, 30, M, MECHANIC, 12/10/1851
1. BRITISH AMERICA 2. U.S. 3. PICTOU

MCDONALD, JOHN, 24, M, NONE, 07/22/1856
1. GREAT BRITAIN 2. U.S. 3. PICTOU

MCDONALD, JOHN, 22, M, HOUSE CARPENTER, 06/25/1856
1. GREAT BRITAIN 2. GREAT BRITAIN 3. PICTOU

MCDONALD, JOHN, 6, M, BOYS, 07/06/1846
1. NOVA SCOTIA 2. U.S. 3. PICTOU

MCDONALD, MAGGIE, 21, F, SERVANT, 11/16/1863
1. PICTOU 2. U.S. 3. PICTOU

MCDONALD, MARGARET, 20, F, HOUSE MAID, 09/17/1860
1. NOVA SCOTIA 2. U.S. 3. PICTOU

MCDONALD, MARGARET, 30, F, SERVANT, 08/27/1846
1. NOVA SCOTIA 2. U.S. 3. PICTOU

MCDONALD, MARGARET, 19, F, SERVANT, 08/21/1852
1. BRITISH AMERICA 2. U.S. 3. PICTOU

MCDONALD, MARGARET, 23, F, DRESSMAKER, 08/08/1857
1. NOVA SCOTIA 2. U.S. 3. PICTOU

MCDONALD, MARIA, 20, F, SERVANT, 06/25/1856
1. GREAT BRITAIN 2. GREAT BRITAIN 3. PICTOU

MCDONALD, MARY, 22, F, NONE, 05/25/1858
1. NOVA SCOTIA 2. U.S. 3. PICTOU

MCDONALD, MARY, 21, F, SERVANT, 09/23/1852
1. BRITISH AMERICA 2. U.S. 3. PICTOU

MCDONALD, MARY, 18, F, SERVANT, 06/25/1856
1. GREAT BRITAIN 2. GREAT BRITAIN 3. PICTOU

MCDONALD, MARY, 20, , HOUSE SERVANT, 09/22/1864
1. NOVA SCOTIA 2. U.S. 3. PICTOU

MCDONALD, MARY, 30, F, LADY, 07/06/1846
1. NOVA SCOTIA 2. U.S. 3. PICTOU

MCDONALD, MARY, 26, F, LADY, 07/06/1846
1. NOVA SCOTIA 2. U.S. 3. PICTOU

MCDONALD, MARY ANN, 18, F, LADY, 08/18/1849
1. BRITISH AMERICA 2. U.S. 3. PICTOU

MCDONALD, MISS, 50, F, NONE, 07/22/1856
1. GREAT BRITAIN 2. U.S. 3. PICTOU

MCDONALD, NANCY, 4, F, CHILDREN, 07/06/1846
1. NOVA SCOTIA 2. U.S. 3. PICTOU

MCDONALD, RONALD, 24, M, HOUSE CARPENTER, 08/19/1859
1. NOVA SCOTIA 2. U.S. 3. PICTOU

MCDONALD, TAVI, 20, F, HOUSEWORK, 09/25/1854
1. PICTOU 2. U.S. 3. PICTOU

MCDONNAU, JOHN, 28, M, MECHANIC, 09/20/1838
1. IRELAND 2. NEW YORK 3. PICTOU

MCDONOUGH, JESSE, 22, M, LABORER, 11/15/1854
1. PICTOU 2. U.S. 3. PICTOU

MCDONOUGH, MARGARET, 18, F, SERVANT, 11/15/1854
1. PICTOU 2. U.S. 3. PICTOU

MCDOUGAL, CATHERINE, 25, F, SERVANT, 07/01/1862
1. NOVA SCOTIA 2. U.S. 3. PICTOU

MCDOUGAL, CATHERINE, 22, F, , 07/06/1857
1. PICTOU 2. U.S. 3. PICTOU

MCDOUGAL, JAMES, 42, M, FARMER, 11/07/1832
1. NOVA SCOTIA 2. U.S. 3. PICTOU

MCDOUGAL, MARY, 22, F, SERVANT, 07/28/1862
1. NOVA SCOTIA 2. U.S. 3. PICTOU

MCDOUGALL, CHARLES, 14, M, SAILOR, 06/25/1832
1. ST. CROIX 2. U.S. 3. ST. CROIX

MCDOUGALL, DAVID, 23, M, FARMER, 09/09/1844
1. NOVA SCOTIA 2. U.S. 3. PICTOU

MCDURMT, DURMET, 24, M, JOINER, 05/22/1857
1. GREAT BRITAIN 2. GREAT BRITAIN 3. PICTOU

MCEACHRAN, DOUGAL, 17, M, LABORER, 06/17/1867
1. NOVA SCOTIA 2. U.S. 3. PICTOU,

MCFARLANE, FLORA, 3, F, CHILD, 07/08/1852
1. BRITISH AMERICA 2. U.S. 3. PICTOU

MCFARLANE, JAMES, 6, M, CHILD, 07/08/1852
1. BRITISH AMERICA 2. U.S. 3. PICTOU

MCFARLANE, MALCOLM, 32, M, FARMER, 07/08/1852
1. BRITISH AMERICA 2. U.S. 3. PICTOU

MCFARLANE, MALCOLM, 8, M, CHILD, 07/08/1852
1. BRITISH AMERICA 2. U.S. 3. PICTOU

MCFARLANE, PERNEL, 28, F, WIFE, 07/08/1852
1. BRITISH AMERICA 2. U.S. 3. PICTOU

MCFARLANE, ROBERT, 1, M, CHILD, 07/08/1852
1. BRITISH AMERICA 2. U.S. 3. PICTOU

MCFEE, BETSEY, 25, F, LADY, 10/08/1849
1. U.S. 2. U.S. 3. PICTOU

MCGARVEY, JANE, 24, F, , 10/10/1853
1. GREAT BRITAIN 2. GREAT BRITAIN 3. PICTOU

MCGILVERY, CATHARINE, 18, F, , 07/11/1850
1. BRITISH AMERICA 2. U.S. 3. PICTOU

MCGILVREY, CATHERINE, 25, F, , 08/29/1853
1. U.S. 2. U.S. 3. PICTOU

MCGILVREY, SARAH, 20, F, , 08/29/1853
1. U.S. 2. U.S. 3. PICTOU

MCGOVERN, ALEXANDER, 23, M, MASON, 07/05/1823
1. SCOTLAND 2. U.S. 3. HONDURAS

MCGRATH, BRIDGET, 35, F, SERVANT, 07/25/1832
1. NOVA SCOTIA 2. U.S. 3. HALIFAX

MCGRATH, MARY, 8, F, , 07/25/1832
1. NOVA SCOTIA 2. U.S. 3. HALIFAX

MCGRATH, WILLIAM, 5, M, , 07/25/1832
1. NOVA SCOTIA 2. U.S. 3. HALIFAX

MCGRAU, JOANNA, 35, F, SERVANT, 09/03/1868
1. BRITISH AMERICA 2. U.S. 3. PICTOU

MCGUNIGLE, ELISABETH, 15, F, SERVANT, 08/22/1850
1. BRITISH AMERICA 2. U.S. 3. PICTOU

MCGUNIGLE, GEORGE, 6, M, CHILD, 08/22/1850
1. BRITISH AMERICA 2. U.S. 3. PICTOU

MCGUNIGLE, JAMES, 10, M, CHILD, 08/22/1850
1. BRITISH AMERICA 2. U.S. 3. PICTOU

MCGUNIGLE, NANCY, 37, F, SERVANT, 08/22/1850
1. BRITISH AMERICA 2. U.S. 3. PICTOU

MCGUNIGLE, WILLIAM, 8, M, CHILD, 08/22/1850
1. BRITISH AMERICA 2. U.S. 3. PICTOU

MCGUYRE, JOHN, 35, M, TAYLOR, 08/13/1829
1. U.S. 2. U.S. 3. MATANZAS

MCHAY, ALEX, 26, M, CARPENTER, 09/13/1844
1. NOVA SCOTIA 2. U.S. 3. PICTOU

MCINTOSH, ALEXANDER, 19, M, , 10/01/1850
1. BRITISH AMERICA 2. U.S. 3. PICTOU

MCINTOSH, ANNA, 26, F, SERVANT, 09/20/1851
1. U.S. 2. U.S. 3. PICTOU

MCINTOSH, CHRISTIANA, 26, F, SERVANT, 09/09/1844
1. NOVA SCOTIA 2. U.S. 3. PICTOU

MCINTOSH, DANIEL F., 5 MONTHS, M, , 06/23/1857
1. PICTOU 2. BOSTON 3. PICTOU

MCINTOSH, DAVID, 2, M, , 06/23/1857
1. PICTOU 2. BOSTON 3. PICTOU

MCINTOSH, JAMES, 19, M, JOINER, 08/16/1851
1. BRITISH AMERICA 2. U.S. 3. PICTOU

MCINTOSH, JOHN, 22, M, , 10/01/1850
1. BRITISH AMERICA 2. U.S. 3. PICTOU

MCINTOSH, JOHN, 18, M, , 10/01/1850
1. BRITISH AMERICA 2. U.S. 3. PICTOU

MCINTOSH, JOHN, 22, M, HARNESSMAKER, 06/23/1857
1. PICTOU 2. BOSTON 3. PICTOU

MCINTOSH, JOHN L., 23, M, LABORER, 07/02/1844
1. NOVA SCOTIA 2. MASSACHUSETTS 3. PICTOU

MCINTOSH, MARGARET, 38, F, NONE, 07/19/1858
1. NOVA SCOTIA 2. NOVA SCOTIA 3. PICTOU

MCINTOSH, MARY ANN, 33, F, DRESSMAKER, 09/10/1858
1. NOVA SCOTIA 2. U.S. 3. PICTOU

MCINTOSH, MARY ANN, 25, F, , 06/23/1857
1. PICTOU 2. BOSTON 3. PICTOU

MCINTOSH, NANCY, 21, F, LADY, 07/20/1844
1. NOVA SCOTIA 2. U.S. 3. PICTOU

MCINTOSH, WILLIAM, 25, M, SHIP CARPENTER, 11/23/1844
1. GREAT BRITAIN 2. U.S. 3. PICTOU

MCISAAC, CATHARINE, 26, F, LADY, 07/06/1846
1. NOVA SCOTIA 2. U.S. 3. PICTOU

MCISAAC, DONALD, 6, M, BOY, 07/06/1846
1. NOVA SCOTIA 2. U.S. 3. PICTOU

MCISAAC, ISABELLA, 50, F, LADY, 07/06/1846
1. NOVA SCOTIA 2. U.S. 3. PICTOU

MCISAAC, JOHN, 22, , BLACKSMITH, 09/16/1869
1. BRITISH AMERICA 2. U.S. 3. LUIZAN

MCISAAC, MARGARET, 2, F, CHILD, 07/06/1846
1. NOVA SCOTIA 2. U.S. 3. PICTOU

MCISAAC, NANCY, 28, F, LADY, 07/06/1846
1. NOVA SCOTIA 2. U.S. 3. PICTOU

MCISAACS, JOHN, 22, , CLERK, 08/17/1868
1. BRITISH AMERICA 2. U.S. 3. PICTOU

MCKAIN, MARGARET, 15, F, SERVANT, 07/28/1862
1. NOVA SCOTIA 2. U.S. 3. PICTOU

MCKALEP, JOHN, 20, M, FARMER, 06/11/1856
1. NOVA SCOTIA 2. NOVA SCOTIA 3. PICTOU

MCKAY, ALEXANDER, 60, M, SCHOOLMASTER, 08/16/1851
1. BRITISH AMERICA 2. BRITISH AMERICA 3. PICTOU

MCKAY, BURTON, 23, M, MECHANIC, 12/10/1851
1. BRITISH AMERICA 2. U.S. 3. PICTOU

MCKAY, CHARLES, 25, M, SHIP JOINER, 07/31/1852
1. BRITISH AMERICA 2. U.S. 3. PICTOU

MCKAY, CHRISTY, 25, F, DOMESTIC, 09/21/1859
1. NOVA SCOTIA 2. U.S. 3. PICTOU

MCKAY, ELIZABETH, 20, F, SERVANT GIRL, 09/02/1845
1. NOVA SCOTIA 2. U.S. 3. PICTOU

MCKAY, HANNAH, 10, F, , 09/13/1859
1. NOVA SCOTIA 2. U.S. 3. PICTOU

MCKAY, JESSIE, 24, F, SERVANT, 09/16/1858
1. NOVA SCOTIA 2. U.S. 3. PICTOU

MCKAY, JESSIE, 22, F, DOMESTIC, 09/21/1859
1. NOVA SCOTIA 2. U.S. 3. PICTOU

MCKAY, MARGARET, 8, F, , 09/13/1859
1. NOVA SCOTIA 2. U.S. 3. PICTOU

MCKAY, MARY, 17, F, IN PURSUIT OF EMPLOY, 08/04/1841
1. BRITISH AMERICA 2. U.S. 3. PICTOU

MCKAY, WILLIAM, 35, M, MECHANIC, 09/19/1842
1. U.S. 2. U.S. 3. PICTOU

MCKAY, WILLIAM, 17, M, CARPENTER, 08/23/1845
1. BRITISH AMERICA 2. U.S. 3. PICTOU

MCKEEN, ELISABETH, 29, F, SERVANT, 09/09/1844
1. NOVA SCOTIA 2. U.S. 3. PICTOU

MCKEIL, BETSEY, 27, F, SPINSTER, 09/18/1845
1. NOVA SCOTIA 2. U.S. 3. PICTOU

MCKEIM, CATHARINE, 15, F, , 07/09/1860
1. NOVA SCOTIA 2. U.S. 3. PICTOU

MCKEIM, ELIZABETH, 18, F, , 07/09/1860
1. NOVA SCOTIA 2. U.S. 3. PICTOU

MCKELLON, DUNCAN, 39, M, CARPENTER, 07/27/1845
1. BRITISH AMERICA 2. U.S. 3. PICTOU

MCKELVIN, JANE, 40, F, NONE, 07/14/1862
1. U.S. 2. U.S. 3. PICTOU

MCKENNA, FLORA, 20, F, SERVANT, 08/23/1850
1. PICTOU 2. PROVIDENCE 3. PICTOU

MCKENNA, FLORA, 16, F, DOMESTIC, 09/21/1859
1. NOVA SCOTIA 2. U.S. 3. PICTOU

MCKENNA, ISABELLE, 23, F, DOMESTIC, 09/21/1859
1. NOVA SCOTIA 2. U.S. 3. PICTOU

MCKENNA, NANCY, 16, F, SERVANT, 08/23/1850
1. PICTOU 2. PROVIDENCE 3. PICTOU

MCKENSIE, ANA, 20, F, SERVANT, 09/09/1844
1. NOVA SCOTIA 2. U.S. 3. PICTOU

MCKENSIE, ANN, 20, F, LADY, 11/02/1847
1. BRITISH AMERICA 2. U.S. 3. PICTOU

MCKENSIE, HECTOR, 20, M, SHIP CARPENTER, 06/03/1844
1. NOVA SCOTIA 2. U.S. 3. PICTOU

MCKENSIE, JOHN, 17, M, CARPENTER, 07/03/1851
1. BRITISH AMERICA 2. U.S. 3. PICTOU

MCKENSIE, MARY, 29, F, , 11/02/1850
1. BRITISH AMERICA 2. U.S. 3. PICTOU

MCKENSIE, NANCY, 30, F, LADY, 07/02/1844
1. PRINCE EDWARD ISLAND 2. MASSACHUSETTS 3. PICTOU

MCKENYEA, COLKIN, 20, M, LABORER, 10/03/1840
1. ENGLAND 2. U.S. 3. PICTOU

MCKENYEA, ELIZABETH ANN, 18, F, SEAMSTRESS, 10/03/1840
1. 2. 3. PICTOU

MCKENZEY, LUNAR, 20, M, , 10/01/1850
1. BRITISH AMERICA 2. U.S. 3. PICTOU

MCKENZIE, ALEXANDER, 65, M, SHIP CARPENTER, 07/01/1858
1. GREAT BRITAIN 2. GREAT BRITAIN 3. PICTOU

MCKENZIE, ANN, 22, F, SERVANT, 11/16/1863
1. PICTOU 2. U.S. 3. PICTOU

MCKENZIE, ANN, 19, F, SERVANT, 06/20/1863
1. NOVA SCOTIA 2. U.S. 3. PICTOU

MCKENZIE, ANNIE, 30, F, MILLINER, 07/18/1857
1. NOVA SCOTIA 2. U.S. 3. PICTOU

MCKENZIE, ARCHIBALD, 42, M, FARMER, 05/09/1859
1. NOVA SCOTIA 2. U.S. 3. PICTOU

MCKENZIE, CATHARINE, 26, F, , 05/23/1857
1. NOVA SCOTIA 2. U.S. 3. PICTOU

MCKENZIE, CATHERINE, 29, F, , 07/06/1857
1. PICTOU 2. U.S. 3. PICTOU

MCKENZIE, CHRISTIE, 21, F, HOUSE MAID, 09/19/1860
1. NOVA SCOTIA 2. U.S. 3. PICTOU

MCKENZIE, CHRISTY, 11, M, , 05/23/1857
1. NOVA SCOTIA 2. U.S. 3. PICTOU

MCKENZIE, DALINA, 18, F, SERVANT, 09/08/1862
1. PICTOU 2. PROVIDENCE 3. PICTOU

MCKENZIE, DANL, 24, M, LABORER, 09/14/1858
1. NOVA SCOTIA 2. U.S. 3. PICTOU

MCKENZIE, DUNCAN, 23, M, MACHINIST, 06/11/1856
1. NOVA SCOTIA 2. NOVA SCOTIA 3. PICTOU

MCKENZIE, ELISABETH, 19, F, SERVANT, 09/29/1852
1. BRITISH AMERICA 2. U.S. 3. PICTOU

MCKENZIE, FLORA, 16, F, SERVANT, 09/15/1854
1. NOVA SCOTIA 2. U.S. 3. PICTOU

MCKENZIE, FLORA, 19, F, SERVANT, 08/20/1857
1. NOVA SCOTIA 2. NOVA SCOTIA 3. PICTOU

MCKENZIE, JAMES, 24, M, CARPENTER, 07/02/1844
1. PRINCE EDWARD ISLAND 2. MASSACHUSETTS 3. PICTOU

MCKENZIE, JAMES, 22, M, JOINER, 05/22/1857
1. GREAT BRITAIN 2. U.S. 3. PICTOU

MCKENZIE, JAMES WILLIAM, 3, M, , 07/06/1857
1. PICTOU 2. U.S. 3. PICTOU

MCKENZIE, JANE, 9, F, , 05/23/1857
1. NOVA SCOTIA 2. U.S. 3. PICTOU

MCKENZIE, JANET, 24, F, , 05/23/1857
1. NOVA SCOTIA 2. U.S. 3. PICTOU

MCKENZIE, JOHN, 30, M, CLERK, 08/08/1857
1. NOVA SCOTIA 2. NOVA SCOTIA 3. PICTOU

MCKENZIE, JOHN, 24, M, BAKER, 07/09/1860
1. NOVA SCOTIA 2. U.S. 3. PICTOU

MCKENZIE, JOHN, 22, M, SHOE MAKER, 05/30/1860
1. PRINCE EDWARD ISLAND 2. MASSACHUSETTS 3. PRINCE EDWARD
ISLAND

MCKENZIE, KATE F., 7, F, , 08/14/1860
1. NOVA SCOTIA 2. U.S. 3. PICTOU

MCKENZIE, MARGARET, 28, F, NONE, 07/19/1858
1. NOVA SCOTIA 2. NOVA SCOTIA 3. PICTOU

MCKENZIE, MARGARET, 20, F, , 08/14/1860
1. NOVA SCOTIA 2. U.S. 3. PICTOU

MCKENZIE, MARGARET, 32, F, SERVICE, 08/10/1838
1. 2. 3. PICTOU

MCKENZIE, MARY, 47, F, HOUSEWIFE, 05/23/1857
1. NOVA SCOTIA 2. U.S 3. PICTOU

MCKENZIE, MARY A., 20, F, TAILORESS, 06/11/1856
1. NOVA SCOTIA 2. NOVA SCOTIA 3. PICTOU

MCKENZIE, MARY ANN, 20, F, , 07/06/1857
1. PICTOU 2. PICTOU 3. PICTOU

MCKENZIE, MRS. A., 34, F, , 08/14/1860
1. NOVA SCOTIA 2. U.S. 3. PICTOU

MCKENZIE, WILLIAM, 48, M, MINER, 05/23/1857
1. NOVA SCOTIA 2. U.S. 3. PICTOU

MCKENZIE, WILLIAM, 21, M, TAYLOR, 05/22/1857
1. GREAT BRITAIN 2. U.S. 3. PICTOU

MCKENZIE, WILLIAM, 24, M, FARMER, 10/22/1859
1. NOVA SCOTIA 2. U.S. 3. PICTOU

MCKENZIE, WM., 22, M, CARPENTER, 08/17/1850
1. PICTOU 2. U.S. 3. PICTOU

MCKERNETH, KENNETH, 43, M, FARMER, 09/13/1841
1. NOVA SCOTIA 2. NOVA SCOTIA 3. PICTOU

MCKINAN, JANE, 24, F, HOUSEWIFE, 07/22/1856
1. GREAT BRITAIN 2. U.S. 3. PICTOU

MCKINNAN, MARY, 21, F, IN PURSUIT OF EMPLOY, 08/04/1841
1. BRITISH AMERICA 2. U.S. 3. PICTOU

MCKINNE, MARY, 20, F, SERVICE, 08/10/1838
1. PICTOU 2. PROVIDENCE 3. PICTOU

MCKINNEN, CRISTHIA, 23, F, SERVANT, 11/11/1844
1. NOVA SCOTIA 2. U.S. 3. PICTOU

MCKINNON, GEORGE, 15, M, SERVANT, 07/27/1845
1. BRITISH AMERICA 2. U.S. 3. PICTOU

MCKINNON, HECTOR, 38, M, LABORER, 09/14/1858
1. NOVA SCOTIA 2. U.S. 3. PICTOU

MCKINNON, JANE, 13, F, SERVANT, 07/27/1845
1. BRITISH AMERICA 2. U.S. 3. PICTOU

MCKINNON, MARGARET, 26, F, , 09/28/1859
1. NOVA SCOTIA 2. NOVA SCOTIA 3. PICTOU

MCKINNON, MARY, 29, F, DOMESTIC, 09/21/1859
1. NOVA SCOTIA 2. U.S. 3. PICTOU

MCKINNON, MARY, 27, F, HOUSE SERVANT, 08/19/1863
1. NOVA SCOTIA 2. U.S. 3. PICTOU

MCKINSIE, JANE, 30, F, LADY, 10/08/1849
1. BRITISH AMERICA 2. U.S. 3. PICTOU

MCKINZEY, ISABELLA, 22, F, SERVANT, 09/20/1851
1. BRITISH AMERICA 2. U.S. 3. PICTOU

MCKINZY, ISABELLA, 23, F, SERVANT, 11/04/1851
1. BRITISH AMERICA 2. U.S. 3. PICTOU

MCKNIBB, JOHN, 30, M, MASON, 08/20/1844
1. NOVA SCOTIA 2. U.S. 3. PICTOU

MCLANE, CATHARINE, 20, F, SERVANT, 08/16/1851
1. BRITISH AMERICA 2. U.S. 3. PICTOU

MCLANE, JAMES, 17, M, TANNER, 08/10/1842
1. SCOTLAND 2. U.S. 3. PICTOU

MCLANE, JANE, 22, F, SERVANT, 08/16/1851
1. BRITISH AMERICA 2. U.S. 3. PICTOU

MCLANE, JESSIE, 16, F, SERVANT, 08/21/1852
1. BRITISH AMERICA 2. U.S. 3. PICTOU

MCLANE, MARY, 27, F, LADY, 06/28/1849
1. U.S. 2. U.S. 3. PICTOU

MCLANE, SANDY, 25, M, ENGINEER, 08/10/1842
1. SCOTLAND 2. U.S. 3. PICTOU

MCLARLAN, (INFANT), 1, M, CHILD, 07/03/1845
1. BRITISH AMERICA 2. U.S. 3. PICTOU

MCLARLAN, ANN, 3, F, CHILD, 07/03/1845
1. BRITISH AMERICA 2. U.S. 3. PICTOU

MCLARLAN, ELIZABETH, 24, F, LABOUR, 07/03/1845
1. BRITISH AMERICA 2. U.S. 3. PICTOU

MCLARLAN, TIMOTHY, 2, M, CHILD, 07/03/1845
1. BRITISH AMERICA 2. U.S. 3. PICTOU

MCLARSEN, MARGARET, 22, F, LADY, 07/20/1844
1. NOVA SCOTIA 2. U.S. 3. PICTOU

MCLAUGHLAN, CHARLES, 19, M, FARMER, 07/20/1848
1. BRITISH AMERICA 2. BRITISH AMERICA 3. PICTOU

MCLAUGHLIN, (INFANT), 2 MONTHS, M, NONE, 10/03/1854
1. U.S. 2. U.S. 3. PICTOU

MCLAUGHLIN, ANN, 17, F, SERVANT, 10/24/1854
1. GREAT BRITAIN 2. U.S. 3. GLASGOW

MCLAUGHLIN, CAROLINE, 7, F, NONE, 10/03/1854
1. U.S. 2. U.S. 3. PICTOU

MCLAUGHLIN, CATHARINE, 20, F, SERVANT, 10/24/1854
1. GREAT BRITAIN 2. U.S. 3. GLASGOW

MCLAUGHLIN, ELIZABETH, 32, F, HOUSEWIFE, 10/03/1854
1. U.S. 2. U.S. 3. PICTOU

MCLAUGHLIN, MARY, 32, F, MILLINER, 09/02/1856
1. U.S. 2. U.S. 3. PICTOU

MCLEAD, DANIEL, 22, M, MECHANIC, 09/27/1841
1. U.S. 2. U.S. 3. PICTOU

MCLEAD, MAY, 15, F, LADY, 09/27/1841
1. U.S. 2. U.S. 3. PICTOU

MCLEAIN, MARY, 26, F, SERVANT, 09/09/1844
1. NOVA SCOTIA 2. U.S. 3. PICTOU

MCLEAN, ANN, 20, F, SERVANT, 07/20/1844
1. NOVA SCOTIA 2. U.S. 3. PICTOU

MCLEAN, CATHERINE, 44, F, HOUSEWIFE, 09/05/1860
1. NOVA SCOTIA 2. U.S. 3. PICTOU

MCLEAN, CATHERINE, 10, F, , 09/05/1860
1. NOVA SCOTIA 2. U.S. 3. PICTOU

MCLEAN, CHRISTY, 6, F, , 09/05/1860
1. NOVA SCOTIA 2. U.S. 3. PICTOU

MCLEAN, DANIEL, 16, M, , 09/05/1860
1. NOVA SCOTIA 2. U.S. 3. PICTOU

MCLEAN, DANL, 26, M, LABORER, 07/26/1855
1. NOVA SCOTIA 2. U.S. 3. PICTOU

MCLEAN, DONNALD, 52, M, FARMER, 09/05/1860
1. NOVA SCOTIA 2. U.S. 3. PICTOU

MCLEAN, HECTOR, 14, M, , 09/05/1860
1. NOVA SCOTIA 2. U.S. 3. PICTOU

MCLEAN, ISABELLA, 3, F, , 09/05/1860
1. NOVA SCOTIA 2. U.S. 3. PICTOU

MCLEAN, JESSEY, 17, F, , 09/05/1860
1. NOVA SCOTIA 2. U.S. 3. PICTOU

MCLEAN, JOHN, 22, M, SHIP CARPENTER, 07/20/1857
1. NOVA SCOTIA 2. U.S. 3. PICTOU

MCLEAN, JOHN, 38, M, SEAMAN, 07/20/1857
1. NOVA SCOTIA 2. U.S. 3. PICTOU

MCLEAN, MARGARET, 20, F, , 07/18/1859
1. NOVA SCOTIA 2. U.S. 3. PICTOU

MCLEAN, MARY, 31, F, SERVANT, 10/24/1860
1. NOVA SCOTIA 2. U.S. 3. PICTOU

MCLEAN, MARY ANN, 12, F, , 09/05/1860
1. NOVA SCOTIA 2. U.S. 3. PICTOU

MCLEAN, NEIL, 25, M, LABORER, 07/27/1845
1. BRITISH AMERICA 2. U.S. 3. PICTOU

MCLEAN, SARAH, 9, F, , 09/05/1860
1. NOVA SCOTIA 2. U.S. 3. PICTOU

MCLELLAN, ANN, 24, F, SERVANT, 08/20/1844
1. U.S. 2. U.S. 3. PICTOU

MCLELLAN, CATHARINE, 19, F, SERVANT OR ASSISTANT, 08/09/1853
1. NOVA SCOTIA 2. U.S. 3. PICTOU

MCLELLAND, EDWARD, 40, M, SCHOOL MASTER, 03/25/1858
1. U.S. 2. U.S. 3. HALIFAX

MCLELU, CHRISTOPHER, 35, F, SERVANT, 09/04/1856
1. PICTOU 2. U.S. 3. PICTOU

MCLENAN, CHRISTINE, 34, F, DOMESTIC, 08/19/1859
1. NOVA SCOTIA 2. U.S. 3. PICTOU

MCLEOD, ETHEBELLIER, 25, F, INDIA RUBBER FACTORY, 10/03/1854
1. PICTOU 2. U.S. 3. PICTOU

MCLEOD, MARY, 19, F, HOUSE SERVANT, 07/07/1865
1. BRITISH AMERICA 2. U.S. 3. PICTOU

MCLEOD, NANCY, 30, F, SERVANT, 09/18/1845
1. NOVA SCOTIA 2. U.S. 3. PICTOU

MCLOCHLIN, DONALD, 20, M, SHIP CARPENTER, 07/12/1850
1. BRITISH AMERICA 2. U.S. 3. PICTOU

MCLOCHLIN, DONALD, 19, M, SHIP CARPENTER, 07/17/1850
1. BRITISH AMERICA 2. U.S. 3. PICTOU

MCLOCHLIN, MRS. DONALD, 27, F, , 07/17/1850
1. BRITISH AMERICA 2. U.S. 3. PICTOU

MCLOCHLIN, GILBERT, 6, M, CHILD, 07/17/1850
1. BRITISH AMERICA 2. U.S. 3. PICTOU

MCLOUD, BARCLAY, 16, F, SERVANT, 11/04/1851
1. BRITISH AMERICA 2. U.S. 3. PICTOU

MCLOUD, KENNETH, 19, , LABORER, 07/01/1865
1. BRITISH AMERICA 2. U.S. 3. COW BAY

MCLOUD, MARY, 22, , SERVANT, 09/30/1868
1. 2. 3. PICTOU

MCLOUD, SUSAN, 29, F, , 09/22/1851
1. BRITISH AMERICA 2. BRITISH AMERICA 3. PICTOU

MCMALLY, GEORGE, 40, , WEAVER, 05/09/1837
1. IRELAND 2. NEW YORK 3. LIVERPOOL

MCMANUS, BRIDGET, 18, , SPINSTER, 05/09/1837
1. IRELAND 2. U.S. 3. LIVERPOOL

MCMICHLAN, MRS., 30, F, HOUSE SERVANT, 07/07/1865
1. BRITISH AMERICA 2. U.S. 3. PICTOU

MCMILLAN, ANNABELLE, 22, F, DOMESTIC, 09/21/1859
1. NOVA SCOTIA 2. U.S. 3. PICTOU

MCMILLAN, FLORA, 66, F, DOMESTIC, 09/21/1859
1. NOVA SCOTIA 2. U.S. 3. PICTOU

MCMILLAN, GRACE, 19, F, SERVANT, 09/09/1844
1. NOVA SCOTIA 2. U.S. 3. PICTOU

MCMILLAN, MARY, 22, F, SERVANT, 11/11/1844
1. NOVA SCOTIA 2. U.S. 3. PICTOU

MCMILLAN, MARY JANE, 20, F, HOUSE SERVANT, 09/14/1863
1. NOVA SCOTIA 2. U.S. 3. PICTOU

MCMILLAN, NORMAN, 25, , LABORER, 07/01/1865
1. BRITISH AMERICA 2. U.S. 3. COW BAY

MCMILLEN, ARABELLA, 20, F, SERVANT, 09/18/1856
1. NOVA SCOTIA 2. U.S. 3. PICTOU

MCMILLEN, CHRISTIE, 24, F, DOMESTIC, 09/28/1859
1. NOVA SCOTIA 2. U.S. 3. PICTOU

MCMILLEN, CHRISTY, 21, F, SERVANT, 06/24/1856
1. NOVA SCOTIA 2. U.S. 3. PICTOU

MCMILLEN, ISABEL, 21, F, , 10/01/1850
1. BRITISH AMERICA 2. U.S. 3. PICTOU

MCMILLEN, MARGARET ANN, 23, F, , 06/23/1857
1. PICTOU 2. PROVIDENCE 3. PICTOU

MCMILLEN, MARY, 26, F, DOMESTIC, 09/28/1859
1. NOVA SCOTIA 2. U.S. 3. PICTOU

MCMILLERD, MARY, 18, F, SERVANT, 09/23/1852
1. BRITISH AMERICA 2. U.S. 3. PICTOU

MCMILLIN, ISABELA, 18, F, NONE, 09/12/1848
1. NOVA SCOTIA 2. AMERICA 3. PICTOU

MCMILLIN, NANCY, 21, F, LADY, 06/27/1849
1. 2. 3. PICTOU

MCMULLIN, CHRITEI, 18, F, SERVANT, 09/03/1853
1. PICTOU 2. U.S. 3. PICTOU

MCNAB, WILLIAM, 21, M, PRINTER, 10/24/1854
1. GREAT BRITAIN 2. U.S. 3. GLASGOW

MCNEAL, NANCY, 18, F, SERVANT, 09/16/1858
1. NOVA SCOTIA 2. U.S. 3. PICTOU

MCNEIL, HANNAH, 19, F, SERVANT, 06/20/1863
1. NOVA SCOTIA 2. U.S. 3. PICTOU

MCNEIL, MARY, 22, F, SERVANT, 07/12/1867
1. BRITISH AMERICA 2. 3. PICTOU

MCNEIL, MARY ANN, 20, F, SERVANT, 08/26/1867
1. NOVA SCOTIA 2. NOVA SCOTIA 3.

MCNEIL, RODERICK, 20, M, BLACKSMITH, 06/20/1863
1. NOVA SCOTIA 2. U.S. 3. PICTOU

MCNEILL, ANN, 36, F, , 10/27/1845
1. NOVA SCOTIA 2. CANADA 3. PICTOU

MCNEILL, GRACE E., 4, F, , 10/27/1845
1. NOVA SCOTIA 2. CANADA 3. PICTOU

MCNEILL, JOHN S., 2, M, , 10/27/1845
1. NOVA SCOTIA 2. CANADA 3. PICTOU

MCNEILL, JOHN T., 36, M, SHIP WRIGHT, 10/27/1845
1. NOVA SCOTIA 2. CANADA 3. PICTOU

MCNEILL, MARY E., 1, , , 10/27/1845
1. NOVA SCOTIA 2. CANADA 3. PICTOU

MCNEILL, MATILDA, 6, F, , 10/27/1845
1. NOVA SCOTIA 2. CANADA 3. PICTOU

MCNEMARA, THOMAS, 20, M, LABORER, 09/09/1844
1. NOVA SCOTIA 2. U.S. 3. PICTOU

MCNIEL, DONALD, 20, M, SHOE MAKER, 07/03/1851
1. BRITISH AMERICA 2. U.S. 3. PICTOU

MCNIEL, KATE, 28, F, , 08/26/1870
1. NOVA SCOTIA 2. 3. PICTOU

MCNORTON, JOHN, 40, M, CHAIR MAKER, 09/04/1854
1. NOVA SCOTIA 2. NOVA SCOTIA 3. PICTOU

MCPHEE, BETSY, 20, F, SERVANT, 09/09/1844
1. NOVA SCOTIA 2. U.S. 3. PICTOU

MCPHERSEN, BETSEY, 25, F, LADY, 08/12/1853
1. NOVA SCOTIA 2. NOVA SCOTIA 3. PICTOU

MCPHERSON, ALMA, 18, F, SERVANT, 08/16/1851
1. BRITISH AMERICA 2. U.S. 3. PICTOU

MCPHERSON, ANN, 20, F, SERVANT OR ASSISTANT, 10/01/1853
1. NOVA SCOTIA 2. U.S. 3. PICTOU

MCPHERSON, BETSEY, 17, F, DOMESTIC, 10/10/1853
1. GREAT BRITAIN 2. U.S. 3. PICTOU

MCPHERSON, ELISABETH, 27, F, LADY, 10/08/1849
1. U.S. 2. U.S. 3. PICTOU

MCPHERSON, ELIZABETH, 18, F, SERVANT, 08/07/1855
1. NOVA SCOTIA 2. U.S. 3. PICTOU

MCPHERSON, HUGH, 21, M, BLOCK MAKER, 08/23/1850
1. PICTOU 2. WARREN, RI 3. PICTOU

MCPHERSON, JANET, 63, F, NONE, 08/05/1858
1. NOVA SCOTIA 2. NOVA SCOTIA 3. PICTOU

MCPHERSON, JENNY, 25, F, , 06/20/1859
1. NOVA SCOTIA 2. U.S. 3. PICTOU

MCPHERSON, MISS JESSIE, 20, F, LADY, 07/11/1850
1. PICTOU 2. U.S. 3. PICTOU

MCPHERSON, MARY, 28, F, COOK, 09/13/1851
1. NOVA SCOTIA 2. U.S. 3. PICTOU

MCPHERSON, NANCY, 24, F, , 09/13/1851
1. 2. 3. PICTOU

MCPHERSON, SUSAN, 19, F, LADY, 08/18/1849
1. BRITISH AMERICA 2. U.S. 3. PICTOU

MCPHERSON, WILLIAM, 21, M, PRINTER, 06/20/1859
1. NOVA SCOTIA 2. U.S. 3. PICTOU

MCQUARIO, FLORA, 35, F, SERVANT, 08/31/1866
1. PICTOU 2. U.S. 3. PICTOU

MCQUEEN, , 50, F, LADY, 11/02/1847
1. BRITISH AMERICA 2. U.S. 3. PICTOU

MCQUEEN, ARCHIBALD, , , , 12/14/1823
1. WORCESTER 2. BARBADOS/DEMERARA 3. PROVIDENCE

MCQUEEN, ELIZABETH, 13, F, SERVANT, 09/08/1843
1. U.S. 2. U.S. 3. PICTOU

MCQUEEN, ISABELLA, 8, F, CHILD, 11/02/1847
1. BRITISH AMERICA 2. U.S. 3. PICTOU

MCQUEEN, JAMES, 17, M, LABORER, 11/11/1844
1. NOVA SCOTIA 2. U.S. 3. PICTOU

MCQUEEN, JANE, 16, F, LADY, 11/02/1847
1. BRITISH AMERICA 2. U.S. 3. PICTOU

MCQUEEN, JOHN, 25, M, FARMER, 09/13/1841
1. NOVA SCOTIA 2. NOVA SCOTIA 3. PICTOU

MCQUEEN, MARGARET, 21, F, NURSE, 09/21/1837
1. NOVA SCOTIA 2. U.S. 3. PICTOU

MCQUEEN, MARY A., 13, F, CHILD, 11/02/1847
1. BRITISH AMERICA 2. U.S. 3. PICTOU

MCQUEEN, THOMAS, 25, M, JOINER, 05/22/1857
1. GREAT BRITAIN 2. U.S. 3. PICTOU

MCQUINY, MARY, 19, F, SERVANT, 09/03/1853
1. PICTOU 2. U.S. 3. PICTOU

MCREA, CHARLOTTE, , , , 12/14/1823
1. NEW HAVEN 2. BARBADOS/DEMERARA 3. PROVIDENCE

MCREA, JOHN, , , CHILD OF CHARLOTTE, 12/14/1823
1. NEW HAVEN 2. BARBADOS/DEMERARA 3. PROVIDENCE

MCREA, MARIA, , , CHILD OF CHARLOTTE, 12/14/1823
1. NEW HAVEN 2. BARBADOS/DEMERARA 3. PROVIDENCE

MCSELEU, ALEXANDER C., 5, M, NONE, 09/04/1856
1. PICTOU 2. U.S. 3. PICTOU

MCVEIKAR, DAN, 17, M, TAILOR, 09/19/1835
1. PICTOU 2. U.S. 3. PICTOU

MCVOY, MARY, 22, , SPINSTER, 05/09/1837
1. IRELAND 2. U.S. 3. LIVERPOOL

MELVILLE, DOCTOR, 45, M, SURGEON, 06/04/1834
1. QUEBEC 2. BOUND TO QUEBEC 3. ST. VINCENT

MENDELL, ISAIAH F., 31, M, SEAMAN, 05/20/1847
1. SALEAHURIO 2. NEW BEDFORD 3.

MENDONCA, MANUEL, 30, M, MARINER, 08/28/1872
1. FLORES 2. PROVIDENCE 3.

MERRILL, ANDREW B., 21, M, MERCHANT, 06/18/1829
1. U.S. 2. U.S. 3. PUONAMBANO

MERRILL, W., 17, M, , 05/06/1857
1. U.S. 2. U.S. 3.

MERRIOR, ANN, 28, F, HOUSEWORK, 09/25/1854
1. PICTOU 2. U.S. 3. PICTOU

METHEUS, JOSE, 20, M, FARMER, 08/28/1872
1. FLORES 2. PROVIDENCE 3.

MICHAEL, ANN, 24, F, , 08/16/1850
1. NOVA SCOTIA 2. U.S. 3. PICTOU

MICHAEL, CHRISTY, 19, F, , 08/16/1850
1. NOVA SCOTIA 2. U.S. 3. PICTOU

MICHAEL, JANE, 30, F, , 08/16/1850
1. NOVA SCOTIA 2. U.S. 3. PICTOU

MICKLES, WILLIAM, 35, M, BOOT MAKER, 07/08/1848
1. PICTOU 2. PROVIDENCE 3. PICTOU

MICULS, WILLIAM, 26, M, RAMTER SINGLE, 1836
1. WESEFORD 2. PROVIDENCE 3. PICTOU

MILDENSTEIN, JACOB, 53, M, PLANTER, 07/15/1834
1. CUBA 2. CUBA 3. MATANZAS

MILES, WILLIAM, 45, M, SECRETED HIMSELF ON BOARD, 08/29/1821
1. ENGLAND 2. STOWAWAY 3. HAMBURG

MILLER, D., 22, M, , 05/24/1841
1. 2. 3. MATANZAS

MILLER, JANE, 20, F, LADY, 10/02/1839
1. NOVA SCOTIA 2. U.S. 3. PICTOU

MILLER, JANE, 20, F, , 08/10/1838
1. 2. 3. PICTOU

MILLER, JOB, 37, M, MACHINIST, 06/11/1845
1. U.S. 2. U.S. 3. CARDENAS

MILLER, JOB, 41, M, ENGINEER, 07/07/1846
1. RHODE ISLAND 2. RHODE ISLAND 3. MATANZAS

MILLER, JOB, 39, M, MACHINIST, 07/22/1847
1. U.S. 2. U.S. 3. MATANZAS

MILLIAN, CATHARINE, 21, F, SERVANT, 10/03/1854
1. NOVA SCOTIA 2. U.S. 3. PICTOU

MILLIKEN, DANIEL, 24, M, MARINER, 05/27/1823
1. U.S. 2. U.S. 3. L. BARTS

MILLS, CEBAS, 34, M, MERCHANT, 07/06/1835
1. NEW YORK 2. --- 3. MATANZAS

MILNE, ISABELLA, 16, F, TAILORESS, 11/03/1835
1. 2. FALL RIVER 3. PICTOU

MILNE, JANE, 18, F, TAILORESS, 11/03/1835
1. 2. FALL RIVER 3. PICTOU

MILNE, JANET, 6, F, , 11/03/1835
1. 2. FALL RIVER 3. PICTOU

MILNE, JOHN, 58, M, MINISTER, 11/03/1835
1. SCOTLAND 2. FALL RIVER 3. PICTOU

MILNE, MARION, 50, F, TAILORESS, 11/03/1835
1. SCOTLAND 2. FALL RIVER 3. PICTOU

MILNE, MARY, 10, F, CHILD, 06/03/1844
1. ENGLAND 2. U.S. 3. PICTOU

MINER, AMELIA, 12, F, , 10/24/1860
1. NOVA SCOTIA 2. U.S. 3. PICTOU

MINER, E.D., 2, M, CHILD, 06/01/1852
1. BRITISH AMERICA 2. U.S. 3. PICTOU

MINER, GEO. W., 36, M, PAINTER, 10/24/1860
1. NOVA SCOTIA 2. U.S. 3. PICTOU

MINER, JACOB G., 30, M, CARPENTER, 06/01/1852
1. BRITISH AMERICA 2. U.S. 3. PICTOU

MINER, JANE, 28, F, WIFE, 06/01/1852
1. BRITISH AMERICA 2. U.S. 3. PICTOU

MINER, JANE, 10, F, , 10/24/1860
1. NOVA SCOTIA 2. U.S. 3. PICTOU

MINER, MARY, 33, F, HOUSEWIFE, 10/24/1860
1. NOVA SCOTIA 2. U.S. 3. PICTOU

MINER, MARY JANE, 8, F, CHILD, 06/01/1852
1. BRITISH AMERICA 2. U.S. 3. PICTOU

MINER, SARAH, 4, F, CHILD, 06/01/1852
1. BRITISH AMERICA 2. U.S. 3. PICTOU

MINER, THOS. W., 6, M, CHILD, 06/01/1852
1. BRITISH AMERICA 2. U.S. 3. PICTOU

MINER, JR., GEO. W., 9, M, , 10/24/1860
1. NOVA SCOTIA 2. U.S. 3. PICTOU

MINTEN, J.V., 60, M, MERCHANT, 10/18/1831
1. SWEDEN 2. U.S. 3. GOTENBURG

MITCHEL, ROBERT, 26, M, LABORER, 09/09/1844
1. ENGLAND 2. U.S. 3. PICTOU

MLELLIN, SARAH, 22, F, NONE, 10/14/1846
1. NOVA SCOTIA 2. U.S. 3. PICTOU

MOLOY, ANN, 8, F, NONE, 10/07/1857
1. GREAT BRITAIN 2. U.S. 3. PICTOU

MOLOY, BRIDGET, 27, F, HOUSEWIFE, 10/07/1857
1. GREAT BRITAIN 2. U.S. 3. PICTOU

MOLOY, JAMES, 24, M, LABORER, 07/24/1849
1. IRELAND 2. U.S. 3. SYDNEY

MOLOY, THOMAS, 2, M, NONE, 10/07/1857
1. GREAT BRITAIN 2. U.S. 3. PICTOU

MOLOY, WILLIAM, 6, M, NONE, 10/07/1857
1. GREAT BRITAIN 2. U.S. 3. PICTOU

MONATIC, FELIS, 25, M, MERCHANT, 02/13/1838
1. CUBA 2. CUBA 3. HAVANA

MONROE, CHRISTIE, 18, F, NONE, 08/20/1857
1. NOVA SCOTIA 2. U.S. 3. PICTOU

MONROE, CHRISTY, 19, F, SERVANT OR ASSISTANT, 08/09/1853
1. NOVA SCOTIA 2. U.S. 3. PICTOU

MONROE, DONALD, 21, M, BLACKSMITH, 05/22/1857
1. GREAT BRITAIN 2. U.S. 3. PICTOU

MONROE, MARY, 17, F, SERVANT, 07/22/1856
1. GREAT BRITAIN 2. U.S. 3. PICTOU

MONSON, WEALTHY A., 20, F, , 04/15/1824
1. U.S. 2. U.S. 3. HAVANA

MONTGOMERY, DAVID, 45, M, MERCHANT, 03/01/1832
1. U.S. 2. U.S. 3. SURINAM

MOONEY, CATHARINE, 18, F, LADY, 08/06/1849
1. BRITISH AMERICA 2. U.S. 3. PICTOU

MOONEY, JAMES, 3, M, NONE, 07/07/1857
1. NOVA SCOTIA 2. U.S. 3. PICTOU

MOONEY, JOSEF, 37, M, , 03/22/1826
1. ENGLAND 2. MASSACHUSETTS 3. LIVERPOOL

MOONEY, MARY, 6, F, NONE, 07/07/1857
1. NOVA SCOTIA 2. U.S. 3. PICTOU

MOONEY, MRS. JAMES, 24, F, NONE, 07/07/1857
1. NOVA SCOTIA 2. U.S. 3. PICTOU

MOONEY, THOMAS, 1, M, NONE, 07/07/1857
1. NOVA SCOTIA 2. U.S. 3. PICTOU

MOONEY, WILLIAM N., 30, M, ENGINEER, 03/10/1842
1. U.S. 2. U.S. 3. MATANZAS

MOOTON, BERIAH, 16, F, NONE, 10/14/1846
1. U.S. 2. U.S. 3. PICTOU

MORE, ELIZABETH, 22, F, SERVANT, 08/25/1834
1. NOVA SCOTIA 2. U.S. 3. PICTOU

MORGAN, JAMES R., 27, M, CARPENTER, 06/16/1832
1. U.S. 2. U.S. 3. HAVANA

MORIARTY, BETSEY, 24, F, , 09/27/1837
1. 2. 3. PICTOU

MORIARTY, ELIZABETH, 22, F, , 09/27/1837
1. 2. 3. PICTOU

MORIARTY, JOHN, 28, M, LABORER, 09/27/1837
1. 2. 3. PICTOU

MORIATY, THOMAS, 23, M, LABORER, 09/27/1837
1. IRELAND 2. BOSTON 3. PICTOU

MORONY, BROSNAN, 28, M, CARPENTER, 04/13/1842
1. U.S. 2. U.S. 3. MATANZAS

MORRIS, ADAM, 14, M, NONE, 06/11/1856
1. SCOTLAND 2. U.S. 3. PICTOU

MORRIS, WILLIAM, 44, M, MARINER, 03/13/1835
1. U.S. 2. U.S. 3. HAVANA

MORRISON, ANGUS, 30, , LABORER, 09/11/1867
1. NOVA SCOTIA 2. U.S. 3. SINGAN

MORRISON, DANIEL, 2, , , 09/11/1867
1. 2. 3. SINGAN

MORRISON, JAMES, 18, , TAILOR, 05/09/1837
1. IRELAND 2. NEW YORK 3. LIVERPOOL

MORRISON, MARY, 24, , , 09/11/1867
1. 2. 3. SINGAN

MORRISON, NANCY, 18, F, SERVANT, 09/09/1844
1. NOVA SCOTIA 2. U.S. 3. PICTOU

MORSE, MASON, 26, M, MERCHANT, 08/11/1823
1. U.S. 2. U.S. 3. ---

MORTON, J.E., 22, M, TRADESMAN, 06/24/1861
1. NOVA SCOTIA 2. U.S. 3. PICTOU

MOSCA, MANUEL, 40, M, MARINER, 08/28/1872
1. SAN MIQUEL 2. BOSTON 3.

MOSES, JOHN, 28, M, DOCTOR, 07/16/1823
1. U.S. 2. U.S. 3. HAVANA

MOSHER, LUCY, 26, F, NONE, 07/22/1856
1. GREAT BRITAIN 2. U.S. 3. PICTOU

MOSS, ROBERT, 38, M, ENGINEER, 06/11/1840
1. U.S. 2. U.S. 3. MATANZAS

MOWRY, EDWIN, 24, M, MERCHANT, 09/18/1823
1. RHODE ISLAND 2. U.S. 3. HONDURAS

MUEN, DAVID, 27, M, MINER, 06/08/1835
1. PICTOU 2. NEW YORK 3. PICTOU

MULLEN, JAMES, 6, M, , 07/27/1835
1. NOVA SCOTIA 2. FALL RIVER 3. PICTOU

MULLEN, MARGARET, 25, F, , 07/27/1835
1. NOVA SCOTIA 2. FALL RIVER 3. PICTOU

MULLEN, MOSES, 2, M, , 07/27/1835
1. NOVA SCOTIA 2. FALL RIVER 3. PICTOU

MULLEN, WM., 4, M, , 07/27/1835
1. NOVA SCOTIA 2. FALL RIVER 3. PICTOU

MULNONAY, WM, 20, M, LABORER, 07/27/1835
1. IRELAND 2. PHILADELPHIA 3. PICTOU

MUNDON, JOHN, 25, M, BLACKSMITH, 04/14/1825
1. U.S. 2. U.S. 3. HAVANA

MUNRO, ALEX, 24, M, JOINER, 05/22/1857
1. GREAT BRITAIN 2. U.S. 3. PICTOU

MUNRO, ALEXANDER, 32, M, MINER, 05/23/1857
1. NOVA SCOTIA 2. U.S. 3. PICTOU

MUNRO, CHRISTY, 7, M, , 05/23/1857
1. NOVA SCOTIA 2. U.S. 3. PICTOU

MUNRO, ELIZABETH, 29, F, HOUSE WIFE, 05/23/1857
1. NOVA SCOTIA 2. U.S. 3. PICTOU

MUNRO, JAMES M., 30, M, COOPER, 06/11/1845
1. U.S. 2. U.S. 3. CARDENAS

MUNRO, JAMES M., 40, M, COOPER, 08/03/1855
1. U.S. 2. U.S. 3. MATANZAS

MUNRO, MARY, 4, F, , 06/29/1840
1. CUBA 2. CUBA 3. MATANZAS

MUNRO, MARY, 3, F, , 05/23/1857
1. NOVA SCOTIA 2. U.S. 3. PICTOU

MUNRO, SARAH, 6, F, , 06/29/1840
1. CUBA 2. CUBA 3. MATANZAS

MUNRO, THOMAS, 27, M, , 05/23/1857
1. NOVA SCOTIA 2. U.S. 3. PICTOU

MUNRO, WILLIAM W., 39, M, GENTLEMAN, 06/11/1845
1. U.S. 2. U.S. 3. CARDENAS

MUNROE, ANN, 19, F, SERVANT, 06/18/1850
1. NOVA SCOTIA 2. NOVA SCOTIA 3. PICTOU

MUNROE, CHRISTIE, 18, F, NONE, 08/20/1857
1. NOVA SCOTIA 2. U.S. 3. PICTOU

MUNROE, HARRIET, 32, F, , 06/29/1840
1. CUBA 2. CUBA 3. MATANZAS

MUNROE, ISABEL, 14, F, NONE, 05/21/1858
1. GREAT BRITAIN 2. U.S. 3. PICTOU

MUNROE, ISSABELLA, 30, F, , 09/19/1850
1. BRITISH AMERICA 2. U.S. 3. PICTOU

MUNROE, MARGARET, 15, F, NONE, 05/21/1858
1. GREAT BRITAIN 2. U.S. 3. PICTOU

MUNROE, MARY, 3, F, CHILD, 09/19/1850
1. BRITISH AMERICA 2. U.S. 3. PICTOU

MUNROE, NANCY, 2, F, , 06/29/1840
1. CUBA 2. CUBA 3. MATANZAS

MUNROE, WILLIAM, 22, M, LABORER, 07/05/1866
1. BRITISH AMERICA 2. U.S. 3. PICTOU

MUNROE, WILLIAM W., 26, M, CARPENTER, 07/18/1827
1. U.S. 2. U.S. 3. MATANZAS

MUNROE, WM, 34, M, MERCHANT, 06/29/1840
1. CUBA 2. CUBA 3. MATANZAS

MUNROE, WM, 8, M, , 06/29/1840
1. CUBA 2. CUBA 3. MATANZAS

MUNROW JR., ALLEN, 22, M, COOPER, 06/17/1839
1. U.S. 2. U.S. 3. MATANZAS

MURDICK, ALEXANDER, 24, M, CARPENTER, 05/08/1838
1. U.S. 2. U.S. 3. HAVANA

MURDOCK, ANN, 4, F, , 06/19/1860
1. NOVA SCOTIA 2. U.S. 3. PICTOU

MURDOCK, ELISABETH, 18, F, , 08/16/1850
1. NOVA SCOTIA 2. U.S. 3. PICTOU

MURDOCK, ELIZA, 28, F, HOUSEWIFE, 06/19/1860
1. NOVA SCOTIA 2. U.S. 3. PICTOU

MURDOCK, JESSIE, 5 MONTHS, F, , 06/19/1860
1. NOVA SCOTIA 2. U.S. 3. PICTOU

MURDOCK, JOHN, 20, M, JOINER, 06/16/1845
1. BRITISH AMERICA 2. U.S. 3. PICTOU

MURDOCK, JOHN, 28, M, CARPENTER, 08/25/1848
1. BRITISH AMERICA 2. U.S. 3. PICTOU

MURDOCK, LEONARD, 10 MONTHS, M, , 05/22/1857
1. GREAT BRITAIN 2. U.S. 3. PICTOU

MURDOCK, MARGARET, 28, F, HOUSEWIFE, 05/22/1857
1. GREAT BRITAIN 2. U.S. 3. PICTOU

MURDOCK, MARTHA, 8, F, , 06/19/1860
1. NOVA SCOTIA 2. U.S. 3. PICTOU

MURDOCK, MARY, 11, F, , 06/19/1860
1. NOVA SCOTIA 2. U.S. 3. PICTOU

MURDOCK, RACHEL, 27, F, SERVANT, 07/08/1867
1. BRITISH AMERICA 2. U.S. 3. PICTOU

MURDOCK, WILLIAM, 32, M, SHOEMAKER, 06/19/1860
1. NOVA SCOTIA 2. U.S. 3. PICTOU

MURDOCK, WILLIAM, 21, M, HOUSE JOINER, 07/08/1844
1. NOVA SCOTIA 2. U.S. 3. PICTOU

MURDUCK, MARY, 29, F, AND 5 CHILDREN, 09/10/1836
1. ENGLAND 2. U.S. 3. PICTOU

MURFEY, HANNAH, 16, F, SERVICE, 08/10/1838
1. PICTOU 2. 3. PICTOU

MURPHY, ELISABETH, 28, F, SERVANT, 09/24/1866
1. BRITISH AMERICA 2. NOVA SCOTIA 3. SINGAN

MURPHY, ELLEN, 30, F, SERVANT, 09/24/1866
1. BRITISH AMERICA 2. NOVA SCOTIA 3. SINGAN

MURPHY, EUNICE, 45, F, LABORER, 08/05/1848
1. BRITISH AMERICA 2. U.S. 3. PICTOU

MURPHY, FRANCIS ---, 35, , M---TA MARINER, 03/25/1841
1. NEWBURYPORT 2. 3. TURKS ISLAND

MURPHY, JOSEPH, 21, M, SHIP CARPENTER, 10/13/1846
1. BRITISH AMERICA 2. U.S. 3. PICTOU

MURPHY, PATRICK, 45, M, LABORER, 08/05/1848
1. BRITISH AMERICA 2. U.S. 3. PICTOU

MURRAY, ANN, 25, F, SERVANT, 07/01/1850
1. BRITISH AMERICA 2. U.S. 3. PICTOU

MURRAY, ANNA, 10, F, CHILDREN, 05/16/1851
1. COLCHESTER 2. U.S. 3. MAITLAND

MURRAY, BRIDGET, 30, , LABORER, 05/09/1837
1. IRELAND 2. NEW YORK 3. LIVERPOOL

MURRAY, GEORGE, 45, M, TAILOR, 09/19/1835
1. PICTOU 2. U.S. 3. PICTOU

MURRAY, GEORGE, 21, M, , 11/02/1847
1. BRITISH AMERICA 2. U.S. 3. PICTOU

MURRAY, GEORGEANNA, 20, F, SERVANT, 07/01/1850
1. BRITISH AMERICA 2. U.S. 3. PICTOU

MURRAY, JAMES, 8, M, CHILDREN, 05/16/1851
1. COLCHESTER 2. U.S. 3. MAITLAND

MURRAY, JOHN, 23, M, LABORER, 08/09/1839
1. NOVA SCOTIA 2. U.S. 3. PICTOU

MURRAY, JOHN, 35, M, JOINER, 05/16/1851
1. COLCHESTER 2. U.S. 3. MAITLAND

MURRAY, JOHN, 5, M, CHILD, 05/16/1851
1. COLCHESTER 2. U.S. 3. MAITLAND

MURRAY, MARGARET, 25, F, SEAMSTRESS, 09/19/1835
1. PICTOU 2. U.S. 3. PICTOU

MURRAY, MARY, 30, F, LADY, 05/16/1851
1. COLCHESTER 2. U.S. 3. MAITLAND

MURRAY, MARY, 19, F, HOUSE SERVANT, 06/02/1856
1. NOVA SCOTIA 2. NOVA SCOTIA 3. PICTOU

MURRAY, PHEBE, 17, F, LADY, 05/16/1851
1. COLCHESTER 2. U.S. 3. MAITLAND

MURRAY, ROBERTINA, 18, F, SERVANT, 08/24/1870
1. PICTOU 2. U.S. 3. PICTOU

MURRAY, THOMAS, 2, M, CHILDREN, 05/16/1851
1. COLCHESTER 2. U.S. 3. MAITLAND

MURRY, JAMES, 30, , LABORER, 05/09/1837
1. IRELAND 2. NEW YORK 3. LIVERPOOL

MURRY, JOHN, 30, M, LABOR MARRIED, 1836
1. COUNTY TIPPERARY, IRE. 2. NEW YORK 3. PICTOU

MURRY, MARY, 26, F, WIFE OF JOHN, 1836
1. COUNTY TIPPERARY, IRE. 2. NEW YORK 3. PICTOU

MURRY, NORRY, 1, , CHILD OF JOHN, 1836
1. COUNTY TIPPERARY, IRE. 2. NEW YORK 3. PICTOU

MURRY, PATRICK, 3, M, CHILD OF JOHN, 1836
1. COUNTY TIPPERARY, IRE. 2. NEW YORK 3. PICTOU

MUSADA, CARLOS LEAL, 19, M, FARMER, 08/28/1872
1. FLORES 2. BOSTON 3.

MYRICK, J.G., 48, M, MARINER, 01/19/1824
1. U.S. 2. U.S. 3. GIBRALTER

NAPIER, JAMES, 28, M, MARINER, 02/19/1823
1. U.S. 2. U.S. 3. CURACOA

NARVIN, ELLEN, 16, , SERVANT, 05/09/1837
1. IRELAND 2. U.S. 3. LIVERPOOL

NASON, , 3, F, NONE, 08/24/1863
1. U.S. 2. U.S. 3. PICTOU

NASON, ---GARET, 30, F, HOUSEWIFE, 08/24/1863
1. U.S. 2. U.S. 3. PICTOU

NASON, BENJAMIN, 30, M, FISHERMAN, 08/24/1863
1. U.S. 2. U.S. 3. PICTOU

NAVEIRO, FILOMENA, 19, F, SEAMSTRESSS, 08/28/1872
1. FLORES 2. PROVIDENCE 3.

NAVEIRO, MARIA, 20, F, SEAMSTRESS, 08/28/1872
1. FLORES 2. BOSTON 3.

NEEDHAM, EDWARD, 24, M, TANNER AND CURRIER, 07/08/1844
1. NOVA SCOTIA 2. U.S. 3. PICTOU

NEILL, FRANCIS, , , , 12/30/1823
1. NEW YORK 2. TRINIDAD 3. PROVIDENCE

NEVAL, ANNA, 16, F, , 08/16/1850
1. NOVA SCOTIA 2. U.S. 3. PICTOU

NEVILL, CATHARINE, 7, F, CHILD, 10/20/1845
1. NOVA SCOTIA 2. U.S. 3. PICTOU

NEVILL, DANIEL, 9, M, CHILD, 10/20/1845
1. NOVA SCOTIA 2. U.S. 3. PICTOU

NEVILL, JAMES, 12, M, CHILD, 10/20/1845
1. NOVA SCOTIA 2. U.S. 3. PICTOU

NEVILL, JUNE, 50, F, FAMILY OF THREE, 10/20/1845
1. NOVA SCOTIA 2. U.S. 3. PICTOU

NEVILLE, HARRIET, 13, F, SERVANT, 11/11/1844
1. NOVA SCOTIA 2. U.S. 3. PICTOU

NEWELL, HOMER, 20, M, GENTLEMAN, 05/03/1841
1. U.S. 2. 3. MATANZAS

NEWELL, STANFORD, 55, M, GENTLEMAN, 05/03/1841
1. U.S. 2. 3. MATANZAS

NEWELL, TIMOTHY, 45, M, JOINER, 09/09/1844
1. NOVA SCOTIA 2. U.S. 3. PICTOU

NICHOLS, CHAS. A., 3, M, CHILD, 10/25/1853
1. U.S. 2. U.S. 3. TALCAHUANO

NICHOLS, JAMES, 16, M, FARMER, 07/20/1848
1. BRITISH AMERICA 2. BRITISH AMERICA 3. PICTOU

NICHOLS, MARY, 37, F, WIFE, 10/25/1853
1. U.S. 2. U.S. 3. TALCAHUANO

NICHOLS, MARY, 16 MONTHS, F, CHILD, 10/25/1853
1. U.S. 2. U.S. 3. TALCAHUANO

NICHOLS, SARAH, 8, F, CHILD, 10/25/1853
1. U.S. 2. U.S. 3. TALCAHUANO

NICHOLS, WM U., 3, M, CHILD, 10/25/1853
1. U.S. 2. U.S. 3. TALCAHUANO

NICKLE, HANNAH, 20, F, SERVANT, 06/03/1844
1. NOVA SCOTIA 2. U.S. 3. PICTOU

NICOLAO, MANUEL F., 24, M, MARINER, 08/28/1872
1. FLORES 2. PROVIDENCE 3.

NILO---, JOSE F., 24, M, MARINER, 08/28/1872
1. FLORES 2. BOSTON 3.

NOBLE, MARGARET, 19, F, SERVANT, 07/28/1862
1. NOVA SCOTIA 2. U.S. 3. PICTOU

NORRAWAY, JOHN M., 17, M, STUDENT, 08/27/1860
1. NOVA SCOTIA 2. U.S. 3. PICTOU

NORTHAM, STEPHEN T., 25, M, MERCHANT, 05/05/1829
1. U.S. 2. U.S. 3. MATANZAS

NORTHAM, JR., STEPHEN L., 25, M, MERCHANT, 11/11/1828
1. U.S. 2. U.S. 3. HAVANA

NORTHEY, JAMES, 26, M, GENTLEMAN, 09/10/1845
1. ENGLAND 2. ENGLAND 3. PICTOU

NORTON, MARY, 25, , LABORER, 05/09/1837
1. IRELAND 2. NEW YORK 3. LIVERPOOL

NOVA, MICHIAL, 22, , LABORER, 05/09/1837
1. IRELAND 2. NEW YORK 3. LIVERPOOL

NOYES, ABIJAH M., 48, F, , 05/09/1832
1. U.S. 2. U.S. 3. MATANZAS

NOYES, MAY, 20, F, , 05/09/1832
1. U.S. 2. U.S. 3. MATANZAS

NUMOUGH, GEORGE, 24, M, HOUSE WRIGHT, 05/08/1838
1. U.S. 2. U.S. 3. HAVANA

NUNES, SOLOMON R., 51, M, MERCHANT, 04/22/1820
1. SURINAM 2. SURINAM 3. SURINAM

NUTTON, ELLENOR, 14, F, BLACKS FROM US RETURNED, 10/06/1828
1. PHILADELPHIA 2. PHILADELPHIA 3. PUERTA PLATA

NYLES, HANNAH, 28, F, , 06/30/1830
1. U.S. 2. U.S. 3. HAVANA

O'BRIEN, CATHARINE, 18, F, LADY, 05/16/1842
1. CUBA 2. CUBA 3. HAVANA

O'LEARY, DENNIS, 21, M, LABORER, 07/08/1853
1. IRELAND 2. U.S. 3. NEWPORT, ENGLAND

OBRIEN, BRIDGET, 17, F, MILLINER, 10/27/1834
1. NOVA SCOTIA 2. BOSTON 3. PICTOU

OLDHAM, JOHN, 23, M, TRADESMAN, 03/22/1826
1. ENGLAND 2. MASSACHUSETTS 3. LIVERPOOL

OLIVA, GABRIEL, 18, M, PLANTER, 07/15/1834
1. CUBA 2. CUBA 3. MATANZAS

OLIVE, CHARLES, 40, M, MERCHANT, 11/11/1864
1. GREAT BRITAIN 2. GREAT BRITAIN 3. SIMONS BAY, C.G.H

OLIVER, ANDRIS M., 28, M, , 05/16/1821
1. SPAIN 2. 3. MATANZAS

OLIVER, CATHARINE, 18, F, DOMESTIC, 10/17/1862
   1. PICTOU 2. PROVIDENCE 3. PICTOU

OLIVER, ELLEN, 19, F, DOMESTIC, 10/17/1862
   1. PICTOU 2. PROVIDENCE 3. PICTOU

OLIVER, MARTHA, 35, F, , 06/23/1830
   1. CUBA 2. CUBA 3. MATANZAS

OLNEY, GEORGE, 25, M, CARPENTER, 06/29/1829
   1. U.S. 2. U.S. 3. HAVANA

OLNEY, GEORGE W., 32, M, MERCHANT, 09/18/1823
   1. RHODE ISLAND 2. U.S. 3. HONDURAS

ORNE, EDWARD, 50, M, MERCHANT, 04/16/1821
   1. U.S. 2. U.S. 3. LISBON

ORR, CATHARINE, 19, F, SERVANT, 08/22/1850
   1. BRITISH AMERICA 2. U.S. 3. PICTOU

OSWELL, BENJAMIN, 25, , GENTLEMAN, 01/27/1842
   1. U.S. 2. U.S. 3. MATANZAS

OTIS, JANE E., 35, F, , 06/23/1830
   1. CUBA 2. CUBA 3. MATANZAS

PACHECO, LUIS, 16, M, SHEPHERD, 08/28/1872
   1. SAN MIQUEL 2. BOSTON 3.

PACKARD, ISAAC, 65, , MERCHANT, 04/20/1841
   1. CUBA 2. 3. MATANZAS

PAGE, MARY, 20, F, DRESS MAKER, 07/09/1839
   1. NOVA SCOTIA 2. RHODE ISLAND 3. PICTOU

PAIGE, MRS., 34, F, , 09/19/1835
   1. NEW HAMPSHIRE 2. 3. PICTOU

PALMER, CHARLES, , , , 12/14/1823
   1. HINGHAM 2. BARBADOS/TRINIDAD 3. PROVIDENCE

PALMER, MARY, 38, F, , 10/22/1834
   1. NOVA SCOTIA 2. U.S. 3. CUMBERLAND, N.S.

PALMER, STEPHEN G., , , , SEAMAN SENT HOME FROM PERNAM,
01/16/1849
   1. 2. 3. SANDWICH ISLANDS

PARIOL, PATRICK, 28, M, LABORER, 07/15/1836
   1. IRELAND 2. U.S. 3. PICTOU

PARKER, EDWARD, 25, M, PLACED ABOARD BY CONSUL, 09/03/1821
1. U.S. 2. U.S. 3. MADEIRA

PARKER, HENRY, 26, M, MARINER, 05/08/1830
1. U.S. 2. U.S. 3. ST. SALVADORE

PARKER, MARY, 30, F, DOMESTIC, 08/19/1859
1. NOVA SCOTIA 2. U.S. 3. PICTOU

PARKER, NOAH, 36, M, MECHANIC, 06/13/1836
1. U.S. 2. U.S. 3. HAVANA

PARTRAGE, ANN, 45, F, LADY, 07/08/1848
1. PICTOU 2. PROVIDENCE 3. PICTOU

PARTRIDGE, MARTHA, 40, F, LADY, 06/03/1844
1. ENGLAND 2. U.S. 3. PICTOU

PARTRIDGE, SUSAN, 18, F, LADY, 06/03/1844
1. ENGLAND 2. U.S. 3. PICTOU

PARTRIDGE, THOMAS, 35, M, MACHINIST, 06/03/1844
1. ENGLAND 2. U.S. 3. PICTOU

PATERSON, MARGARET, 22, F, DRESS MAKER, 07/12/1855
1. NOVA SCOTIA 2. U.S. 3. PICTOU

PATHE, R.N., 50, M, MECHANIC, 06/22/1840
1. U.S. 2. U.S. 3. MATANZAS

PATISON, ANN, 44, F, SEAMSTRESS, 09/27/1852
1. BRITISH AMERICA 2. U.S. 3. PICTOU

PATTERSON, ANN, 30, F, LADY, 09/27/1848
1. PICTOU 2. PROVIDENCE 3. PICTOU

PATTERSON, ANN, 40, F, SEAMSTRESS, 10/03/1853
1. PICTOU 2. U.S. 3. PICTOU

PATTERSON, ANNE, 50, F, DRESSMAKER, 09/26/1859
1. NOVA SCOTIA 2. U.S. 3. PICTOU

PATTERSON, BARBARY, 20, F, HOUSEWIFE, 08/30/1855
1. U.S. 2. U.S. 3. PICTOU

PATTERSON, ELLA, 20, F, HOUSE SERVANT, 09/14/1863
1. NOVA SCOTIA 2. U.S. 3. PICTOU

PATTERSON, GEORGE, 22, M, SHIP JOINTER, 06/03/1844
1. NOVA SCOTIA 2. U.S. 3. PICTOU

PATTERSON, GEORGE, 20, M, CLERK, 07/20/1857
1. NOVA SCOTIA 2. U.S. 3. PICTOU

PATTERSON, JOHN, 24, M, ENGRAVER, 08/30/1855
1. U.S. 2. U.S. 3. PICTOU

PATTERSON, MARGARET, 27, F, SERVANT, 10/07/1840
1. PICTOU 2. U.S. 3. PICTOU

PATTERSON, MARGARET, 29, F, SERVANT, 07/20/1844
1. NOVA SCOTIA 2. U.S. 3. PICTOU

PATTERSON, MARION, 20, , SERVANT, 07/18/1864
1. NOVA SCOTIA 2. 3. PICTOU

PATTERSON, MELVILLE, 4, M, , 10/07/1840
1. PICTOU 2. U.S. 3. PICTOU

PATTERSON, THOMAS H., 41, M, LABORER, 10/07/1840
1. PICTOU 2. U.S. 3. PICTOU

PATTISON, STEWART, 18, M, PRINTER, 08/20/1847
1. NOVA SCOTIA 2. NOVA SCOTIA 3. PICTOU

PATTON, WILLIAM C., 34, M, SURGEON U.S. NAVY, 05/29/1835
1. U.S. 2. VIRGINIA 3. N---

PAULIN, JOHN, 21, M, , 09/13/1859
1. NOVA SCOTIA 2. U.S. 3. PICTOU

PAYNE, ARTEMAS, 34, M, MASTER MARINER, 01/16/1849
1. U.S. 2. U.S. 3. NASSAU

PEACH, (CHILD),4, F, , 06/23/1830
1. NEW YORK 2. NEW YORK 3. MATANZAS

PEACH, JOSEPH, 55, M, CARPENTER, 06/23/1830
1. NEW YORK 2. NEW YORK 3. MATANZAS

PEACH, MRS., 34, F, , 06/23/1830
1. NEW YORK 2. NEW YORK 3. MATANZAS

PEARCE, WILLIAM, 21, M, CARPENTER, 07/16/1821
1. U.S. 2. U.S. 3. MATANZAS

PEARL, MARY A., 35, F, , 08/31/1853
1. U.S. 2. U.S. 3. ARICHAT

PEARSON, CHARLES H., 25, M, COOPER, 06/13/1844
1. U.S. 2. U.S. 3. CARDENAS

PEASE, BARZILLAI, 52, M, MARINER, 09/11/1826
1. U.S. 2. U.S. 3. ST. PIERRE

PECK, ERASTUS, 18, M, EXHIBITOR OF WILD ANIMALS, 06/29/1826
1. U.S. 2. U.S. 3. HAVANA

PECK, ROBERT A., 28, M, ENGINEER, 05/29/1855
1. U.S. 2. U.S. 3. CARDENAS

PEDRO, ANTONIO, 16, M, TAILOR, 08/28/1872
1. SAN MIQUEL 2. BOSTON 3.

PEDRO, CAITONO, 26, M, MARINER, 08/28/1872
1. FLORES 2. BOSTON 3.

PENDEGRAS, MARGARET, 28, F, , 07/27/1835
1. IRELAND 2. PROVIDENCE 3. PICTOU

PEREIRA, JACINTO, 20, M, FARMER, 08/28/1872
1. SAN MIQUEL 2. BOSTON 3.

PEREIRA, MANUEL, 28, M, MARINER, 08/28/1872
1. FLORES 2. BOSTON 3.

PERKINS, JAMES, 34, M, MARINER, 08/28/1823
1. U.S. 2. U.S. 3. HONDURAS

PERRIN, JACOB, 22, M, MOULDER, 07/16/1867
1. NOVA SCOTIA 2. U.S. 3. PICTOU

PERROCHER, , 39, M, MERCHANT, 05/20/1839
1. FRANCE 2. MEXICO 3. HAVANA

PERRY, SAMUEL, 30, M, ENGINEER, 08/05/1839
1. U.S. 2. U.S. 3. HAVANA

PERTRERNS, ROBERT, 21, M, , 08/01/1859
1. NOVA SCOTIA 2. U.S. 3. PICTOU

PETERS, DIANA, 21, F, SERVANT, 07/20/1844
1. NOVA SCOTIA 2. U.S. 3. PICTOU

PETERSON, CHARLES W., 23, M, MERCHANT, 09/10/1858
1. U.S. 2. U.S. 3. TURKS ISLAND

PETERSON, GEORGE O., 27, M, MARINER, 08/14/1858
1. U.S. 2. U.S. 3. SAINT JOHN

PHAN, MARY, 24, F, LADY, 08/05/1847
1. BRITISH AMERICA 2. U.S. 3. PICTOU

PHILLIPLANE, DEXTER T., 22, M, MECHANIC, 12/13/1837
1. U.S. 2. U.S. 3.

PHILLIPS, WILLIAM, 50, M, SHIP MASTER, 06/23/1827
1. U.S. 2. U.S. 3. OMOA

PHILPOT, SUSAN, 22, F, SERVANT, 07/30/1866
1. CAPE BRETON 2. U.S. 3. PICTOU

PICKENS, LUTHER, , , DISTRESSED SEAMEN, 01/16/1849
1. 2. 3. NASSAU

PINKHAM, CHARLES H., 15, M, , 05/28/1861
1. PICTOU 2. U.S. 3. PICTOU

PINKHAM, GEORGE, 13, M, HOUSE SERVANT, 09/14/1863
1. NOVA SCOTIA 2. U.S. 3. PICTOU

PINKHAM, JOHN, 1, M, , 05/28/1861
1. PICTOU 2. U.S. 3. PICTOU

PINKHAM, MARGARET, 36, F, , 05/28/1861
1. PICTOU 2. U.S. 3. PICTOU

PINKHAM, MARGARET, 22, F, SPINSTER, 09/18/1845
1. NOVA SCOTIA 2. U.S. 3. PICTOU

PINKHAM, MARGARET F., 6, F, , 05/28/1861
1. PICTOU 2. U.S. 3. PICTOU

PINKHAM, SARAH JANE, 4, F, , 05/28/1861
1. PICTOU 2. U.S. 3. PICTOU

PINKHAM, WILLIAM, 8, M, , 05/28/1861
1. PICTOU 2. U.S. 3. PICTOU

PINKIM, JOHN, 3, M, CHILD, 07/17/1850
1. BRITISH AMERICA 2. U.S. 3. PICTOU

PIRES, DOMINQUES, 42, , , 05/18/1868
1. 2. 3. BRAVA

POLLOCK, LEWIS, 27, M, MERCHANT, 06/21/1838
1. U.S. 2. U.S. 3. MATANZAS

POND, ARNOLD, 40, M, COOPER, 06/02/1856
1. U.S. 2. U.S. 3. PICTOU

POOLER, HENRIETTA, 1, F, , 08/19/1859
1. NOVA SCOTIA 2. U.S. 3. PICTOU

POOLER, STEPHEN, 2, M, , 08/19/1859
1. NOVA SCOTIA 2. U.S. 3. PICTOU

PORTER, JOHN, 20, , LABORER, 06/08/1864
1. NOVA SCOTIA 2. U.S. 3. PICTOU

PORTER, MARY, 20, F, SERVANT OR ASSISTANT, 10/01/1853
1. NOVA SCOTIA 2. U.S. 3. PICTOU

POTTER, AMASA, 22, M, COOPER, 04/29/1828
1. U.S. 2. U.S. 3. HAVANA

POTTER, JOHN D., 23, M, MARINER, 10/13/1820
1. PROVIDENCE 2. U.S. 3. HAVANA

POTTER, R.N., 50, M, ENGINEER, 06/18/1839
1. U.S. 2. U.S. 3. MATANZAS

POTTER, STEPHEN, 47, M, MARINER, 06/23/1828
1. U.S. 2. U.S. 3. HAVANA

POTTINGER, MARGARET, 16, F, , 08/02/1850
1. BRITISH AMERICA 2. U.S. 3. PICTOU

POWEL, LAWRENCE, 34, , LABORER, 05/09/1837
1. IRELAND 2. NEW YORK 3. LIVERPOOL

POWEL, MARGARIT, 27, , WIFE, 05/09/1837
1. IRELAND 2. NEW YORK 3. LIVERPOOL

POWEL, STEPHEN, 1, , CHILD, 05/09/1837
1. IRELAND 2. NEW YORK 3. LIVERPOOL

POWELL, MARY, 26, F, HOUSEWIFE, 10/13/1846
1. BRITISH AMERICA 2. U.S. 3. PICTOU

POWELL, WM, 3, M, CHILD, 10/13/1846
1. BRITISH AMERICA 2. U.S. 3. PICTOU

PRATT, A., 24, M, MERCHANT, 09/18/1834
1. U.S. 2. U.S. 3. HAVANA

PREBBLE, CHARLES, 24, M, MARINER, 08/26/1822
1. U.S. 2. U.S. 3. CANTON

PREIRA, CONSTANTINA, 35, F, LADY, 10/17/1867
1. CAPE VERDE IS. 2. U.S. 3. FLORES

PRESCOTT, O., 18, M, STUDENT, 05/23/1832
1. U.S. 2. U.S. 3. HAVANA

PRINGEL, MARY, 38, F, LADY, 11/11/1844
1. ENGLAND 2. U.S. 3. PICTOU

PRITCHARD, JAMES CARR., 3, M, , 09/18/1845
1. NOVA SCOTIA 2. U.S. 3. PICTOU

PRITCHARD, JANE, 24, F, SPINSTER, 09/18/1845
1. NOVA SCOTIA 2. U.S. 3. PICTOU

PRITCHARD, JOHN WILLIAM, 1, M, , 09/18/1845
1. NOVA SCOTIA 2. U.S. 3. PICTOU

PUJOL, ANTONIO, 2, M, , 07/02/1829
1. ST. DOMINGO, HAITI 2. HAVRE DE GRACE 3. ST. DOMINGO, HAITI

PUJOL, D. PABLO, 43, M, MERCHANT, 07/02/1829
   1. BARCELONA, SPAIN 2. HAVRE DE GRACE 3. ST. DOMINGO, HAITI

PUJOL, MARIA DOLORES, 9, F, , 07/02/1829
   1. ST. DOMINGO, HAITI 2. HAVRE DE GRACE 3. ST. DOMINGO, HAITI

PUJOL, MARIA LAO, 10, F, , 07/02/1829
   1. ST. DOMINGO, HAITI 2. HAVRE DE GRACE 3. ST. DOMINGO, HAITI

PUJOL, JR., PABLO, 7, M, , 07/02/1829
   1. ST. DOMINGO, HAITI 2. HAVRE DE GRACE 3. ST. DOMINGO, HAITI

PUTNAM, MRS., 26, F, HOUSEWIFE, 07/22/1856
   1. GREAT BRITAIN 2. U.S. 3. PICTOU

PUTNAM, NANCY, 19, , , 08/22/1852
   1. BRITISH AMERICA 2. BRITISH AMERICA 3. PICTOU

QUINN, BETSEY, 18, , , 06/25/1838
   1. 2. 3. PICTOU

QUINN, CARNEALUS, 12, , FACTORY EMPLOYMENT, 06/25/1838
   1. SCOTLAND 2. 3. PICTOU

QUINN, ELIZABETH, 17, F, , 08/18/1837
   1. U.S. 2. U.S. 3. PICTOU

QUINN, HANNAH, 52, F, MANUFACTURER, 06/25/1838
   1. 2. 3. PICTOU

QUINN, JOHN, 50, M, FACTORY EMPLOYMENT, 06/25/1838
   1. 2. 3. PICTOU

QUINN, JOSEPH, 22, , FACTORY EMPLOYMENT, 06/25/1838
   1. 2. U.N.S. 3. PICTOU

QUINN, MAREY, 16, , , 06/25/1838
   1. 2. 3. PICTOU

QUINN, MARY, 15, F, , 08/18/1837
   1. U.S. 2. U.S. 3. PICTOU

QUINN, PEETER, 19, , FACTORY EMPLOYMENT, 06/25/1838
   1. 2. 3. PICTOU

QUINN, THERESA, 20, F, , 08/18/1837
   1. U.S. 2. U.S. 3. PICTOU

QUINN, THERESA, 25, , , 06/25/1838
   1. 2. 3. PICTOU

QUINN, JR., JOHN, 10, , MANUFACTURING, 06/25/1838
   1. 2. 3. PICTOU

RABEL, ANNA J., 30, F, SEAMSTRESS, 08/28/1872
1. FLORES 2. PROVIDENCE 3.

RABEL, MARIA E., 15, F, TAILORESS, 08/28/1872
1. S. MIQUEL 2. BOSTON 3.

RABEL, MARIA I., 20, F, SEAMSTRESS, 08/28/1872
1. FLORES 2. BOSTON 3.

RAFAIEL, MANUEL J., 28, M, FARMER, 1872
1. FLORES 2. BOSTON 3.

RAMKEN, MARGARET, 29, F, SERVANT, 09/20/1851
1. BRITISH AMERICA 2. U.S. 3. PICTOU

RAMOS, FRANCISCO, 17, M, FARMER, 08/28/1872
1. FLORES 2. PROVIDENCE 3.

RANKIN, JOHN, 24, M, HOUSE JOINER, 08/23/1850
1. PICTOU 2. PROVIDENCE 3. PICTOU

RANKIN, MARY, 38, F, SERVANT, 08/31/1866
1. PICTOU 2. U.S. 3. PICTOU

RANKIN, MARY, 28, F, DOMESTIC, 09/21/1859
1. NOVA SCOTIA 2. U.S. 3. PICTOU

RANO, CHRISTINE, 18, F, DOMESTIC, 08/19/1859
1. NOVA SCOTIA 2. U.S. 3. PICTOU

RANOLD, ISAAC, 30, M, FARMER, 07/06/1846
1. NOVA SCOTIA 2. U.S. 3. PICTOU

RASICHLEN, FELIX M., 21, , CLERK, 05/09/1837
1. IRELAND 2. NEW YORK 3. LIVERPOOL

RAUBINO, ANTONIO JOSEPH, 20, M, MARINER, 10/17/1867
1. CAPE DE VERDE IS. 2. U.S. 3. FLORES

RAUL, GEORGE, 22, M, BLACKSMITH, 05/08/1838
1. U.S. 2. U.S. 3. HAVANA

READ, JOSEPH H., 37, M, MASTER MARINER, 01/16/1849
1. U.S. 2. U.S. 3. NASSAU

READ, MARGARET, 16, F, , 05/22/1857
1. GREAT BRITAIN 2. U.S. 3. PICTOU

READ, WILLIAM T., 24, M, ENGINEER, 04/16/1842
1. U.S. 2. U.S. 3. MATANZAS

REED, SAML, 53, M, MARINER, 06/18/1839
1. U.S. 2. U.S. 3.

REED, JR., GEORGE, , , , 12/14/1823
  1. PHILADELPHIA 2. BARBADOS/ DEMERARA 3. PROVIDENCE

REIY, JOHN, 35, M, BLACKSMITH, 11/23/1844
  1. U.S. 2. U.S. 3. PICTOU

REMINGTON, DEXTER S., 38, M, MECHANIC, 03/11/1841
  1. U.S. 2. U.S. 3. HAVANA

RENNAM, DANIEL, 21, M, STUDENT, 10/10/1862
  1. CAPE BRETON 2. U.S. 3. ARICHAT

RENTON, JESSY, 15, M, NONE, 08/01/1855
  1. NOVA SCOTIA 2. NOVA SCOTIA 3. PICTOU

RENTON, MARY ANN, 17, F, SERVANT, 08/01/1855
  1. NOVA SCOTIA 2. NOVA SCOTIA 3. PICTOU

REYNOLDS, JAMES, 25, M, CURRIER, 05/22/1857
  1. GREAT BRITAIN 2. U.S. 3. PICTOU

REYNOLDS, JOSEPH O., 24, M, CARPENTER, 07/08/1829
  1. U.S. 2. U.S. 3. MATANZAS

RHODES, J., 27, M, MARINER, 09/10/1824
  1. U.S. 2. U.S. 3. HAVANA

RHODES, JAMES E., 25, M, CARPENTER, 04/21/1820
  1. U.S. 2. U.S. 3. MATANZAS

RHODES, JOSIAH, 26, M, MARINER, 09/24/1823
  1. CONNECTICUT 2. U.S. 3. HAVANA

RHODINS, J.A.H., , , , 12/30/1823
  1. PROVIDENCE 2. DEMERARA 3. PROVIDENCE

RHODINS, J.D.A., , , , 12/30/1823
  1. PROVIDENCE 2. DEMERARA 3. PROVIDENCE

RHODINS, M.C., , , , 12/30/1823
  1. PROVIDENCE 2. DEMERARA 3. PROVIDENCE

RICE, HARRIET, 2, F, CHILD, 08/29/1845
  1. BRITISH AMERICA 2. U.S. 3. PICTOU

RICE, MARGARET, 28, F, HOUSE KEEPER, 08/29/1845
  1. BRITISH AMERICA 2. U.S. 3. PICTOU

RICHARDSON, THOMAS P., 43, M, MERCHANT, 07/28/1826
  1. U.S. 2. U.S. 3. CURACOA

RILEY, BRIDGET, 20, , SPINSTER, 05/09/1837
  1. IRELAND 2. U.S. 3. LIVERPOOL

RILEY, JAMES, 28, M, MERCHANT, 09/11/1825
1. U.S. 2. U.S. 3. HONDURAS

RILEY, MR., 28, M, LABORER, 08/08/1837
1. NOVA SCOTIA 2. NEW YORK 3. PICTOU

RING, W.T., 23, M, BRITISH ARMY, 05/28/1834
1. IRELAND 2. WORLD 3. HAVANA

ROACH, JOAN, 38, F, SERVICE, 08/10/1838
1. PICTOU 2. BOSTON 3. PICTOU

ROACH, JOAN, 11, F, SERVICE, 08/10/1838
1. PICTOU 2. 3. PICTOU

ROACH, PATRICK, 11, M, SERVICE, 08/10/1838
1. PICTOU 2. 3. PICTOU

ROACH, WILLIAM, 22, M, CARPENTER, 07/12/1855
1. NOVA SCOTIA 2. U.S. 3. PICTOU

ROATH, BENJAMIN T., 31, M, GENTLEMAN, 04/25/1840
1. U.S. 2. U.S. 3. MATANZAS

ROBERTS, ELIZABETH, 23, F, , 03/22/1826
1. 2. 3. LIVERPOOL

ROBERTS, WILLIAM, 20, M, GENTLEMAN, 04/16/1842
1. U.S. 2. U.S. 3. MATANZAS

ROBERTSON, JOHN, 45, M, CARPENTER, 10/02/1843
1. BRITISH AMERICA 2. U.S. 3. PICTOU

ROBERTSON, MARGARET, 21, F, SERVANT, 09/09/1844
1. NOVA SCOTIA 2. U.S. 3. PICTOU

ROBERTSON, MARY, 19, F, SERVANT, 11/04/1851
1. BRITISH AMERICA 2. U.S. 3. PICTOU

ROBERTSON, ROBERT, 37, M, MINER, 06/11/1856
1. SCOTLAND 2. U.S. 3. PICTOU

ROBINSON, CATHARINE, 38, F, HOUSEWIFE, 07/09/1860
1. NOVA SCOTIA 2. U.S. 3. PICTOU

ROBINSON, ELLEN, 30, F, , 07/06/1857
1. PICTOU 2. U.S. 3. PICTOU

ROBINSON, H.S., 28, M, CLERK, 07/07/1841
1. MATANZAS 2. MATANZAS 3. MATANZAS

ROBINSON, JAMES, 21, M, MILLER, 07/20/1844
1. NOVA SCOTIA 2. U.S. 3. PICTOU

ROBINSON, JAMES, 10, M, , 07/09/1860
1. NOVA SCOTIA 2. U.S. 3. PICTOU

ROBINSON, JANE, 18, F, DRESS MAKER, 06/03/1844
1. NOVA SCOTIA 2. U.S. 3. PICTOU

ROBINSON, JANE, 12, F, , 07/09/1860
1. NOVA SCOTIA 2. U.S. 3. PICTOU

ROBINSON, JOHN, 45, M, CARPENTER, 05/07/1859
1. NOVA SCOTIA 2. NOVA SCOTIA 3. PICTOU

ROBINSON, JOHN, 45, M, SHIP CARPENTER, 07/09/1860
1. NOVA SCOTIA 2. U.S. 3. PICTOU

ROBINSON, JOHN, 7, M, , 07/09/1860
1. NOVA SCOTIA 2. U.S. 3. PICTOU

ROBINSON, MARY, 22, F, SERVANT, 10/27/1854
1. U.S. 2. U.S. 3. PICTOU

ROBINSON, MARY E., 23, , SERVANT, 10/19/1868
1. BRITISH AMERICA 2. U.S. 3. PICTOU

ROBINSON, NORMAN, 23, M, MERCHANT, 10/27/1826
1. U.S. 2. U.S. 3. MATANZAS

ROBINSON, REBECCA, 19, , SERVANT, 10/19/1868
1. BRITISH AMERICA 2. U.S. 3. PICTOU

ROBINSON, SANDFORD, 25, M, MERCHANT, 03/19/1827
1. U.S. 2. U.S. 3. MATANZAS

ROBINSON, SUTIA, 48, F, LADY, 07/20/1844
1. NOVA SCOTIA 2. U.S. 3. PICTOU

ROBINSON, WILLIAM, 20, M, STEWARD, 06/22/1848
1. BOSTON 2. PROVIDENCE 3. MATANZAS

ROBLEY, SOPHIA, 25, F, SERVANT, 10/24/1860
1. NOVA SCOTIA 2. U.S. 3. PICTOU

RODRIGUES, JOSEPH, 14, M, , 10/17/1867
1. CAPE DE VERDE IS. 2. U.S. 3. FLORES

RODRIQUES, MANUEL, 23, M, FARMER, 08/28/1872
1. FLORES 2. BOSTON 3.

RODRIQUES, THOMAS, 20, M, MARINER, 08/28/1872
1. FLORES 2. BOSTON 3.

ROGERS, DANIEL R., 25, M, MERCHANT, 03/22/1824
1. U.S. 2. U.S. 3. HAVANA

ROGERS, WM., 32, M, MARINER, 11/03/1835
1. U.S. 2. PROVIDENCE 3. PICTOU

ROLLA, JOHN, 12, M, SERVANT, 06/08/1843
1. AFRICA CAPE COAST 2. CAPE COAST AFRICA 3. AFRICA

ROMANO, ROSA, 54, F, TAILORESS, 08/28/1872
1. SAN MIQUEL 2. BOSTON 3.

RORIQUL, STEPHEN, 19, M, TO GO TO SCHOOL, 06/26/1837
1. CUBA 2. SPAIN 3. PROVIDENCE

ROSA, MARIA, 27, F, LADY, 10/17/1867
1. CAPE DE VERDE IS. 2. U.S. 3. FLORES

ROSS, ABBY, 19, F, DRESS MAKER, 09/05/1846
1. SCOTLAND 2. U.S. 3. PICTOU

ROSS, ALEXANDER, 28, M, SHIP CARPENTER, 07/03/1845
1. SCOTLAND 2. U.S. 3. PICTOU

ROSS, ALICE, 18, F, SERVANT, 07/20/1844
1. NOVA SCOTIA 2. U.S. 3. PICTOU

ROSS, CHARLES, 22, M, CLERK, 08/14/1852
1. BRITISH AMERICA 2. U.S. 3. PICTOU

ROSS, CHRISTINA, 19, F, SERVANT, 08/05/1856
1. NOVA SCOTIA 2. NOVA SCOTIA 3. PICTOU

ROSS, DAVID, 20, M, TAILOR, 11/04/1851
1. BRITISH AMERICA 2. U.S. 3. PICTOU

ROSS, ELIZABETH, 19, F, DRESS MAKER, 08/29/1854
1. NOVA SCOTIA 2. U.S. 3. PICTOU

ROSS, ETHEBELLIER, 25, F, DRESS MAKER, 09/25/1854
1. PICTOU 2. U.S. 3. PICTOU

ROSS, ISABELLA, 26, F, LADY, 07/31/1845
1. NOVA SCOTIA 2. NOVA SCOTIA 3. PICTOU

ROSS, JAMES, 33, M, CLERGYMAN, 07/31/1845
1. NOVA SCOTIA 2. NOVA SCOTIA 3. PICTOU

ROSS, JAMES DUNCAN, 5, M, CHILD, 07/31/1845
1. NOVA SCOTIA 2. NOVA SCOTIA 3. PICTOU

ROSS, JOHN, 35, M, CARPENTER, 08/17/1850
1. PICTOU 2. U.S. 3. PICTOU

ROSS, JOHN, 16, M, SERVANT, 09/20/1851
1. BRITISH AMERICA 2. U.S. 3. PICTOU

ROSS, JOHN T., 51, M, MERCHANT, 04/02/1827
   1. NEWBURYPORT 2. U.S. 3. HAVANA

ROSS, MARIION, 21, F, NONE, 10/07/1857
   1. NOVA SCOTIA 2. U.S. 3. PICTOU

ROSS, MARY, 16, F, SERVANT, 07/05/1866
   1. BRITISH AMERICA 2. U.S. 3. PICTOU

ROSS, RODERIC, 20, M, TINSMITH, 10/04/1848
   1. 2. U.S. 3. PICTOU

ROSS, THOMAS, 32, M, COPPER SMITH, 05/24/1839
   1. AMERICA 2. NEW ORLEANS 3. PICTOU

ROSS, WILLIAM, 15, M, , 09/17/1860
   1. NOVA SCOTIA 2. U.S. 3. PICTOU

ROUDEN, PETER, 15, M, NONE, 08/03/1855
   1. SPAIN 2. SPAIN 3. MATANZAS

ROUENBERGH, WM. F., 20, M, STUDENT, 11/08/1859
   1. GERMANY 2. U.S. 3. PICTOU

ROUSELEAU, CHARLES F., 28, M, MECANNIC, 04/07/1831
   1. U.S. 2. U.S. 3. HAVANA

ROWE, JOHN, 30, M, MARINER, 03/13/1826
   1. U.S. 2. U.S. 3. HAVANA

RUAN, MARY, , , , 12/14/1823
   1. NEW YORK 2. ST. CROIX 3. PROVIDENCE

RUGGLES, SPOONER, 43, M, MERCHANT, 10/16/1824
   1. U.S. 2. U.S. 3. SURINAM

RUGGLES, SPOONER, 45, M, MERCHANT, 10/17/1825
   1. U.S. 2. U.S. 3. SURINAM

RUGGLES, SPOONER, 44, M, MERCHANT, 11/02/1826
   1. U.S. 2. U.S. 3. SURINAM

RUSELS, GEORGE, 28, M, SHOEMAKER, 10/22/1834
   1. NOVA SCOTIA 2. U.S. 3. CUMBERLAND, N.S.

RUSH, GEORGE W., 27, M, TRAVELING, 09/11/1839
   1. GREAT BRITAIN 2. ENGLAND 3. PICTOU

RUSSELL, ANDREW, 24, M, SURGEON, 10/11/1828
   1. SCOTLAND 2. U.S. 3. SANTIAGO, CUBA

RUSSELL, BETSEY, 25, F, , 03/08/1833
   1. U.S. 2. U.S. 3. HAVANA

RUSSELL, CATHARINE, 31, F, , 08/29/1836
1. SCOTLAND 2. NEW YORK 3. PICTOU

RUSSELL, CHARLES, 44, M, MARINER, 12/23/1823
1. U.S. 2. U.S. 3. HONDURAS

RUSSELL, EDWARD T., 60, M, , 09/17/1860
1. U.S. 2. U.S. 3. PICTOU

RUSSELL, GEORGE F., 36, M, MARINER, 05/08/1830
1. U.S. 2. U.S. 3. ST. SALVADORE, BRAZIL

RUSSELL, JOSEPH W., 24, M, TRAVELLER, 11/17/1870
1. GREAT BRITAIN 2. GREAT BRITAIN 3. PICTOU

RUSSELL, MARY, 20, F, MAID SERVANT, 11/25/1854
1. GREAT BRITAIN 2. U.S. 3. ARDROSSAN

RYAN, CHRISTINA, 10, F, CHILD, 08/02/1850
1. BRITISH AMERICA 2. U.S. 3. PICTOU

RYAN, ISABELLA, 46, F, , 08/02/1850
1. BRITISH AMERICA 2. U.S. 3. PICTOU

RYAN, ISABELLA, 17, F, , 08/02/1850
1. BRITISH AMERICA 2. U.S. 3. PICTOU

RYAN, JANE, 11, F, CHILD, 08/02/1850
1. BRITISH AMERICA 2. U.S. 3. PICTOU

RYAN, JOHN, 6, M, CHILD, 08/02/1850
1. BRITISH AMERICA 2. U.S. 3. PICTOU

RYAN, WILLIAM, 9, M, CHILD, 08/02/1850
1. BRITISH AMERICA 2. U.S. 3. PICTOU

RYAN, WM., 21, , LABORER, 05/09/1837
1. IRELAND 2. NEW YORK 3. LIVERPOOL

RYDER, WM, 25, M, MARINA, 05/06/1867
1. U.S. 2. U.S. 3. ARDROSSAN

SABASTIAN, MANUEL P., 35, M, MARINER, 08/28/1872
1. FLORES 2. BOSTON 3.

SABIN, JOHN, 22, M, CARPENTER, 07/16/1821
1. U.S. 2. U.S. 3. MATANZAS

SABIN, N. S., 30, , FARMER, 04/20/1841
1. RANDOLPH, OHIO 2. 3. MATANZAS

SAFFORD, WILLIAM F., 33, M, MERCHANT, 07/07/1841
1. CARDENAS 2. CARDENAS 3. MATANZAS

SAGUNOLAS, BENARDO, 35, M, MERCHANT, 11/11/1828
1. SPAIN 2. SPAIN 3. HAVANA

SALMOND, ELIZABETH, 26, F, , 05/30/1860
1. PRINCE EDWARD ISLAND 2. PRINCE EDWARD ISLAND 3. PRINCE EDWARD ISLAND

SANBORN, BENJAMIN, 26, M, PHYSICIAN, 06/18/1827
1. U.S. 2. U.S. 3. HAVANA

SANBURN, MATHEW, 25, , CARPENTER, 07/18/1839
1. KENTUCKY 2. NEW YORK 3. HAVANA

SANFORD, JOHN W., 25, , TAILOR, 07/18/1827
1. 2. 3. MATANZAS

SAPARTA, JOHN, 40, M, GENTLEMAN, 07/19/1833
1. SPAIN 2. SPAIN 3. HAVANA

SARGENT, JAMES, 31, M, MERCHANT, 07/20/1826
1. BOSTON 2. U.S. 3. MATANZAS

SARGENT, JR., JAS, 31, M, MERCHANT, 06/23/1830
1. BOSTON 2. BOSTON 3. MATANZAS

SAUNDERS, EDWARD, 19, M, LABORER, 11/02/1831
1. IRELAND 2. U.S. 3. SYDNEY

SAVAGE, CHARLES, 47, M, U.S. CONSOL, 08/15/1825
1. U.S. 2. BOSTON 3. HAVANA

SCARBOROUGH, LYDIA, 23, F, SERVANT, 09/15/1854
1. NOVA SCOTIA 2. U.S. 3. PICTOU

SCEANLEW, PATRICK, 40, , LABORER, 05/09/1837
1. IRELAND 2. U.S. 3. LIVERPOOL

SCHELLY, RACHEL, 18, F, , 09/20/1851
1. U.S. 2. U.S. 3. PICTOU

SCHERMAN, CAROLINE, 20, F, WIFE OF WILLIAM, 08/08/1827
1. SWEDEN 2. U.S. 3. GOTENBURG

SCHERMAN, WILLIAM, 34, M, MECHANIC, 08/08/1827
1. SWEDEN 2. U.S. 3. GOTENBURG

SCHILLIE, RACHEL, 25, F, SERVANT, 09/16/1858
1. NOVA SCOTIA 2. U.S. 3. PICTOU

SCHMILOER, PETER ALBAT, 30, M, GENTLEMAN, 12/02/1828
1. SURINAM 2. U.S. 3. SURINAM

SCOTT, ARCHIBALD, 23, M, SEAMAN, 05/16/1853
1. IRELAND 2. IRELAND 3. ARDROSSAN

SCOTT, JOSEPH, 32, M, SHIP CARPENTER, 11/05/1834
1. AMERICA 2. NEW YORK NAVY YARD 3. PICTOU

SCOTT, MARY, 28, F, DRESS MAKER, 11/05/1834
1. NOVA SCOTIA 2. NEW YORK 3. PICTOU

SCUDER, FAMES, 25, M, MARINER, 05/27/1823
1. U.S. 2. U.S. 3. L. BARTS

SCULLEN, PETER, 30, M, CARPENTER, 06/17/1829
1. IRELAND 2. ENGLAND 3. HAVANA

SECHEM, JOHN, 22, , LABORER, 05/09/1837
1. IRELAND 2. NEW YORK 3. LIVERPOOL

SELLAR, ANN, 4 MONTHS, F, CHILD OF RICHARD, 06/16/1828
1. ENGLAND 2. U.S. 3. LIVERPOOL

SELLAR, BETSEY, 2, F, CHILD OF RICHARD, 06/16/1828
1. ENGLAND 2. U.S. 3. LIVERPOOL

SELLAR, JANE, 35, F, WF OF RICHARD, 06/16/1828
1. ENGLAND 2. U.S. 3. LIVERPOOL

SELLAR, JANE, 9, F, CHILD OF RICHARD, 06/16/1828
1. ENGLAND 2. U.S. 3. LIVERPOOL

SELLAR, MARY, 7, F, CHILD OF RICHARD, 06/16/1828
1. ENGLAND 2. U.S. 3. LIVERPOOL

SELLAR, RICHARD, 40, M, GARDENER, 06/16/1828
1. ENGLAND 2. U.S. 3. LIVERPOOL

SENSABAUGH, CHARLOTTE, 30, F, NONE, 07/01/1858
1. GREAT BRITAIN 2. U.S. 3. PICTOU

SERENA, GODENCIO GOMES, 18, M, FARMER, 10/17/1867
1. CAPE DE VERDE IS. 2. U.S. 3. FLORES

SERENA, MARIA GOMES, 25, F, LADY, 10/17/1867
1. CAPE DE VERDE IS. 2. U.S. 3. FLORES

SEXTON, LOREN, , , SEAMAN SENT HOME BY CONSUL, 01/16/1849
1. 2. 3. SANDWICH ISLANDS

SHAW, BENJAMIN, 70, M, MERCHANT, 07/22/1822
1. U.S. 2. U.S. 3. HAVANA

SHAW, THOMAS, 30, M, CARPENTER, 08/26/1822
1. U.S. 2. U.S. 3. CANTON

SHEA, CATHARINE, 26, F, SERVANT, 10/19/1836
1. MADONMISHE 2. BOSTON 3. PICTOU

SHEA, JOHN, 4, M, , 10/18/1836
1. MADONMISHE 2. BOSTON 3. PICTOU

SHEA, PATRICK, 1, M, , 10/18/1836
1. MADONMISHE 2. BOSTON 3. PICTOU

SHEARMAN, GEORGE M., 36, , JEWELER, 05/09/1837
1. GERMANY 2. U.S. 3. LIVERPOOL

SHERIDAN, ANNA, 20, , SPINSTER, 05/09/1837
1. IRELAND 2. NEW YORK 3. LIVERPOOL

SHERIDAN, MARY, 21, , SPINSTER, 05/09/1837
1. IRELAND 2. NEW YORK 3. LIVERPOOL

SHERIDEN, MARY, 17, , SPINSTER, 05/09/1837
1. IRELAND 2. U.S. 3. LIVERPOOL

SHERMAN, MRS. HENRY J., 46, F, HOUSE KEEPER, 07/05/1864
1. U.S. 2. U.S. 3. PICTOU

SHERMAN, JOHN, , M, , 10/06/1848
1. BRITISH AMERICA 2. U.S. 3. PICTOU

SILISIG, MARY, 6, , , 05/18/1868
1. 2. 3. BRAVA

SILISIG, MICHALA, 28, , , 05/18/1868
1. 2. 3. BRAVA

SILISKEY, MARIA J., 22, F, SERVANT, 07/20/1844
1. NOVA SCOTIA 2. U.S. 3. PICTOU

SILVA, MARIAMMA DE, 35, F, LADY, 10/17/1867
1. CAPE DE VERDE IS. 2. U.S. 3. FLORES

SILVER, BRIDGET, 17, F, SERVANT, 09/06/1855
1. GREAT BRITAIN 2. U.S. 3. PICTOU

SIMMONS, AMEY, 20, F, , 06/24/1861
1. PICTOU 2. U.S. 3. PICTOU

SIMMONS, WALTER W., 25, M, SHIP WRIGHT, 05/08/1838
1. U.S. 2. U.S. 3. HAVANA

SIMPSON, ALEXANDER, 30, M, LABORER, 08/03/1855
1. GREAT BRITAIN 2. U.S. 3. LIVERPOOL

SIMPSON, ALEXANDER, 30, M, TAILOR, 09/15/1856
1. GREAT BRITAIN 2. U.S. 3. PICTOU

SIMPSON, ALPHRED, 21, M, COACH BUILDER, 10/27/1845
1. NOVA SCOTIA 2. CANADA 3. PICTOU

SIMPSON, CATHERINE, 34, F, LADY, 06/27/1849
1. BRITISH AMERICA 2. U.S. 3. PICTOU

SIMPSON, DILSOA, 51, , , 06/27/1849
1. BRITISH AMERICA 2. U.S. 3. PICTOU

SIMPSON, JAMES, 27, M, WATCHMAKER, 09/15/1856
1. GREAT BRITAIN 2. U.S. 3. PICTOU

SIMPSON, JOHN, 1, , , 10/27/1845
1. NOVA SCOTIA 2. CANADA 3. PICTOU

SIMPSON, JOHN F., 42, M, MECHANIC, 06/27/1849
1. BRITISH AMERICA 2. U.S. 3. PICTOU

SIMPSON, MARY ANN, 7, , CHILD, 06/27/1849
1. BRITISH AMERICA 2. U.S. 3. PICTOU

SIMPSON, MRS. ALEXANDER, 25, F, HOUSEWIFE, 09/15/1856
1. GREAT BRITAIN 2. U.S. 3. PICTOU

SIMPSON, SARAH, 20, F, , 10/27/1845
1. NOVA SCOTIA 2. CANADA 3. PICTOU

SIMUROLA, MR., 32, M, MERCHANT, 03/20/1835
1. MARTINIQUE 2. FRANCE 3. MARTINIQUE

SINCLAIR, ALEXANDER, 18, M, FARMER, 07/27/1845
1. BRITISH AMERICA 2. U.S. 3. PICTOU

SINCLAIR, ROBERT, 32, M, FARMER, 07/27/1845
1. BRITISH AMERICA 2. U.S. 3. PICTOU

SINGLETON, JOHN, 25, M, COOPER, 09/26/1831
1. BOSTON 2. U.S. 3. HAVANA

SINGLETON, JOHN, 60, M, COOPER, 06/23/1834
1. U.S. 2. U.S. 3. HAVANA

SKELLEY, JANE, 17, F, , 09/13/1859
1. NOVA SCOTIA 2. U.S. 3. PICTOU

SKELLY, ARCHIBALD, 22, M, MOULDER, 07/26/1855
1. NOVA SCOTIA 2. U.S. 3. PICTOU

SKELLY, CHARLES, 7, M, NONE, 07/26/1855
1. NOVA SCOTIA 2. U.S. 3. PICTOU

SKELLY, ISABELLA, 10, F, NONE, 07/26/1855
1. NOVA SCOTIA 2. U.S. 3. PICTOU

SKELLY, JANE, 46, F, HOUSEWIFE, 07/26/1855
1. NOVA SCOTIA 2. U.S. 3. PICTOU

SKELLY, JANE, 13, F, NONE, 07/26/1855
1. NOVA SCOTIA 2. U.S. 3. PICTOU

SKELLY, WILLIAM, 15, M, MOULDER, 07/26/1855
1. NOVA SCOTIA 2. U.S. 3. PICTOU

SKELTON, ANN, 16, F, SERVANT, 09/25/1843
1. IRELAND 2. U.S. 3. PICTOU

SKELTON, ISAAC, 10, M, BOY, 09/25/1843
1. IRELAND 2. U.S. 3. PICTOU

SKELTON, JAMES, 8, M, BOY, 09/25/1843
1. IRELAND 2. U.S. 3. PICTOU

SKELTON, SARAH, 58, F, SERVANT, 09/25/1843
1. IRELAND 2. U.S. 3. PICTOU

SKIDMORE, JAMES, 27, M, COAL MINER, 07/11/1850
1. PICTOU 2. U.S. 3. PICTOU

SKIDMORE, JR., JOSEPH, 15, M, COAL MINER, 07/11/1850
1. PICTOU 2. U.S. 3. PICTOU

SKIDMORE, SR., JOSEPH, 45, M, COAL MINER, 07/11/1850
1. PICTOU 2. U.S. 3. PICTOU

SMALL, ALEXANDER, 30, M, SHIP CARPENTER, 07/20/1857
1. NOVA SCOTIA 2. U.S. 3. PICTOU

SMALL, ANDREW, 3 MONTHS, M, , 05/23/1857
1. NOVA SCOTIA 2. U.S. 3. PICTOU

SMALL, EDWARD, 31, M, MINER, 05/23/1857
1. NOVA SCOTIA 2. U.S. 3. PICTOU

SMALL, ELLEN, 24, F, SERVANT, 11/04/1851
1. BRITISH AMERICA 2. U.S. 3. PICTOU

SMALL, JOHN ROBERT, 8, M, , 05/23/1857
1. NOVA SCOTIA 2. U.S. 3. PICTOU

SMALL, MARGARET, 26, F, HOUSE WIFE, 05/23/1857
1. NOVA SCOTIA 2. U.S. 3. PICTOU

SMALL, WILLIAM, 6, M, , 05/23/1857
1. NOVA SCOTIA 2. U.S. 3. PICTOU

SMITH, ALEXANDER, 56, M, FARMER, 09/22/1851
1. BRITISH AMERICA 2. BRITISH AMERICA 3. PICTOU

SMITH, ANN, 60, F, , 05/09/1832
1. U.S. 2. U.S. 3. MATANZAS

SMITH, ANN, 28, F, SERVANT, 07/01/1870
1. NOVA SCOTIA 2. U.S. 3. PICTOU

SMITH, ANNIE, 24, F, NONE, 10/03/1854
1. GREAT BRITAIN 2. NOVA SCOTIA 3. GLASGOW

SMITH, BARBARA, 23, F, LADY, 10/08/1849
1. BRITISH AMERICA 2. U.S. 3. PICTOU

SMITH, CATHARINE, 25, F, SERVANT, 09/03/1868
1. BRITISH AMERICA 2. U.S. 3. PICTOU

SMITH, CHRISTIANA, 13, F, SERVANT, 06/18/1850
1. NOVA SCOTIA 2. U.S. 3. PICTOU

SMITH, CHRISTIANNA, 50, F, , 09/22/1851
1. BRITISH AMERICA 2. BRITISH AMERICA 3. PICTOU

SMITH, ELIZABETH, 24, F, LADY (LISEY), 09/20/1847
1. NOVA SCOTIA 2. U.S. 3. PICTOU

SMITH, MRS. ELIZABETH, 25, F, , 09/19/1851
1. U.S. 2. U.S. 3. PICTOU

SMITH, ELLEN, 21, F, LADY, 08/06/1849
1. BRITISH AMERICA 2. U.S. 3. PICTOU

SMITH, ISABELLA, 25, F, SERVANT, 09/09/1844
1. NOVA SCOTIA 2. U.S. 3. PICTOU

SMITH, JAMES, 25, M, LABORER, 09/09/1847
1. IRELAND 2. CANADA 3. PICTOU

SMITH, JAMES U., 17, M, CLERK, 12/10/1851
1. BRITISH AMERICA 2. U.S. 3. PICTOU

SMITH, JOHN, 24, M, CABINET MAKER, 07/11/1827
1. U.S. 2. U.S. 3. HAVANA

SMITH, JOHN, 54, M, LABORER, 09/02/1845
1. NOVA SCOTIA 2. U.S. 3. PICTOU

SMITH, JOHN, 45, M, CARPENTER, 09/20/1847
1. NOVA SCOTIA 2. U.S. 3. PICTOU

SMITH, JOHN, 25, M, CARPENTER, 09/12/1848
1. AMERICA 2. AMERICA 3. PICTOU

SMITH, JOHN, 42, M, HOUSE CARPENTER, 09/29/1848
1. BRITISH AMERICA 2. U.S. 3. PICTOU

SMITH, JOHN, 30, M, SHIP CARPENTER, 07/01/1850
1. BRITISH AMERICA 2. U.S. 3. PICTOU

SMITH, MRS JOHN, 60, F, , 05/12/1834
1. U.S. 2. U.S. 3. MATANZAS

SMITH, LILLIE, 22, F, SERVANT, 09/09/1844
1. NOVA SCOTIA 2. U.S. 3. PICTOU

SMITH, LOUISA, 18, F, NONE, 10/03/1854
1. GREAT BRITAIN 2. NOVA SCOTIA 3. GLASGOW

SMITH, MARGARET, 59, F, SERVANT, 07/30/1846
1. SCOTLAND 2. U.S. 3. PICTOU

SMITH, MARGARET, 16, F, SERVANT GIRL, 08/29/1854
1. NOVA SCOTIA 2. U.S. 3. PICTOU

SMITH, MARK A., 22, M, MARINER, 04/25/1820
1. U.S. 2. U.S. 3. HAVANA

SMITH, MARY ANN, 20, F, SERVANT, 09/08/1862
1. PICTOU 2. PROVIDENCE 3. PICTOU

SMITH, REBECCA, 30, F, LABORER, 09/09/1847
1. IRELAND 2. CANADA 3. PICTOU

SMITH, RICHARD, 40, M, CARPENTER, 04/16/1821
1. U.S. 2. U.S. 3. MATANZAS

SMITH, ROBERT, 35, M, SHIP CARPENTER, 07/26/1848
1. BRITISH AMERICA 2. BRITISH AMERICA 3. PICTOU

SMITH, SANFORD, 34, M, ENGINEER, 04/13/1842
1. U.S. 2. U.S. 3. MATANZAS

SMITH, SANFORD, , M, , 07/05/1853
1. U.S. 2. U.S. 3. CARDENAS

SMITH, SARAH, 60, F, , 06/09/1834
1. U.S. 2. U.S. 3. MATANZAS

SMITH, SARAH M. D., 28, F, , 05/09/1832
1. U.S. 2. U.S. 3. MATANZAS

SMITH, SM., 30, M, CARPENTER, 09/20/1847
1. NOVA SCOTIA 2. U.S. 3. PICTOU

SMITH, THOMAS, 40, M, MERCHANT, 08/01/1839
1. SPAIN 2. 3. MATANZAS

SMITH, WILLIAM, 21, M, MECHANIC, 09/22/1851
1. BRITISH AMERICA 2. BRITISH AMERICA 3. PICTOU

SMITH, WILLIAM, 50, M, MARINER, MASTER OF VESSEL, 11/25/1853
1. U.S. 2. U.S. 3. TURKS ISLAND

SMITH, WILLIAM, 28, M, MUSICIAN, 07/10/1857
1. U.S. 2. U.S. 3. PICTOU

SMITH, WILLIAM C., 25, M, HOUSE CARPENTER, 05/25/1858
1. NOVA SCOTIA 2. U.S. 3. PICTOU

SMITH, WILLIAM R., 21, M, CARPENTER, 10/04/1848
1. BRITISH AMERICA 2. U.S. 3. PICTOU

SMYTH, JOHN, 32, M, CARPENTER, 04/27/1871
1. GREAT BRITAIN 2. U.S. 3.

SOIJ, JAMES, 26, M, GRANSTONE CUTTER, 10/22/1834
1. NOVA SCOTIA 2. U.S. 3. CUMBERLAND, N.S.

SOLLOMOM, MICHAL, 56, M, CORN DOCTORS/UPHOLSTERER, 04/24/1821
1. AMSTERDAM 2. BOSTON 3. PARAMARIBO

SORRENZEN, J., 23, M, HOUSE JOINER, 06/28/1855
1. NOVA SCOTIA 2. U.S. 3. WEYMOUTH, N.S.

SOTO, PETER, 11, M, SCHOOL BOY, 05/19/1839
1. HAVANA 2. HAVANA, CUBA 3. HAVANA

SOUSA, ADELINA, 4, F, TAILORESS, 08/28/1872
1. SAN MIQUEL 2. BOSTON 3.

SOUSA, ALBERTO, 3, M, NONE, 08/28/1872
1. SAN MIQUEL 2. BOSTON 3.

SOUTHERLAND, CRISTIANNA, 6, F, CHILD, 07/03/1845
1. BRITISH AMERICA 2. U.S. 3. PICTOU

SOUTHERLAND, DAVID, 51, M, LABORER, 07/03/1845
1. BRITISH AMERICA 2. U.S. 3. PICTOU

SOUTHERLAND, ELLEN, 48, F, LABORER, 07/03/1845
1. BRITISH AMERICA 2. U.S 3. PICTOU

SOUTHERLAND, HANNAH, 16, F, LABORER, 07/03/1845
1. BRITISH AMERICA 2. U.S. 3. PICTOU

SOUTHERLAND, JOHN, 12, M, LABORER, 07/03/1845
1. BRITISH AMERICA 2. U.S. 3. PICTOU

SOUTHERLAND, MARY, 9, F, CHILD, 07/03/1845
1. BRITISH AMERICA 2. U.S. 3. PICTOU

SOUTHERLAND, WILLIAM, 14, M, LABORER, 07/03/1845
1. BRITISH AMERICA 2. U.S. 3. PICTOU

SOUTHWORTH, , 36, M, FISHERMAN, 10/14/1861
1. U.S. 2. U.S. 3. PICTOU

SPALDING, H., 25, M, MERCHANT, 06/14/1859
1. U.S. 2. U.S. 3. ZANZIBAR

SPALDING, HENRY, 35, M, MERCHANT, 05/05/1862
1. U.S. 2. U.S. 3. ZANZIBAR

SPARROW, JOHN, 27, M, MACHINIST, 06/08/1843
1. U.S. 2. U.S. 3. HAVANA

SPEEDY, ANDREW, 7, M, CHILD, 11/03/1849
1. BRITISH AMERICA 2. U.S. 3. PICTOU

SPEEDY, ISABEL, 28, F, LADY, 11/03/1849
1. BRITISH AMERICA 2. U.S. 3. PICTOU

SPEEDY, MATTHEW, 28, M, MACHINIST, 11/03/1849
1. BRITISH AMERICA 2. U.S. 3. PICTOU

SPENCER, JAMES, 45, M, JINGINEAR, 08/08/1837
1. AMERICAN 2. U.S. 3. HAVANA

SPLANE, TIMOTHY, 23, M, LABORER, 07/31/1857
1. GREAT BRITAIN 2. U.S. 3. PICTOU

SPOONER, H. N., 29, M, MASON, 05/23/1831
1. U.S. 2. U.S. 3. HAVANA

SPRAGUE, JOHN, 22, M, PLACED ABOARD BY CONSUL, 08/29/1821
1. U.S. 2. STOWAWAY 3. HAMBURG

SPRATT, JOHN, 24, M, CARPENTER, 07/19/1833
1. U.S. 2. U.S. 3. HAVANA

STAFFEN, ANNA, 24, F, LADY, 08/06/1849
1. BRITISH AMERICA 2. U.S. 3. PICTOU

STAFFORD, ANN, 24, F, SERVANT, 09/09/1844
1. NOVA SCOTIA 2. U.S. 3. PICTOU

STAMAS, C. J., 55, M, NONE, 11/07/1856
1. GREAT BRITAIN 2. GREAT BRITAIN 3. TURKS ISLAND

STANHOPE, HANNAH, 4, F, , 05/19/1839
1. U.S. 2. U.S. 3. HAVANA

STANHOPE, HARRIET, 32, F, , 06/30/1830
1. U.S. 2. U.S. 3. HAVANA

STANHOPE, HARRIET, 38, F, MARINER, 05/19/1839
1. U.S. 2. U.S. 3. HAVANA

STANHOPE, HARRIET, 17, F, , 05/19/1839
1. U.S. 2. U.S. 3. HAVANA

STANHOPE, JOHN, 45, M, SHIPMASTER, 08/02/1827
1. NEWPORT 2. NEWPORT 3. MATANZAS

STANHOPE, JOHN R., 41, M, MARINER, 07/02/1832
1. U.S. 2. U.S. 3. HAVANA

STANLEY, WILLIAM, 22, M, MASON, 08/05/1848
1. U.S. 2. U.S. 3. PICTOU

STANWOOD, THEODORE, 19, M, MARINER, 04/25/1820
1. U.S. 2. U.S. 3. HAVANA

STAPLES, JAMES D., 2, M, NONE, 09/02/1856
1. U.S. 2. U.S. 3. PICTOU

STAPLES, MARY A., 24, F, HOUSEWIFE, 09/02/1856
1. U.S. 2. U.S. 3. PICTOU

STAPLETON, RACHAEL, 40, F, LADY, 06/03/1844
1. ENGLAND 2. U.S. 3. PICTOU

STAPLETON, SUSAN, 16, F, LADY, 06/03/1844
1. ENGLAND 2. U.S. 3. PICTOU

STAPLETON, WILLIAM, 45, M, SHIP CARPENTER, 06/03/1844
1. ENGLAND 2. U.S. 3. PICTOU

STARK, LEWIS, 24, M, MECHANIC, 05/22/1837
1. PORTSMOUTH 2. U.S. 3. MATANZAS

STEEN, JOHN, 24, M, MERCHANT, 10/16/1824
1. IRELAND 2. U.S. 3. SURINAM

STERNS, MARIA, 24, F, DOMESTIC, 07/15/1836
1. NOVA SCOTIA 2. U.S. 3. PICTOU

STEVENSON, ELISABETH, 38, F, SERVANT, 09/09/1844
1. NOVA SCOTIA 2. U.S. 3. PICTOU

STEVENSON, ELISABETH, 30, F, LADY, 11/02/1847
1. BRITISH AMERICA 2. U.S. 3. PICTOU

STEVENSON, ELIZABETH, 55, F, , 05/28/1861
1. PICTOU 2. U.S. 3. PICTOU

STEWART, CATHARINE, 19, F, SERVANT, 08/21/1852
1. BRITISH AMERICA 2. U.S. 3. PICTOU

STEWART, CATHARINE, 27, F, NONE, 07/28/1857
1. U.S. 2. U.S. 3. MATANZAS

STEWART, JAMES, 40, M, FARMER, 07/11/1850
1. PICTOU 2. U.S. 3. PICTOU

STEWART, MARY, 18, F, DOMESTIC, 08/19/1859
1. NOVA SCOTIA 2. U.S. 3. PICTOU

STEWART, MISS, 16, , , 04/20/1841
1. NEW YORK 2. 3. MATANZAS

STEWART, MRS., 31, , , 04/20/1841
1. NEW YORK 2. 3. MATANZAS

STEWART, WILLIAM, 20, M, FARMER, 08/16/1850
1. NOVA SCOTIA 2. U.S. 3. PICTOU

STEWERT, NICAL, 22, M, FARMER, 06/25/1838
1. IRELAND 2. U.S. 3. PICTOU

STILFOX, THOMAS, 25, M, CARPENTER, 05/19/1839
1. U.S. 2. U.S. 3. HAVANA

STOCKMAN, JAMES, 40, M, MARINER, 02/29/1828
1. U.S. 2. U.S. 3. HAVANA

STOCKWELL, LYSANDER, 25, M, SOAP BOILER, 05/28/1835
1. U.S. 2. U.S. 3. HAVANA

STROBEL, CATHARINE, 18, F, LADY, 04/17/1845
1. U.S. 2. U.S. 3. AFRICA

STROBRIDGE, R.P., , , DISTRESSSED SEAMEN, 01/16/1849
1. 2. 3. NASSAU

STUART, JOHN, 25, M, MINER, 06/22/1857
1. NOVA SCOTIA 2. U.S. 3. PICTOU

STUTSON, JEREMIAH, 18, M, CARPENTER, 04/21/1820
1. U.S. 2. U.S. 3. MATANZAS

SULIVEN, DENNIS, 29, , LABORER, 05/09/1837
1. IRELAND 2. U.S. 3. LIVERPOOL

SUNDERLAND, ELIZABTH, 15, F, NONE, 08/27/1846
1. BOSTON 2. BOSTON 3. PICTOU

SUTEINS, JOHN, 31, M, MINER, 08/19/1840
1. ENGLAND 2. U.S. 3. SYDNEY

SUTHERLAND, ALEX, 25, M, MASON, 07/17/1850
1. BRITISH AMERICA 2. U.S. 3. PICTOU

SUTHERLAND, ALEXANDER, 26, M, LABORER, 10/03/1854
1. U.S. 2. U.S. 3. PICTOU

SUTHERLAND, CATHARINE, 29, F, SERVANT, 07/12/1864
1. BRITISH AMERICA 2. U.S. 3. PICTOU

SUTHERLAND, CATHARINE, 16, F, LADY, 08/05/1847
1. BRITISH AMERICA 2. U.S. 3. PICTOU

SUTHERLAND, ELISABETH, 26, F, SERVANT, 09/09/1844
1. NOVA SCOTIA 2. U.S. 3. PICTOU

SUTHERLAND, FLORA, 18, F, SERVANT, 07/01/1862
1. NOVA SCOTIA 2. U.S. 3. PICTOU

SUTHERLAND, JANET, 18, F, SERVANT, 09/08/1862
1. PICTOU 2. PROVIDENCE 3. PICTOU

SUTHERLAND, JOHN, 19, M, SEAMAN, 07/23/1870
1. BRITISH AMERICA 2. U.S. 3. PORT CALEDONIA

SUTHERLAND, MARGARET, 16, F, SERVANT, 07/20/1844
1. NOVA SCOTIA 2. U.S. 3. PICTOU

SUTHERLAND, WALTER, 21, M, HOUSE JOINER, 07/08/1844
1. NOVA SCOTIA 2. U.S. 3. PICTOU

SUTHERLAND, WILLIAM, 22, M, LABORER, 08/11/1834
1. NOVA SCOTIA 2. U.S. 3. PICTOU

SWEET, HENRY, 28, M, ENGINEER, 04/13/1842
1. U.S. 2. U.S. 3. MATANZAS

SWEET, MINRA A., 26, M, CARPENTER, 04/21/1820
1. U.S. 2. U.S. 3. MATANZAS

SWIFT, WILLIAM, 33, M, CABINET MAKER, 05/07/1824
1. U.S. 2. U.S. 3. HAITI

SYLVESTER, MARGARET, 20, F, SERVANT, 07/20/1844
1. NOVA SCOTIA 2. U.S. 3. PICTOU

TAFT, THOMAS F., 34, M, ENGINEER, 04/16/1842
1. U.S. 2. U.S. 3. MATANZAS

TALBERT, MARGARET, 25, F, LADY, 07/08/1848
1. PICTOU 2. PROVIDENCE 3. PICTOU

TALBOT, B. H., 24, M, MERCHANT, 07/10/1821
1. U.S. 2. U.S. 3. HAVANA

TALBOT, JAMES, 18, M, SHIP CARPENTER, 10/07/1857
1. NOVA SCOTIA 2. NOVA SCOTIA 3. PICTOU

TALBOT, SUSAN, 24, , HOUSEKEEPER, 09/30/1868
1. BRITISH AMERICA 2. 3. PICTOU

TALLMAN, FRANCIS, 25, M, CARPENTER, 05/12/1835
1. U.S. 2. U.S. 3. HAVANA

TALLMAN, MOSES, 45, M, CARPENTER, 03/13/1826
1. U.S. 2. U.S. 3. HAVANA

TANNER, ELIZA, 23, F, NONE, 05/24/1858
1. NOVA SCOTIA 2. U.S. 3. PICTOU

TANNER, ELIZABETH, 2, F, , 07/27/1835
1. NOVA SCOTIA 2. PROVIDENCE 3. PICTOU

TANNER, ELIZABETH, 20, F, SERVANT OR ASSISTANT, 10/01/1853
1. NOVA SCOTIA 2. U.S. 3. PICTOU

TANNER, HENRY, 4, M, , 07/27/1835
1. NOVA SCOTIA 2. PROVIDENCE 3. PICTOU

TANNER, RACHEL, 25, F, , 07/27/1835
1. NOVA SCOTIA 2. PROVIDENCE 3. PICTOU

TARRIOT, JEFFREY, 26, M, SEAMAN, 08/31/1853
1. U.S. 2. U.S. 3. ARICHAT

TARRIOT, VICTOR, 23, M, SEAMAN, 08/31/1853
1. U.S. 2. U.S. 3. ARICHAT

TAVARES, JOSE, 13, M, CARPENTER, 08/28/1872
1. SAN MIQUEL 2. BOSTON 3.

TAVARES, JULIO, 16, M, CARPENTER, 08/28/1872
1. SAN MIQUEL 2. BOSTON 3.

TAYLOR, ELIZABETH, 27, F, LADY, 09/20/1847
1. NOVA SCOTIA 2. U.S. 3. PICTOU

TAYLOR, FRANCES, O2, F, CHILD, 09/20/1847
1. NOVA SCOTIA 2. U.S. 3. PICTOU

TAYLOR, JAMES, 25, M, MERCHANT, 09/27/1855
1. GREAT BRITAIN 2. GREAT BRITAIN 3. TURKS ISLAND

TAYLOR, LILLIS, 23, F, SPINSTER, 09/18/1845
1. NOVA SCOTIA 2. U.S. 3. PICTOU

TAYLOR, MARY, 18, F, LADY, 05/16/1842
1. U.S. 2. U.S. 3. HAVANA

TAYLOR, REUBEN, 25, , MARINER, 03/25/1841
1. YARMOUTH 2. 3. TURKS ISLAND

TEARINON, BRIDGET, 19, , SPINSTER, 05/09/1837
1. IRELAND 2. U.S. 3. LIVERPOOL

TEBALA, MANUEL, 17, M, BOY, 04/14/1828
1. CENTRAL AMERICA 2. U.S. FOR EDUCATION 3. OMOA

TEBALA, VICTOR, 15, M, BOY, 04/14/1828
1. CENTRAL AMERICA 2. U.S. FOR EDUCATION 3. OMOA

TENNA, MARIA ROSA, 25, F, LADY, 10/17/1867
1. CAPE DE VERDE IS. 2. U.S. 3. FLORES

TERRY, THOMAS, 21, M, MINER, 06/11/1856
1. ENGLAND 2. U.S. 3. PICTOU

THANE, ALEX, 35, M, PAINTER, 05/22/1857
1. GREAT BRITAIN 2. U.S. 3. PICTOU

THAYER, ELIZABETH, 20, F, NONE, 07/07/1857
1. NOVA SCOTIA 2. U.S. 3. PICTOU

THAYER, JR., WILLIAM, 25, M, MERCHANT, 04/23/1821
1. U.S. 2. RHODE ISLAND 3. HAVANA

THAYNE, ISABELLE, 28, F, SERVANT, 08/20/1845
1. SCOTLAND 2. U.S. 3. PICTOU

THEODORO, JOAO, 32, M, MARINER, 08/28/1872
1. FLORES 2. BOSTON 3.

THOM, JOHN, 27, M, EXHIBITOR OF WILD ANIMALS, 06/29/1826
1. U.S. 2. U.S. 3. HAVANA

THOMAS, CAITONO, 40, M, MARINER, 08/28/1872
1. FLORES 2. BOSTON 3.

THOMAS, JOSE, 35, M, MARINER, 08/28/1872
1. FLORES 2. PROVIDENCE 3.

THOMAS, MANUEL, 20, M, FARMER, 08/28/1872
1. FLORES 2. BOSTON 3.

THOMAS, STEPHEN, 30, M, LABORER, 11/25/1844
1. GREAT BRITAIN 2. U.S. 3. PICTOU

THOMASIA, ANNA, 25, F, SEAMSTRESS, 08/28/1872
1. FLORES 2. BOSTON 3.

THOMPSON, ALICE, 23, F, , 03/22/1826
1. ENGLAND 2. MASSACHUSETTS 3. LIVERPOOL

THOMPSON, ANN, 19, F, , 07/09/1860
1. NOVA SCOTIA 2. U.S. 3. PICTOU

THOMPSON, ASA, , M, , 07/05/1853
1. U.S. 2. U.S. 3. CARDENAS

THOMPSON, CREA, 2, F, , 03/22/1826
   1. 2. 3. LIVERPOOL

THOMPSON, END., 1, F, , 03/22/1826
   1. 2. 3. LIVERPOOL

THOMPSON, JOHN, 33, M, , 03/22/1826
   1. 2. 3. LIVERPOOL

THOMPSON, JOHN, 29, M, ENGINEER, 06/11/1840
   1. U.S. 2. U.S. 3. MATANZAS

THOMPSON, JOHN, 21, M, LABORER, 10/03/1854
   1. NOVA SCOTIA 2. U.S. 3. PICTOU

THOMPSON, MRS., 36, F, GENTLEWOMAN, 07/23/1828
   1. ENGLAND 2. U.S. 3. SANTIAGO

THOMPSON, REBECCA, 33, F, , 03/22/1826
   1. 2. 3. LIVERPOOL

THOMPSSON, FRACE, 21, F, , 07/09/1860
   1. NOVA SCOTIA 2. U.S. 3. PICTOU

THORNTON, JOHN, 28, M, DOCTOR, 04/16/1823
   1. SCOTLAND 2. LONDON 3. HONDORUS

THORPE, JOSEPH T., 38, M, MERCHANT, 09/22/1828
   1. ENGLAND 2. U.S. 3. LIVERPOOL

THURSTON, SARAH, , , , 12/30/1823
   1. PROVIDENCE 2. NEW PROVIDENCE 3. PROVIDENCE

THURSTON, T., 25, M, MECHANIC, 06/22/1840
   1. U.S. 2. U.S. 3. MATANZAS

THURSTON, THOMAS, 25, , CARPENTER, 04/20/1841
   1. NEWPORT 2. 3. MATANZAS

TIERNEY, CATHARINE G., 16, F, SERVANT, 09/21/1846
   1. NOVA SCOTIA 2. BRITISH AMERICA 3. PICTOU

TIERNEY, MARY ANN, 15, F, SERVANT, 09/21/1846
   1. NOVA SCOTIA 2. BRITISH AMERICA 3. PICTOU

TILTON, JOHN, 35, M, MARINER, 02/11/1859
   1. U.S. 2. U.S. 3. ZANZIBAR

TITHERTON, ELLEN, 27, F, , 08/17/1850
   1. PICTOU 2. U.S. 3. PICTOU

TIZZARD, WILLIAM A., 46, M, MARINER, 06/27/1827
   1. U.S. 2. U.S. 3. GOTENBURG

TOLEDO, PHILIP, 12, M, SCHOOLBOY, 09/11/1825
1. GUATELMALA 2. GUATEMALA 3. HONDURAS

TOLOR, JAIMS, 32, M, PLACED ABOARD BY CONSUL, 09/03/1821
1. U.S. 2. U.S. 3. MADEIRA

TOMLINE, FAUSTINA, 20, F, SERVANT, 04/28/1842
1. MATANZAS 2. U.S. 3. MATANZAS

TOWEY, MANUEL, 19, M, CARPENTER, 09/15/1847
1. ST. MICHAELS 2. U.S. 3. PICTOU

TOWLE, ELISHA, 36, M, SAWYER, 09/13/1841
1. AMERICAN 2. U.S. 3. PICTOU

TOWNSEND, SAMUEL, 22, M, CLERK, 05/18/1840
1. U.S. 2. AMERICA 3. MATANZAS

TRAVERS, MAY, 29, F, LADY, 10/02/1839
1. NOVA SCOTIA 2. U.S. 3. PICTOU

TRICOX, JOSEPH, 25, M, LABORER, 09/27/1841
1. U.S. 2. U.S. 3. PICTOU

TRINIDADE, JOAQUINA, 17, F, SEAMSTRESS, 08/28/1872
1. FLORES 2. BOSTON 3.

TROY, CATHARINE, 21, F, , 06/24/1861
1. PICTOU 2. U.S. 3. PICTOU

TRUMAN, MRS., 23, F, , 06/07/1841
1. U.S. 2. 3. HAVANA

TRUMAN, NATHAN, 27, M, MERCHANT, 06/07/1841
1. U.S. 2. 3. HAVANA

TRYON, MOSES, 44, M, MERCHANT, 09/15/1825
1. U.S. 2. U.S. 3. MATANZAS

TUCKER, JOHN W., 25, M, MASTER MARINER, 08/02/1858
1. U.S. 2. U.S. 3. SUNDERLAND

TUCKER, JR., JAMES, 34, M, MARINER, 11/03/1835
1. U.S. 2. PROVIDENCE 3. PICTOU

TURNBELL, SARAH, 25, F, LADY, 07/08/1848
1. PICTOU 2. PROVIDENCE 3. PICTOU

TURNBULL, ANN MCKAY, 23, F, TAILORESS, 09/06/1860
1. NOVA SCOTIA 2. U.S. 3. PICTOU

TURNBULL, MARGARET, 22, F, SERVANT, 06/03/1844
1. NOVA SCOTIA 2. U.S. 3. PICTOU

TURNER, BENJAMIN, 8, M, BOY CHILD OF HANNAH, 09/02/1845
1. NOVA SCOTIA 2. U.S. 3. PICTOU

TURNER, C., 19, F, , 09/25/1863
1. U.S. 2. U.S. 3. PICTOU

TURNER, DAVID, 6, M, BOY CHILD OF HANNAH, 09/02/1845
1. NOVA SCOTIA 2. U.S. 3. PICTOU

TURNER, HANNAH, 34, F, LADY, 09/02/1845
1. NOVA SCOTIA 2. U.S. 3. PICTOU

TURNER, HANNAH, 37, F, LADY, 09/12/1848
1. ENGLAND 2. U.S. 3. PICTOU

TURNER, JOHN, 38, M, MERCHANT, 09/25/1863
1. U.S. 2. U.S. 3. PICTOU

TURNER, MARTHA, 4, F, CHILD OF HANNAH, 09/02/1845
1. NOVA SCOTIA 2. U.S. 3. PICTOU

TURNER, MARTHA, 6, F, CHILD, 09/12/1848
1. BRITISH AMERICA 2. U.S. 3. PICTOU

TURNER, MARY, 5, F, CHILD, 09/12/1848
1. BRITISH AMERICA 2. U.S. 3. PICTOU

TURNER, MARY ANN, 2, F, CHILD OF HANNAH, 09/02/1845
1. NOVA SCOTIA 2. U.S. 3. PICTOU

TURNER, MR., , , MACHINIST, 09/02/1845
1. 2. 3. PICTOU

TURNER, WILLIAM, 10, M, BOY CHILD OF HANNAH, 09/02/1845
1. NOVA SCOTIA 2. U.S. 3. PICTOU

TYLER, WILLIAM, 40, M, GENTLEMAN, 04/16/1842
1. U.S. 2. U.S. 3. MATANZAS

UANGOVYA, DUDU, 10, , SERVANT, 10/24/1855
1. ZANZIBAR 2. U.S. 3. ZANZIBAR, MOZAMBIQUE

UDECK, CATHARINE, 22, F, HOUSEWIFE, 06/11/1858
1. GERMANY 2. U.S. 3. MAITLAND

UDECK, FREDERICK, 1, M, , 06/11/1858
1. GERMANY 2. U.S. 3. MAITLAND

UDECK, JACOB, 28, M, MINER, 06/11/1858
1. GERMANY 2. U.S. 3. MAITLAND

UHRBACK, CARLO, 26, M, MERCHANT, 07/07/1841
1. MATANZAS 2. MATANZAS 3. MATANZAS

UNDERHILL, EDWIN, 3, M, CHILD, 07/31/1845
1. ENGLAND 2. U.S. 3. PICTOU

UNDERHILL, ELISABETH, 22, F, SERVANT, 11/11/1844
1. ENGLAND 2. U.S. 3. PICTOU

UNDERHILL, ELIZABETH, 28, F, SPINSTER, 07/31/1845
1. ENGLAND 2. U.S. 3. PICTOU

UNDERHILL, JAMES, 32, M, LABORER, 07/31/1845
1. ENGLAND 2. U.S. 3. PICTOU

UNDERHILL, JAMES, 5, M, CHILD, 07/31/1845
1. ENGLAND 2. U.S. 3. PICTOU

UNDERHILL, NIMROD, 7, M, LAD, 07/31/1845
1. ENGLAND 2. U.S. 3. PICTOU

UNDERWOOD, CHRISTOPHER, 20, M, FARMER, 06/18/1850
1. NOVA SCOTIA 2. NOVA SCOTIA 3. PICTOU

URQUHART, ELIZABETH, 11, F, NONE, 08/05/1858
1. NOVA SCOTIA 2. U.S. 3. PICTOU

URQUHART, JAMES, 45, M, LABORER, 07/20/1857
1. NOVA SCOTIA 2. U.S. 3. PICTOU

URQUHART, JANE, 49, F, HOUSEWIFE, 08/14/1858
1. NOVA SCOTIA 2. U.S. 3. PICTOU

URQUHART, JANET, 37, F, LABORESS, SERVANT, 08/05/1858
1. NOVA SCOTIA 2. U.S. 3. PICTOU

URQUHART, JOHN W., 9, M, NONE, 08/05/1858
1. NOVA SCOTIA 2. U.S. 3. PICTOU

USHER, ALLEN, 35, M, MARINER, 10/03/1834
1. U.S. 2. U.S. 3. HAVANA

VALISON, JOHN, 41, M, MARINER, 04/16/1821
1. U.S. 2. U.S. 3. LISBON

VARNEY, SAMUEL, 56, M, SHIP MASTER, 01/16/1849
1. U.S. 2. U.S. 3. SANDWICH ISLANDS

VEDELL, MADAM, 40, F, WIDOW OF AN APOTHECARY, 07/16/1828
1. FRANCE 2. U.S. 3. OMOA

VELLACE, LUCIUS, 9, M, , 10/19/1858
1. AFRICA 2. U.S. 3. QUILEMANE

VICENTE, ANTONIO J., 28, M, MARINER, 08/28/1872
1. FLORES 2. BOSTON 3.

VICKERY, RICHARD, 26, M, MILLER, 07/20/1844
1. NOVA SCOTIA 2. U.S. 3. PICTOU

VIEIRA, ANTONIO C., 33, M, MARINER, 08/28/1872
1. FLORES 2. PROVIDENCE 3.

VIERA, ANTONIO R., 30, M, MARINER, 08/28/1872
1. FLORES 2. BOSTON 3.

VIERIA, FRANCISCO, 32, M, MARINER, 08/28/1872
1. FLORES 2. PROVIDENCE 3.

VILLIER, HENRY, 32, M, CLERK, 08/29/1854
1. NOVA SCOTIA 2. U.S. 3. PICTOU

VINTON, AMOS M., 24, M, MERCHANT, 04/12/1823
1. U.S. 2. U.S. 3. CANTON

VOIMEL, JOHN, 63, M, GENTLEMAN, 06/28/1825
1. GERMANY 2. U.S. 3. SURINAM

VOLL, AUGUSTUS, 29, M, MASON, 06/11/1858
1. GERMANY 2. U.S. 3. MAITLAND

VORHEES, SAMUEL, 35, M, MARINER, 03/11/1828
1. U.S. 2. U.S. 3. PEMAMBUS

WADDEN, JAMES, 35, M, MINER, 10/13/1865
1. BRITISH AMERICA 2. U.S. 3. COW BAY

WADDEN, JAMES, 6, M, , 10/13/1865
1. BRITISH AMERICA 2. U.S. 3. COW BAY

WADDEN, JOSEPH, 6 MONTHS, M, , 10/13/1865
1. BRITISH AMERICA 2. U.S. 3. COW BAY

WADDEN, MARY, 34, F, HOUSEWIFE, 10/13/1865
1. BRITISH AMERICA 2. U.S. 3. COW BAY

WADDEN, POLLY, 8, F, , 10/13/1865
1. BRITISH AMERICA 2. U.S. 3. COW BAY

WADE, E., 27, M, MERCHANT, 09/30/1826
1. U.S. 2. U.S. 3. HAVANA

WADE, E., 32, M, MERCHANT, 06/23/1834
1. U.S. 2. U.S. 3. HAVANA

WADE, EBEN, 22, M, MERCHANT, 08/13/1823
1. U.S. 2. U.S. 3. HAVANA

WADE, EBEN, 33, M, MERCHANT, 07/06/1835
1. U.S. 2. U.S. 3. HAVANA

WADE, EBEN., 28, M, MERCHANT, 11/02/1830
1. U.S. 2. U.S. 3. HAVANA

WADE, EBENEZER, 27, M, MERCHANT, 06/29/1829
1. U.S. 2. U.S. 3. HAVANA

WADE, EBENEZER, 29, M, MERCHANT, 07/14/1832
1. U.S. 2. U.S. 3. HAVANA

WADE, EBENZ., 22, M, MERCHANT, 07/10/1824
1. U.S. 2. U.S. 3. HAVANA

WADE, LEWIS, 25, M, WEAVER, 06/04/1858
1. U.S. 2. U.S. 3. MATANZAS

WADE, SARAH, 24, F, , 07/14/1832
1. U.S. 2. U.S. 3. HAVANA

WADE, THOMAS, 14, M, SERVANT, 07/14/1832
1. U.S. 2. U.S. 3. HAVANA

WADE, THOMAS, 14, M, SERVANT, 06/23/1834
1. SPAIN 2. SPAIN 3. HAVANA

WADE, WM, 20, M, COOPER, 07/05/1837
1. U.S. 2. U.S. 3. HAVANA

WAITHMEN, JANETTE, MRS., 22, F, , 09/05/1839
1. PROVIDENCE 2. PROVIDENCE 3. PICTOU

WALCH, ELLEN, 25, F, SERVANT, 09/13/1841
1. IRELAND 2. U.S. 3. PICTOU

WALES, ANDREW, 20, M, MECHANIC, 06/07/1841
1. U.S. 2. 3. HAVANA

WALES, HENRY, 26, M, MECHANIC, 06/07/1841
1. U.S. 2. 3. HAVANA

WALKER, ELIZABETH, 42, F, HOUSEWIFE, 07/26/1855
1. NOVA SCOTIA 2. U.S. 3. PICTOU

WALKER, ELLEN, 22, F, HOUSEWIFE, 07/20/1857
1. NOVA SCOTIA 2. U.S. 3. PICTOU

WALKER, HUGH, 11, M, NONE, 07/26/1855
1. NOVA SCOTIA 2. U.S. 3. PICTOU

WALKER, JAMES, 4, M, NONE, 07/20/1857
1. NOVA SCOTIA 2. U.S. 3. PICTOU

WALKER, JANE, 38, F, LADY, 10/18/1836
1. SCOTLAND 2. NEW YORK 3. PICTOU

WALKER, JOHN, 41, M, GENTLEMAN, 10/18/1836
   1. SCOTLAND 2. NEW YORK 3. PICTOU

WALKER, JOHN, 15, M, NONE, 07/26/1855
   1. NOVA SCOTIA 2. U.S. 3. PICTOU

WALKER, JOHN, 2, M, NONE, 07/20/1857
   1. NOVA SCOTIA 2. U.S. 3. PICTOU

WALKER, JOSEPH, 18, M, TEACHER, 07/01/1862
   1. NOVA SCOTIA 2. U.S. 3. PICTOU

WALKER, MARY, 13, F, NONE, 07/26/1855
   1. NOVA SCOTIA 2. U.S. 3. PICTOU

WALKER, MATILDA, 23, F, SERVANT, 10/27/1854
   1. U.S. 2. U.S. 3. PICTOU

WALKER, WILLIAM, 7, M, NONE, 07/26/1855
   1. NOVA SCOTIA 2. U.S. 3. PICTOU

WALKER, WILLIAM, 5 MONTHS, M, NONE, 07/20/1857
   1. NOVA SCOTIA 2. U.S. 3. PICTOU

WALLACE, ANNA, 20, F, HOUSE SERVANT, 08/05/1858
   1. NOVA SCOTIA 2. U.S. 3. PICTOU

WALLACE, LUCY, 20, F, SERVANT, 09/29/1852
   1. BRITISH AMERICA 2. U.S. 3. PICTOU

WALLACE, MARGARET, 17, F, SERVANT, 09/29/1852
   1. BRITISH AMERICA 2. U.S. 3. PICTOU

WALLACE, MARY, 16, F, HOUSE SERVANT, 08/05/1858
   1. NOVA SCOTIA 2. U.S. 3. PICTOU

WALLACE, WILLIAM E., 12, M, CLERK, 04/25/1826
   1. U.S. 2. U.S. 3. HAVANA

WALLEN, CATHARINE, 18, F, SERVANT, 07/20/1844
   1. NOVA SCOTIA 2. U.S. 3. PICTOU

WALLEN, MARY, 19, F, LADY, 06/27/1849
   1. 2. 3. PICTOU

WALLER, EDMUND, 17, M, NONE, 10/31/1854
   1. GREAT BRITAIN 2. BRITISH AMERICA 3. BOMBAY, ADEN AND
   ZANZIBAR

WALLER, JOSELYN, 16, M, NONE, 10/31/1854
   1. GREAT BRITAIN 2. BRITISH AMERICA 3. BOMBAY, ADEN AND
   ZANZIBAR

WALLEY, EDWARD, 22, M, OYSTERMAN, 07/28/1862
1. NOVA SCOTIA 2. U.S. 3. PICTOU

WALLEY, MRS. EDWARD, 25, F, HOUSEWIFE, 07/28/1862
1. NOVA SCOTIA 2. U.S. 3. PICTOU

WARD, JAMES, 22, M, CARPENTER, 04/26/1831
1. U.S. 2. U.S. 3. HAVANA

WARDSWORTH, GEO. P., 22, M, MARINA, 05/06/1867
1. U.S. 2. U.S. 3. ARDROSSAN

WARDSWORTH, WILLIAM, 24, M, MARINA, 05/06/1867
1. U.S. 2. U.S. 3. ARDROSSAN

WARDWELL, NANCY, 38, F, , 11/22/1838
1. U.S. 2. U.S. 3. MATANZAS

WARING, STEPHEN, 30, M, CARPENTER, 07/17/1835
1. U.S. 2. U.S. 3. HAVANA

WARNER, JOHN, 26, M, CARPENTER, 05/23/1831
1. U.S. 2. U.S. 3. HAVANA

WATERS, DAVID, 10, M, , 07/31/1863
1. PICTOU 2. PICTOU 3. PICTOU

WATERS, MARY, 35, F, LADY, 07/31/1863
1. PICTOU 2. PICTOU 3. PICTOU

WATSON, AGNES, 20, F, HOUSEWIFE, 06/11/1856
1. NOVA SCOTIA 2. U.S. 3. PICTOU

WATSON, CHARLES H., 35, M, MACHINIST, 06/22/1863
1. PICTOU 2. U.S. 3. PICTOU

WATSON, MRS. CHARLES H., 35, F, LADY, 06/22/1863
1. PICTOU 2. U.S. 3. PICTOU

WATSON, ELLEN, 1, F, NONE, 06/11/1856
1. NOVA SCOTIA 2. U.S. 3. PICTOU

WATSON, JAMES, 8, M, NONE, 06/11/1856
1. NOVA SCOTIA 2. U.S. 3. PICTOU

WATSON, JANE, 15, F, , 06/22/1857
1. NOVA SCOTIA 2. U.S. 3. PICTOU

WATSON, JANET, 3, F, NONE, 06/11/1856
1. NOVA SCOTIA 2. U.S. 3. PICTOU

WATSON, JOHN, 28, M, MINER, 06/11/1856
1. NOVA SCOTIA 2. U.S. 3. PICTOU

WATSON, MRS. JOHN, 26, F, HOUSEWIFE, 06/11/1856
1. NOVA SCOTIA 2. U.S. 3. PICTOU

WATSON, MRS. JOHN, 56, F, HOUSE WIFE, 06/22/1857
1. NOVA SCOTIA 2. U.S. 3. PICTOU

WATSON, LYDIA, 4, F, NONE, 06/11/1856
1. NOVA SCOTIA 2. U.S. 3. PICTOU

WATSON, MARGARET, 6, F, NONE, 06/11/1856
1. NOVA SCOTIA 2. U.S. 3. PICTOU

WATSON, MARY, 4 MONTHS, F, NONE, 06/11/1856
1. NOVA SCOTIA 2. U.S. 3. PICTOU

WATSON, MISS, 4, F, , 06/22/1857
1. NOVA SCOTIA 2. U.S. 3. PICTOU

WATSON, REBECCA, 9, F, NONE, 06/11/1856
1. NOVA SCOTIA 2. U.S. 3. PICTOU

WATSON, ROBERT, 17, M, MINER, 06/22/1857
1. NOVA SCOTIA 2. U.S. 3. PICTOU

WATSON, THOMAS, 20, M, MINER, 06/11/1856
1. NOVA SCOTIA 2. U.S. 3. PICTOU

WATSON, THOMAS, 25, M, LABOUR, 09/07/1838
1. U.S. 2. U.S. 3. PICTOU

WATSON, W., 12, M, , 06/22/1857
1. NOVA SCOTIA 2. U.S. 3. PICTOU

WATSON, WILLIAM, 23, M, MINER, 06/11/1856
1. NOVA SCOTIA 2. U.S. 3. PICTOU

WAUNE, JOHN, 26, M, NONE, 10/31/1854
1. GREAT BRITAIN 2. BRITISH AMERICA 3. BOMBAY, ADEN AND ZANZIBAR

WAYLAND, MARGARET, 28, F, SERVANT, 06/03/1862
1. NOVA SCOTIA 2. U.S. 3. PICTOU

WEAVER, JOSIAH B., , , DISTRESSED SEAMEN, 01/16/1849
1. 2. 3. NASSAU

WEBB, JOHN DAVID, 46, M, PLANTER, 09/03/1824
1. GREAT BRITAIN 2. UNCERTAIN 3. ST. CHRISTOPHER

WEBSTER, CHARLES, 26, M, CARPENTER, 07/28/1857
1. U.S. 2. U.S. 3. MATANZAS

WEBSTER, MARIE, 35, F, AND FOUR CHILDREN, 07/20/1826
1. MIDDLETOWN, CT. 2. CONNECTICUT 3. MATANZAS

WEBSTER, W.E., 39, M, PLANTER, 07/20/1826
1. MIDDLETOWN, CT. 2. CONNECTICUT 3. MATANZAS

WEEDEN, ROSA, 10, F, BLACKS FROM US RETURNED, 10/06/1828
1. PHILADELPHIA 2. PHILADELPHIA 3. PUERTA PLATA

WEEKS, BENJAMIN, 32, M, MARINER, 05/13/1820
1. U.S. 2. U.S. 3. GIBRALTAR

WEIR, DANIEL, 15, M, SAIL MAKER, 06/28/1859
1. U.S. 2. U.S. 3. SAINT JOHN

WEIR, DUNCAN, 28, M, MINER, 08/29/1836
1. SCOTLAND 2. NEW YORK 3. PICTOU

WEIR, ELIZABETH, 26, F, , 08/29/1836
1. SCOTLAND 2. NEW YORK 3. PICTOU

WEIR, JOHN, 25, , MINER, 08/27/1835
1. GRUNOCK 2. 3. PICTOU

WELCH, MARY ANN, 18, F, SERVANT, 09/09/1844
1. NOVA SCOTIA 2. U.S. 3. PICTOU

WELCH, WM E., 31, M, MARINER, 08/03/1857
1. U.S. 2. U.S. 3. TURKS ISLAND

WESTON, S.P., 40, M, MERCHANT, 08/18/1837
1. U.S. 2. 3. BONAIRE

WHALAND, MARGARET, 30, F, SERVANT, 09/15/1856
1. GREAT BRITAIN 2. U.S. 3. PICTOU

WHALEN, ANNIE, 18, F, NONE, 08/20/1857
1. NOVA SCOTIA 2. U.S. 3. PICTOU

WHALEN, ANNIE, 18, F, NONE, 08/20/1857
1. NOVA SCOTIA 2. U.S. 3. PICTOU

WHALEN, CATHARINE, 20, F, SERVANT OR ASSISTANT, 08/09/1853
1. NOVA SCOTIA 2. U.S. 3. PICTOU

WHALEN, ELLEN, 18, F, SERVANT OR ASSISTANT, 08/09/1853
1. NOVA SCOTIA 2. U.S. 3. PICTOU

WHALLEN, CHARLES, 30, M, PAINTER, 04/27/1871
1. U.S. 2. U.S. 3.

WHEELER, EDWARD P., 30, M, MARINER, 06/15/1840
1. U.S. 2. U.S. 3. MATANZAS

WHEELOCK, PETER, 35, M, LAWYER, 06/14/1821
1. U.S. 2. 3. HAVANA

WHITAKER, ALBERT, 20, M, ENGINEER, 04/13/1842
1. U.S. 2. U.S. 3. MATANZAS

WHITE, ANN, 6 MONTHS, F, DAUGHTER OF RICHARD, 03/22/1826
1. ENGLAND 2. MASSACHUSETTS 3. LIVERPOOL

WHITE, MRS. GEORGE F., 28, F, HOUSEWIFE, 10/31/1854
1. U.S. 2. U.S. 3. BOMBAY, ADEN AND ZANZIBAR

WHITE, JOHN, 50, M, PLANTER, 08/01/1825
1. GREAT BRITAIN 2. U.S. 3. BARBADOS

WHITE, JOHN, 3, M, SON OF RICHARD, 03/22/1826
1. ENGLAND 2. MASSACHUSETTS 3. LIVERPOOL

WHITE, JOSEPH, 32, M, ENGINEER, 05/23/1859
1. U.S. 2. U.S. 3. MATANZAS

WHITE, MARY, 23, F, WIFE OF RICHARD, 03/22/1826
1. ENGLAND 2. MASSACHUSETTS 3. LIVERPOOL

WHITE, MARY, 21, F, SERVANT, 07/02/1845
1. BRITISH AMERICA 2. U.S. 3. PICTOU

WHITE, RICHARD, 30, M, CALICO PRINTER, 03/22/1826
1. ENGLAND 2. MASSACHUSETTS 3. LIVERPOOL

WHITMAN, HENRY, 41, M, ARTIST, 08/03/1857
1. U.S. 2. U.S. 3. TURKS ISLAND

WIER, ALLEN, 19, M, , 06/23/1857
1. PICTOU 2. PETERILL 3. PICTOU

WILBOUR, WILLIAM, 26, M, MASON, 04/21/1820
1. U.S. 2. U.S. 3. MATANZAS

WILDEN, MARY ANN, 27, , , 07/24/1858
1. LIVERPOOL, ENGLAND 2. YARMOUTH 3. ARDROSSAN

WILDEN, POLLY, 3, , , 07/24/1858
1. LIVERPOOL, ENGLAND 2. YARMOUTH 3. ARDROSSAN

WILIE, AGNES, 23, F, SERVANT GIRL, 08/12/1853
1. NOVA SCOTIA 2. U.S. 3. PICTOU

WILKINS, WM.P., 22, M, MERCHANT, 04/25/1824
1. SURINAM 2. SURINAM 3. SURINAM

WILKINSON, ARTHUR, 35, M, SEAMAN, 06/24/1861
1. U.S. 2. U.S. 3. PICTOU

WILKINSON, MISS, 3, F, , 03/11/1841
1. U.S. 2. U.S. 3. HAVANA

WILKINSON, MRS., 24, F, , 03/11/1841
1. U.S. 2. U.S. 3. HAVANA

WILLARD, HEZEKIAH, 32, M, MARINER (CAPT.), 08/01/1839
1. U.S. 2. U.S. 3. MATANZAS

WILLCOX, CHARLES, 36, M, MARINER, 07/24/1821
1. U.S. 2. NEWPORT 3. HAVANA

WILLIAMS, ANN E., 24, F, GENTLEWOMAN, 09/22/1825
1. GREAT BRITAIN 2. CANADA 3. GIBRALTAR

WILLIAMS, DANIEL, 25, M, SEAMAN, 12/30/1853
1. U.S. 2. U.S. 3. MATANZAS

WILLIAMS, ELIZABETH, 5, F, , 08/29/1859
1. NEW BRUNSWICK 2. NEW BRUNSWICK 3. PICTOU

WILLIAMS, J., , , SERVANT, 12/30/1823
1. PROVIDENCE 2. DEMERARA 3. PROVIDENCE

WILLIAMS, JOHN, 27, M, MARINER, 06/11/1836
1. U.S. 2. U.S. 3. HAVANA

WILLIAMS, MARY, 30, F, , 08/29/1859
1. NEW BRUNSWICK 2. NEW BRUNSWICK 3. PICTOU

WILLIAMS, MRS. N., 38, F, GENTLEWOMAN, 07/14/1829
1. BOSTON 2. U.S. 3. HAVANA

WILLIAMS, THOMAS, 31, M, TAILOR, 09/07/1838
1. U.S. 2. U.S. 3. PICTOU

WILSON, (CHILD), 2, M, , 06/22/1857
1. NOVA SCOTIA 2. U.S. 3. PICTOU

WILSON, CATHARINE, 30, F, TAILORESS, 11/09/1835
1. ST. JOHN 2. NEW YORK 3. CUMBERLAND, N.S.

WILSON, JAMES, 27, M, COOPER, 06/17/1842
1. U.S. 2. U.S. 3. MATANZAS

WILSON, JANET, 20, F, HOUSEWIFE, 07/20/1857
1. NOVA SCOTIA 2. U.S. 3. PICTOU

WILSON, JOHN, 24, M, MINER, 06/22/1857
1. NOVA SCOTIA 2. U.S. 3. PICTOU

WILSON, JOHN L., 17, M, , 05/12/1834
1. U.S. 2. U.S. 3. MATANZAS

WILSON, MARGARET, 7, F, CHILD, 08/06/1849
1. BRITISH AMERICA 2. U.S. 3. PICTOU

WILSON, MRS., 25, F, LADY, 08/06/1849
1. BRITISH AMERICA 2. U.S. 3. PICTOU

WILSON, MRS., 22, F, HOUSE WIFE, 06/22/1857
1. NOVA SCOTIA 2. U.S. 3. PICTOU

WILSON, THOMAS, 2, M, NONE, 07/20/1857
1. NOVA SCOTIA 2. U.S. 3. PICTOU

WILSON, WILLIAM W., 1, M, CHILD, 08/06/1849
1. BRITISH AMERICA 2. U.S. 3. PICTOU

WINN, JOSEPH, 52, M, MERCHANT, 06/14/1859
1. U.S. 2. U.S. 3. ZANZIBAR

WINSLOW, SMITH, 45, M, COOPER, 06/18/1839
1. U.S. 2. U.S. 3. MATANZAS

WISON, AA., 18, M, SERVANT, 04/25/1824
1. SURINAM 2. SURINAM 3. SURINAM

WOLFE, ALLEN S., 28, M, MERCHANT, 03/22/1837
1. U.S. 2. U.S. 3. HAVANA

WOLFE, MARTHA S., 22, F, , 03/22/1837
1. U.S. 2. U.S. 3. HAVANA

WOLFE, MRS. S., 52, F, , 03/22/1837
1. U.S. 2. U.S. 3. HAVANA

WOOD, BENJM., 38, M, TOBACCONIST, 07/10/1821
1. U.S. 2. U.S. 3. HAVANA

WOOD, CHRISTINA, 17, F, NONE, 06/11/1855
1. GREAT BRITAIN 2. U.S. 3. PICTOU

WOOD, DAVID, 28, M, MINER, 06/08/1835
1. PICTOU 2. NEW YORK 3. PICTOU

WOOD, JAMES, 24, M, MERCHANT, 05/23/1822
1. HONDURAS 2. HONDURAS 3. HONDURAS

WOOD, MRS., , F, AND SEVEN CHILDREN, 07/10/1821
1. 2. 3. HAVANA

WOODBURY, L.A., 28, M, , 05/16/1821
1. U.S. 2. 3. MATANZAS

WOODS, WILLIAM, 25, M, LABORER, 06/16/1828
1. IRELAND 2. U.S. 3. LIVERPOOL

WOODWARD, MR., 34, M, MECHANIC, 03/22/1837
1. U.S. 2. U.S. 3. HAVANA

WREN, JOHN, 40, M, ENGINEER, 07/01/1850
1. U.S. 2. U.S. 3. SAGUA LE GRANDE

WREN, MARGARET, 40, F, LADY, 07/01/1850
1. U.S. 2. U.S. 3. SAGUA LE GRANDE

WRIGHT, CLARK, , , DISTRESSED SEAMAN, 01/16/1849
1. 2. 3. NASSAU

WRIGHT, DANIEL, 26, M, EXHIBITOR OF WILD ANIMALS, 06/29/1826
1. U.S. 2. U.S. 3. HAVANA

WRIGHT, JOHN, 45, M, ENGINEER, 05/10/1842
1. U.S. 2. U.S. 3. MATANZAS

WRIGHT, JR., JOHN, 16, M, ENGINEER, 05/10/1842
1. U.S. 2. U.S. 3. MATANZAS

WROTH, JAS, 42, M, MERCHANT, 05/20/1839
1. FRANCE 2. MEXICO 3. HAVANA

WYLEY, ANDREW, 46, M, , 10/01/1850
1. BRITISH AMERICA 2. U.S. 3. PICTOU

WYLIE, CATHARINE M., 32, F, ---, 06/04/1825
1. U.S. 2. U.S. 3. MATANZAS

WYLLIE, GRACE, 16, F, SERVANT, 08/22/1850
1. BRITISH AMERICA 2. U.S. 3. PICTOU

YATES, SAML., 20, M, PLACED ABOARD BY CONSUL, 08/29/1821
1. U.S. 2. STOWAWAY 3. HAMBURG

YOUNG, JAMES, 22, M, SPINNER, 06/16/1828
1. ENGLAND 2. U.S. 3. LIVERPOOL

CUSTOMS PASSENGER LISTS

❦

PORTS OF BRISTOL AND WARREN, 1820–1871

KEY: NAME, AGE, SEX, OCCUPATION, DATE OF
ARRIVAL
(1) COUNTRY TO WHICH THEY BELONG
(2) COUNTRY TO WHICH THEY INTEND TO
BECOME INHABITANTS
(3) TAKEN ON BOARD AT

JULIANA, 18, F, , 09/27/1841
1. CUBA 2. CUBA 3. MATANZAS

UFO, , 14, M, SERVANT, 03/31/1860
1. CANTON 2. 3. ST. HELENA

ADAM, DANIEL, 39, M, SEAMAN, 06/23/1821
1. CHARLESTOWN 2. CHARLESTOWN 3. HAVANA

ADAMS, ALEXANDER, 20, M, , 03/13/1846
1. U.S. 2. U.S. 3. SYDNEY

ADAMS, JOHN, 32, M, MARINER, 04/24/1849
1. U.S. 2. U.S. 3. SAN SALVADOR

ADAMS, MARY JANE, 18, F, , 03/13/1846
1. U.S. 2. U.S. 3. SYDNEY

ADAMS, REV. M.T., 50, M, SEAMAN'S CHAPLAIN, 03/13/1846
1. U.S. 2. U.S. 3. SYDNEY

ALEXANDER, JOHN, 23, M, MARINER, 04/24/1849
1. U.S. 2. U.S. 3. SAN SALVADOR

ALLEN, CHARLES, 22, M, CARPENTER, 06/22/1820
1. U.S. 2. U.S. 3. MATANZAS

ALLEN, CHARLES, 25, M, MECHANIC, 05/17/1823
1. RHODE ISLAND 2. AMERICA 3. MATANZAS

ALLEN, MATHEW, 23, M, MECHANIC, 05/17/1823
1. RHODE ISLAND 2. AMERICA 3. MATANZAS

ALLEN, MATHEW, 26, M, CARPENTER, 07/13/1826
1. U.S. 2. U.S. 3. MATANZAS

ALLEN, MATTHEW, 20, M, CARPENTER, 06/14/1820
1. U.S. 2. U.S. 3. MATANZAS

ALLEN, WILLIAM, 26, M, PAINTER, 02/13/1821
1. U.S. 2. U.S. 3. HAVANA

ALLEN, WILLIAM, 36, M, MARINER, 1845
1. U.S. 2. U.S. 3. MATANZAS

ALMAN, WILLIAM, 31, M, COOPER, 08/20/1832
1. NEWPORT 2. U.S. 3.

ANTHONY, HENRY, 25, M, CARPENTER, 05/21/1830
1. U.S. 2. U.S. 3. MATANZAS

ANTHONY, JOSEPH, 40, M, MARINER, 06/11/1821
1. BRISTOL 2. BRISTOL 3. HAVANA

ARNO, JAMES, 48, M, MERCHANT, 06/21/1822
 1. NEW YORK 2. U.S. 3. HAVANA

ATWATER, N. M., 45, M, MERCHANT, 06/08/1846
 1. U.S. 2. U.S. 3. CARDENAS

B., A., 35, M, MERCHANT, 01/13/1824
 1. FRANCE 2. U.S. 3. HAVANA

B., A., 38, M, MARINER, 02/13/1824
 1. PORTUGAL 2. U.S. 3. HAVANA

BAKER, JOSEPH, 40, M, CARPENTER, 04/19/1821
 1. U.S. 2. U.S. 3. MATANZAS

BARKER, NOAH, 32, M, CARPENTER, 08/03/1825
 1. U.S. 2. U.S. 3. HAVANA

BARNES, TOD, 35, M, MERCHANT, 10/12/1832
 1. U.S. 2. U.S. 3. NEW YORK

BARREO, SAMUEL, 24, M, MARINER, 07/03/1822
 1. CHARLESTON 2. 3. MATANZAS

BARRETT, JOSEPH W., 36, M, COOPER, 09/17/1847
 1. U.S. 2. U.S. 3. MATANZAS

BEATIE, WILLIAM H., 35, M, MERCHANT, 06/30/1864
 1. U.S. 2. 3. SAGUA LA GRANDE

BEEMAN, HENRY, 35, M, ENGINEER, 05/22/1845
 1. U.S. 2. NEW YORK 3. CARDENAS

BEYMANN, EUNICE, 48, F, WIFE OF SEYMOUR, 06/25/1852
 1. U.S. 2. U.S. 3. MATANZAS

BISHOP, HENRY, 40, M, SERVANT, 04/23/1835
 1. U.S. 2. U.S. 3. HAVANA

BISHOP, NATHAN A., 45, M, COOPER, 07/11/1854
 1. U.S. 2. U.S. 3. MATANZAS

BLANCHARD, N.G., 25, M, MERCHANT, 07/01/1821
 1. U.S. 2. U.S. 3. MATANZAS

BONAPARTE, ANTONIO, 46, M, GENTLEMAN, 09/06/1832
 1. ITALY 2. COLUMBIA 3. NEW YORK

BOTT, ANN, 48, F, , 1822
 1. U.S. 2. U.S. 3. TRINIDAD

BOTT, JAMES, 10 MONTHS, M, ,1822
 1. U.S. 2. U.S. 3. TRINIDAD

BOWEN, ABRAHAM, 25, M, CARPENTER, 06/14/1827
1. U.S. 2. U.S. 3. MATANZAS

BOWEN, JOHN, 26, M, MARINER, 06/22/1820
1. U.S. 2. U.S. 3. MATANZAS

BOWEN, NATHANIEL, 40, M, MARINER, 11/23/1824
1. U.S. 2. U.S. 3. HAVANA

BOWEN, NATHANIEL J., 26, M, MARINER, 1845
1. U.S. 2. U.S. 3. MATANZAS

BRADFORD, ELIZABETH, 06, F, , 05/22/1828
1. 2. 3. HAVANA

BRADFORD, HENRY, 56, M, MERCHANT, 04/14/1827
1. U.S. 2. U.S. 3. MATANZAS

BRADFORD, JEMIMA G., 30, F, , 05/22/1828
1. BRISTOL 2. BRISTOL 3. HAVANA

BRAND, ANNAGNESS, 19, F, SEAMSTRESS, 04/20/1823
1. NEW YORK 2. U.S. 3. MATANZAS

BRODIE, WALTER, 30, M, MERCHANT, 08/14/1843
1. ENGLAND 2. ENGLAND 3. BAY OF ISLANDS

BROWN, A., 40, M, ENGINEER, 06/30/1867
1. U.S. 2. 3. CUBA

BROWN, THOMAS A., 25, M, MARINER, 07/03/1822
1. NEW YORK 2. 3. MATANZAS

BROWN, WILLIAM R., 29, M, MERCHANT, 12/18/1820
1. U.S. 2. U.S. 3. MATANZAS

BURDICK, BENJAMIN, 24, M, COOPER, 05/28/1824
1. U.S. 2. U.S. 3. HAVANA

BUTLER, JAMES H., 23, M, CARPENTER, 06/05/1834
1. U.S. 2. U.S. 3. HAVANA

BUTLER, WILLIAM, 25, M, LABOURER, 09/18/1834
1. IRELAND 2. U.S. 3. PICTOU

CADY, STEPHEN, 25, M, BAKER, 02/16/1822
1. 2. U.S. 3. ST. THOMAS

CAMBEL, FELIX, 32, M, MERCHANT, 08/20/1832
1. TRINIDAD 2. U.S. 3.

CAMEDIO, LOUIS INACIO, 16, M, SCHOOL BOY, 05/09/1848
1. CUBA 2. CUBA 3. MATANZAS

CAN, JR., WILLIAM, 30, M, MARINER, 04/19/1825
1. U.S. 2. U.S. 3. MATANZAS

CANTORO, JUSTICE, 17, M, GENTLEMAN, 08/19/1831
1. TRINIDAD 2. TRINIDAD 3. TRINIDAD

CAREW, JOHN A., 25, M, , 05/19/1825
1. U.S. 2. U.S. 3. MATANZAS

CARNELL, ALFRED, 35, M, COOPER, 04/26/1850
1. U.S. 2. U.S. 3. MATANZAS

CARR, GEORGE W., 40, M, MARINER, 05/15/1851
1. U.S. 2. 3. HAVANA

CATTON, CALVIN S., 24, M, MARINER, 1845
1. U.S. 2. U.S. 3. MATANZAS

CHAMBERLINE, STEPHEN, 26, M, CARPENTER, 06/25/1850
1. U.S. 2. 3. MATANZAS

CHAPPEN, EDWIN L., 28, M, CARPENTER, 09/24/1832
1. U.S. 2. U.S. 3. MATANZAS

CHASE, HENRY, 22, M, MASON, 01/26/1825
1. U.S. 2. U.S. 3. MATANZAS

CHEELTZ, CLAIRE, 21, F, WIFE OF JOHN, 01/02/1845
1. CANADA 2. CANADA 3. DEMERARA

CHEELTZ, FREDERIC, 5, M, , 01/02/1845
1. CANADA 2. CANADA 3. DEMERARA

CHEELTZ, GEORGE, 3, M, , 01/02/1845
1. CANADA 2. CANADA 3. DEMERARA

CHEELTZ, HENRY, 1 1/2, M, , 01/02/1845
1. CANADA 2. CANADA 3. DEMERARA

CHEELTZ, JOHN, 31, M, FARMER, 01/02/1845
1. CANADA 2. CANADA 3. DEMERARA

CHURCH, CHARLES, 30, M, CARPENTER, 06/05/1834
1. U.S. 2. U.S. 3. HAVANA

CHURCH, CHARLES, 23, M, SEAMAN, 06/09/1830
1. U.S. 2. U.S. 3. SEA

CHURCHILL, CAROLINE E., 2, F, , 1822
1. U.S. 2. U.S. 3. TRINIDAD

CHURCHILL, WILLIAM E., O3, M, , 1822
1. U.S. 2. U.S. 3. TRINIDAD

CLAPP, DARIUS, 22, , MERCHANT, 08/11/1823
1. BOSTON 2. U.S. 3. HAVANA

CLARK, MRS., 54, , , 05/31/1824
1. U.S. 2. U.S. 3. HAVANA

CLARK, PELEG, , M, MECHANIC, 05/19/1829
1. U.S. 2. U.S. 3. HAVANA

CLARKE, DAVID, 22, M, ENGINEER, 06/25/1850
1. U.S. 2. 3. CARDENAS

CLARKE, HARTFORD T., 21, M, MERCHANT, 07/01/1848
1. U.S. 2. U.S. 3. MATANZAS

CLIFFORD, BENJAMIN, 22, M, MERCHANT, 07/29/1824
1. U.S. 2. U.S. 3. MATANZAS

COGGESHALL, GEORGE, 48, M, MERCHANT, 05/22/1828
1. BRISTOL 2. BRISTOL 3. HAVANA

COLDENO, CLAFINA, 35, M, TOBACCONIST, 08/23/1832
1. SPAIN 2. 3. HAVANA

COLLINS, CHARLES, 50, M, MERCHANT, 05/05/1821
1. U.S. 2. U.S. 3. MATANZAS

COLLISON, WILLIAM E., 31, M, MARINER, 07/03/1822
1. PHILADELPHIA 2. 3. MATANZAS

COLON, B.W., 32, M, MERCHANT, 07/01/1821
1. U.S. 2. U.S. 3. MATANZAS

CONGDON, , 38, F, LADY, 07/01/1848
1. U.S. 2. U.S. 3. MATANZAS

CONGDON, DANIEL, 40, M, CARPENTER, 05/05/1848
1. U.S. 2. U.S. 3. MATANZAS

CONGDON, DANIEL, 21, M, CARPENTER, 06/08/1825
1. U.S. 2. U.S. 3. MATANZAS

COOK, JAMES, 25, M, SEAMAN, 06/09/1830
1. U.S. 2. U.S. 3. SEA

COOK, WILLIAM, 33, M, SEAMAN, 06/09/1830
1. U.S. 2. U.S. 3. SEA

COPE, PHILIP, 49, M, COOPER, 07/18/1845
1. U.S. 2. U.S. 3. MATANZAS

CORNELL, ALFRED, 35, M, COOPER, 04/26/1850
1. U.S. 2. 3. MATANZAS

CORTES, JOHN E., , M, SCHOLAR, 04/23/1832
   1. U.S. 2. U.S. 3. HAVANA

COTTRELL, JESSE, 23, M, CARPENTER, 06/30/1823
   1. WICKFORD 2. U.S. 3. MATANZAS

CRAMER, CHARLES, 25, M, MERCHANT, 09/17/1824
   1. RUSSIA 2. RUSSIA 3. ST. PETERSBURG

CRANSTON, THOMAS, 35, M, MARINER, 06/30/1860
   1. U.S. 2. 3. HONOLULU

CROW, BASIL, 55, M, PLANTER, 05/12/1822
   1. LOUISIANA 2. U.S. 3. HAVANNA

CUNINGHORN, JAMES, 33, M, CARPENTER, 06/13/1820
   1. U.S. 2. U.S. 3. MATANZAS

D'WOLF, ABBY, 43, F, , 07/27/1849
   1. U.S. 2. U.S. 3. MATANZAS

D'WOLF, CHARLES, 53, M, MERCHANT, 07/05/1833
   1. U.S. 2. U.S. 3. HAVANA

D'WOLF, GEORGE, 43, M, MERCHANT, 05/21/1821
   1. U.S. 2. U.S. 3. MATANZAS

D'WOLF, JOHN, 48, M, MERCHANT, 09/17/1824
   1. U.S. 2. U.S. 3. ST. PETERSBURG

D., C., 28, F, , 01/13/1824
   1. RUSSIA 2. RUSSIA 3. HAVANA

D., C., 45, M, MECHANIC, 02/13/1824
   1. ENGLAND 2. U.S. 3. HAVANA

DARLING, WILLIAM, 30, M, BLACKSMITH, 05/09/1837
   1. U.S. 2. U.S. 3. MATANZAS

DASLLION, DOM. JOHN, 38, M, MERCHANT, 08/23/1858
   1. SPAIN 2. SPAIN 3. CARDENAS

DAVENPORT, GIDEON, 33, M, CARPENTER, 06/23/1821
   1. PROVIDENCE 2. PROVIDENCE 3. HAVANA

DELETU, AN, 30, F, SERVANT, 09/27/1841
   1. CUBA 2. CUBA 3. MATANZAS

DELOURE, ALDOLPHO, 30, M, PLANTER, 05/03/1845
   1. U.S. 2. U.S. 3. CARDENAS

DENNIS, JOHN, 35, M, MARINER, 1824
   1. PORTSMOUTH 2. U.S. 3. HAVANA

DESHOAN, DANIEL, 22, M, MERCHANT, 04/08/1844
1. U.S. 2. MASSACHUSETTS 3. MATANZAS

DEWEY, GEORGE R., 22, M, CARPENTER, 06/14/1820
1. U.S. 2. U.S. 3. MATANZAS

DIMAN, JOHN, 50, M, COOPER, 10/01/1844
1. U.S. 2. U.S. 3. MATANZAS

DIMAN, JOHN, 55, M, COOPER, 05/15/1849
1. U.S. 2. U.S. 3. MATANZAS

DIMAN, MARIA P., 31, F, , 04/04/1825
1. U.S. 2. U.S. 3. HAVANA

DIMAN, CHILD, 04/04/1825
1. U.S. 2. U.S. 3. HAVANA

DISNEY, JOHN, 40, M, MARINER, 04/24/1849
1. U.S. 2. U.S. 3. SAN SALVADOR

DIXON, LEWIS H., 19, M, MARINER, 04/23/1850
1. U.S. 2. 3. ST. HELENA

DOMINQUEZ, DELORES, 41, F, LADY, 10/08/1855
1. OLD SPAIN 2. 3. HAVANA

DONNENBERG, G.H., 32, M, MERCHANT, 06/12/1822
1. GERMAN 2. 3.

DOTY, BENJAMIN, 42, M, COOPER, 05/05/1848
1. U.S. 2. U.S. 3. MATANZAS

DOTY, BENJAMIN, 37, M, COOPER, 03/10/1847
1. U.S. 2. U.S. 3. MATANZAS

DOTY, GEORGE, 21, M, COOPER, 05/28/1824
1. U.S. 2. U.S. 3. HAVANA

DRAKE, DANIEL, 21, M, SEAMAN, 06/27/1848
1. U.S. 2. U.S. 3. ST. HELENA

DUNCAN, JAMES, 25, M, CARPENTER, 08/19/1831
1. NEW YORK 2. TRINIDAD 3. TRINIDAD

DUNHAM, CHARLES, 16, M, , 04/24/1845
1. PROVIDENCE 2. U.S. 3. MATANZAS

DUNHAM, CHARLES C., 42, M, ENGINEER, 04/24/1845
1. PROVIDENCE 2. U.S. 3. MATANZAS

DUNHAM, MARIA, 36, F, , 04/24/1845
1. PROVIDENCE 2. U.S. 3. MATANZAS

DWYER, JOHN, 23, M, MARINER, 07/22/1857
1. U.S. 2. U.S. 3. HONOLULU

EASTERBROOKS, WILLIAM, 31, M, COOPER, 05/12/1855
1. U.S. 2. U.S. 3. MATANZAS

EDDY, JAMES, 38, M, ENGINEER, 06/25/1850
1. U.S. 2. 3. CARDENAS

EDDY, JR., BENJAMIN, 21, M, MARINER, 05/28/1824
1. U.S. 2. U.S. 3. HAVANA

ELDRIDGE, STEPHEN R.B., 35, M, MARINER, 11/23/1852
1. U.S. 2. 3. ST. HELENA

ELTS, PHILIP, 40, M, MERCHANT, 04/23/1832
1. U.S. 2. U.S. 3. HAVANA

EMERY, SAMUEL, 35, M, MARINER, 07/03/1822
1. BALTIMORE 2. 3. MATANZAS

ESTERY, J.A., 22, M, BLACKSMITH, 05/15/1820
1. U.S. 2. HARTFORD 3. MATANZAS

F., E., 37, M, YEOMAN, 01/13/1824
1. SWEDEN 2. U.S. 3. HAVANA

F., E., 27, F, , 02/13/1824
1. U.S. 2. U.S. 3. HAVANA

FAIRBANKS, MARSHAL, 25, M, TRANSPORTATION AGENT, 08/13/1850
1. U.S. 2. 3. CAPE HAYTIEN

FALES, CHS. J., 40, M, MERCHANT, 06/30/1864
1. U.S. 2. 3. SAGUA LA GRANDE

FALES, GEO. A., 27, M, MERCHANT, 05/03/1845
1. U.S. 2. U.S. 3. CARDENAS

FALES, THOMAS, 11, M, SCHOOL BOY, 07/13/1826
1. U.S. 2. U.S. 3. MATANZAS

FALES, WILLIAM, 42, M, MERCHANT, 05/03/1845
1. U.S. 2. U.S. 3. CARDENAS

FARLANE, M., 35, M, GOLD DIGGER, 05/15/1849
1. U.S. 2. U.S. 3. OAHU

FARNIER, JOHN F., 25, M, SEAMAN, 03/31/1860
1. U.S. 2. U.S. 3. ST. HELENA

FAY, SAMUEL, 25, M, ENGINEER, 07/05/1832
1. U.S. 2. U.S. 3. HAVANA

FENNER, RUBEN, 35, M, CARPENTER, 05/09/1837
1. U.S. 2. U.S. 3. MATANZAS

FITCH, CHARLES, 42, M, CLERK, 04/19/1856
1. U.S. 2. U.S. 3. LAHAINA

FOLE, PATRICK, 31, M, MARINER, 07/19/1822
1. BROOKLYN 2. BROOKLYN 3. TRINIDAD

FORBES, THOMAS, 35, M, MERCHANT, 05/17/1823
1. NEW YORK 2. AMERICA 3. MATANZAS

FORSYTH, ALEXANDER, 16, M, , 09/01/1845
1. RUM KEY 2. U.S. 3. RUM KEY

FOUYUN, DON, 30, M, PLANTER, 06/05/1833
1. CUBA 2. 3. HAVANA

FOX, HENRY, 23, M, CARPENTER, 05/21/1830
1. U.S. 2. U.S. 3. MATANZAS

FREDERICK, MATTHIAS, 48, M, COOPER, 05/12/1855
1. U.S. 2. 3. MATANZAS

FREEBODY, CHARLES, 24, M, SHOEMAKER, 05/09/1821
1. U.S. 2. U.S. 3. HAVANA

FREEBODY, WILLIAM, 11, M, SHOEMAKER, 05/09/1821
1. U.S. 2. U.S. 3. HAVANA

FREEMAN, B. S., 38, M, MARINER, 01/29/1852
1. U.S. 2. U.S. 3. LAHAINA

FRIGE, BASILIO ANTONIO, 23, M, CLERK, 05/11/1827
1. SPAIN 2. 3. MATANZAS

FRINK, RUFUS, 30, M, , 02/27/1828
1. U.S. 2. U.S. 3. HAVANA

FULLER, DANIEL, 40, M, CARPENTER, 06/14/1820
1. U.S. 2. U.S. 3. MATANZAS

GALE, CAPT. LEVI H., 30, M, MARINER, 05/31/1824
1. U.S. 2. U.S. 3. HAVANA

GARDNER, JOHN, 40, M, CARPENTER, 06/14/1820
1. U.S. 2. U.S. 3. MATANZAS

GARDNER, JOHN, 38, M, CARPENTER, 04/19/1821
1. U.S. 2. U.S. 3. MATANZAS

GAULT, ROBERT, , M, SEAMAN, 07/07/1829
1. U.S. 2. U.S. 3. RIO DE JANEIRO

GEORGE, JOHN, 40, M, , 08/31/1846
1. U.S. 2. U.S. 3. MATANZAS

GIFFORD, FREDERICK, 30, M, ENGINEER, 05/08/1837
1. U.S. 2. U.S. 3. MATANZAS

GLADDING, SAMUEL, 44, M, COOPER, 08/18/1851
1. U.S. 2. 3. MATANZAS

GLADDING, SAMUEL, 45, M, COOPER, 06/25/1850
1. U.S. 2. 3. MATANZAS

GOFF, NATHANIEL, 20, M, ORDINARY, 05/31/1820
1. BRISTOL 2. COUNTY OF BRISTOL 3. TRINIDAD

GOLDSMITH, MOSES, 40, M, MERCHANT, 06/05/1827
1. GREAT BRITAIN 2. U.S. 3. BARCELONA

GOODING, LEWIS, 24, M, , 08/03/1825
1. U.S. 2. CUBA 3. HAVANA

GOODRIDGE, SAMUEL, 25, M, COOPER, 05/25/1822
1. U.S. 2. U.S. 3. HAVANA

GOODWIN, CALEB, 26, M, MARINER, 04/24/1849
1. U.S. 2. U.S. 3. SAN SALVADOR

GOODWIN, JOSEPH, 50, M, PLANTER, 06/05/1833
1. CUBA 2. U.S. 3. HAVANA

GORHAM, EDWARD, 24, M, SEAMAN, 04/15/1834
1. U.S. 2. U.S. 3. HAVANA

GOUDRY, SUSANNAH, 29, F, , 08/09/1838
1. NOVA SCOTIA 2. OHIO 3. PICTOU

GRAB, CHARLES, 17, M, , 07/03/1826
1. ENGLAND 2. 3. MATANZAS

GRAB, JOHN N., 50, M, PLANTER, 07/03/1826
1. ENGLAND 2. 3. MATANZAS

GRACE, JOHN, 35, M, MERCHANT, 04/08/1823
1. HAVANA 2. HAVANA 3. HAVANA

GRAHAM, CHARLES H., , M, MERCHANT, 04/23/1832
1. U.S. 2. U.S. 3. HAVANA

GRANIUS, THOMAS, 31, M, MARINER, 04/24/1852
1. U.S. 2. 3. LAHAINA

GRAY, GEORGE A., 35, M, PLANTER, 08/01/1838
1. U.S. 2. U.S. 3. MATANZAS

GREENE, ANTHONY H., 19, M, CARPENTER, 05/21/1830
1. U.S. 2. U.S. 3. MATANZAS

GREENMAN, ESICK, 32, M, MARINER, 06/23/1820
1. U.S. 2. U.S. 3. MATANZAS

GRIFFITHS, JOHN, 30, M, ENGINEER, 07/05/1832
1. U.S. 2. U.S. 3. HAVANA

GRONAS, FRANCIS, 10, M, SERVANT, 02/12/1856
1. FAYAL 2. U.S. 3. ST. HELENA

GROSVENOR, LEMUEL, 50, M, , 05/21/1821
1. U.S. 2. U.S. 3. MATANZAS

GURCEN, LAUATON, 43, M, , 04/27/1837
1. SPAIN 2. 3. HAVANA

HADLEY, GEORGE, 23, M, SEAMAN, 08/14/1843
1. AMERICA 2. AMERICA 3. BAY OF ISLANDS

HAIL, COOMER, 20, M, SEAMAN, 05/31/1820
1. BRISTOL 2. COUNTY OF BRISTOL 3. TRINIDAD

HALE, JOHN, 35, M, MERCHANT, 08/05/1825
1. GREAT BRITAIN 2. U.S. 3. PONCA

HANSON, THOMAS, 31, M, HAND SERVANT, 06/12/1822
1. BOSTON 2. BOSTON 3.

HARRIS, JOHN, , M, SEAMAN, 07/07/1829
1. U.S. 2. U.S. 3. RIO DE JANEIRO

HARRIS, MRS, 27, F, , 11/18/1831
1. U.S. 2. U.S. 3. ST. THOMAS

HARVARD, EDWIN F., 55, M, SEAMAN, 07/01/1859
1. U.S. 2. U.S. 3. ST. HELENA

HARVEY, J., 25, M, MARINER, 06/04/1849
1. U.S. 2. U.S. 3. CARDENAS

HASKING, E.N., 35, , MARINER, 08/11/1823
1. PLYMOUTH 2. U.S. 3. HAVANA

HATCH, FRANCIS M., 27, M, ENGINEER, 06/25/1850
1. U.S. 2. 3. CARDENAS

HATCH, WILLIAM, 25, M, MARINER, 02/17/1824
1. BRISTOL 2. U.S. 3. HAVANA

HATHAWAY, FRANCIS W., 28, M, SEAMAN, 05/09/1859
1. U.S. 2. U.S. 3. ST. HELENA

HATHAWAY, JOHN, 28, M, BRICKLAYER, 04/19/1821
  1. U.S. 2. U.S. 3. MATANZAS

HATHAWAY, WILLIAM H., 45, M, MACHINIST, 01/14/1858
  1. U.S. 2. 3. HAVANA

HAVEN, EDWIN F., 55, M, , 05/09/1859
  1. U.S. 2. U.S. 3. ST. HELENA

HAVENS, HENRY, 27, M, MARINER, 09/06/1853
  1. U.S. 2. U.S. 3. IAHANNA

HAYWOOD, DANIEL, 27, M, CARPENTER, 04/17/1822
  1. U.S. 2. U.S. 3. TRINIDAD

HEALE, FRAN J., 30, M, MERCHANT, 04/27/1837
  1. U.S. 2. U.S. 3. HAVANA

HEARSE, JOHN, 23, M, MASON, 06/16/1831
  1. U.S. 2. U.S. 3. TRINIDAD

HENRY, CLARK, 23, M, MARINER, 04/19/1825
  1. U.S. 2. U.S. 3. MATANZAS

HENRY, DAVID, 22, M, MARINER, 07/22/1857
  1. U.S. 2. U.S. 3. HONOLULU

HERRICK, JAMES D., 23, M, MECHANIC, 05/17/1823
  1. RHODE ISLAND 2. AMERICA 3. MATANZAS

HINCKLEY, E., 28, , MARINER, 08/11/1823
  1. BOSTON 2. U.S. 3. HAVANA

HINKLY, GEORGE, 22, M, MARINER, 04/10/1855
  1. U.S. 2. U.S. 3. LAHAINA

HOOD, NOBLE, 38, M, COOPER, 05/18/1823
  1. WARREN 2. U.S. 3. MATANZAS

HOOPER, ELLIS, 35, M, ENGINEER, 06/25/1850
  1. U.S. 2. 3. CARDENAS

HOOPER, ROBT. C., 29, M, MERCHANT, 06/05/1830
  1. U.S. 2. U.S. 3. HAVANA

HOPKINS, HIRAM, 32, M, ENGINEER, 07/05/1832
  1. U.S. 2. U.S. 3. HAVANA

HOPKINS, LAYD, 20, M, MARINER, 07/22/1857
  1. U.S. 2. U.S. 3. HONOLULU

HORTON, MISS MARTHA M., 25, F, , 05/20/1837
  1. U.S. 2. U.S. 3. MATANZAS

HOTA, JOHN, 16, M, , 05/21/1830
1. U.S. 2. U.S. 3. MATANZAS

HOTTLE, HENRY, 25, M, SEAMAN, 04/15/1834
1. U.S. 2. U.S. 3. HAVANA

HOUGH, JOSEPH B., 50, M, MERCHANT, 12/18/1820
1. U.S. 2. U.S. 3. MATANZAS

HOWANA, JOHN, 27, M, PLANTER, 04/19/1821
1. U.S. 2. U.S. 3. MATANZAS

HOWARD, BENJAMIN, 31, M, COOPER, 05/25/1822
1. U.S. 2. U.S. 3. HAVANA

IDE, W., 23, M, MERCHANT, 07/01/1821
1. U.S. 2. U.S. 3. MATANZAS

INGRAHAM, ALLEN, 27, M, , 06/11/1821
1. BRISTOL 2. BRISTOL 3. HAVANA

INGRAHAM, ALLEN, , M, SEAMAN, 07/07/1829
1. U.S. 2. U.S. 3. RIO DE JANEIRO

INGRAHAM, ALLEN, 32, M, COOPER, 04/04/1825
1. U.S. 2. U.S. 3. HAVANA

INGRAHAM, JOHN, 48, M, COOPER, 05/12/1855
1. U.S. 2. U.S. 3. MATANZAS

INGRAHAM, JOHN, 22, M, COOPER, 04/04/1825
1. U.S. 2. U.S. 3. HAVANA

INMAN, AARON C., 33, M, GOLD DIGGER, 06/06/1849
1. U.S. 2. U.S. 3. OAHU

INMAN, MRS., 45, F, AND TWO CHILDREN, 06/06/1849
1. U.S. 2. U.S. 3. OAHU

IVES, FREDERICK G., 19, M, GENTLEMAN, 04/08/1844
1. U.S 2. U.S. 3. VALPARAISO

JACKSON, ANN, 9, F, SERVANT, 1822
1. U.S. 2. U.S. 3. TRINIDAD

JACKSON, JANE, 43, F, SERVANT, 1822
1. U.S. 2. U.S. 3. TRINIDAD

JAMES, RICHARD, 16, M, MARINER, 06/30/1864
1. U.S. 2. 3. REMEDIOS

JESPHER, WILLIAM, 35, M, COOPER, 08/23/1839
1. U.S. 2. U.S. 3. MATANZAS

JOHNSON, FRANK, 33, M, GENTLEMAN, 10/24/1843
1. GREAT BRITAIN 2. GREAT BRITAIN 3. TALCHUANNO

JOHNSON, NEAL, 23, M, CABINET MAKER, 09/17/1824
1. U.S. 2. U.S. 3. ST. PETERSBURG

JOHNSON, PETER, 22, M, MARINER, 08/13/1850
1. U.S. 2. 3. CAPE HAYTIEN

JOHNSTON, JOHN, 28, M, GOLD DIGGER, 05/15/1849
1. U.S. 2. U.S. 3. OAHU

JOSIAH, HENRY, 27, M, MERCHANT, 10/20/1820
1. HAVANA 2. UNCERTAIN 3. HAVANA

KELTON, M. G., 53, M, ENGINEER, 06/30/1867
1. U.S. 2. 3. CUBA

KENTEY, S.W., 31, M, LABOURER, 05/15/1820
1. IRELAND 2. U.S. 3. MATANZAS

KIDWELL, WILLIAM, 16, M, MARINER, 09/08/1827
1. U.S. 2. U.S. 3. BARCELONA

KILPATRICK, WILLIAM, 25, M, MECHANIC, 06/13/1827
1. U.S. 2. U.S. 3. MATANZAS

KING, JOSEPH, 25, M, SEAMAN, 06/27/1848
1. U.S. 2. U.S. 3. ST. HELENA

KING, MARTIN, 45, M, COOPER, 04/26/1850
1. U.S. 2. 3. MATANZAS

KING, RUEBEN M., , M, MERCHANT, 05/17/1825
1. U.S. 2. U.S. 3. MATANZAS

KING, WILLIAM, 27, M, COOPER, 06/29/1825
1. U.S. 2. U.S. 3. HAVANA

LAFFONT, WILLIAM, 18, M, MARINER, 04/10/1855
1. U.S. 2. U.S. 3. LAHAINA

LAMBERT, WILLIAM, 28, M, SEAMAN, 06/09/1830
1. U.S. 2. U.S. 3. SEA

LANE, SAMUEL, 25, M, MARINER, 08/13/1850
1. U.S. 2. 3. CAPE HAYTIEN

LAWRENCE, JAMES, 31, M, JEWELLER, 07/18/1845
1. U.S. 2. U.S. 3. MATANZAS

LEAVITT, ANDREW, 27, M, MECHANIC, 04/26/1834
1. U.S. 2. U.S. 3. MATANZAS

LEONARD, JOHN, 58, M, MERCHANT, 06/05/1827
1. U.S. 2. U.S. 3. BARCELONA

LEONARD, JOHN, 8, M, , 05/18/1848
1. U.S. 2. U.S. 3. TALCAHUANO

LEONARD, MRS., 38, F, , 05/18/1848
1. U.S. 2. U.S. 3. TALCAHUANO

LEONARD 2ND, JOHN, 13, M, BOY, 06/05/1827
1. U.S. 2. U.S. 3. BARCELONA

LEWIS, JOSEPH, 33, M, MARINER, 10/20/1820
1. U.S. 2. U.S. 3. HAVANA

LEWIS, ROBERT, 24, M, CARPENTER, 04/19/1821
1. U.S. 2. U.S. 3. MATANZAS

LEYBURN, ISAAC D., 26, M, MARINER, 08/13/1850
1. U.S. 2. 3. CAPE HAYTIEN

LEYBURN, MARY ANN, 22, F, WIFE OF ISAAC, 08/13/1850
1. U.S. 2. 3. CAPE HAYTIEN

LINDY, JOAB, 30, M, CARPENTER, 05/20/1821
1. U.S. 2. U.S. 3. HAVANA

LINNEY, RICHARD, 30, M, MARINER, 07/22/1857
1. U.S. 2. U.S. 3. HONOLULU

LINSEY, SAMUEL, 50, M, ENGINEER, 05/15/1841
1. U.S. 2. U.S. 3. MATANZAS

LINZ, GEORGE, 40, M, CARPENTER, 10/01/1841
1. U.S. 2. U.S. 3. MATANZAS

LINZ, JANE MARIA, 13, F, , 10/01/1841
1. U.S. 2. U.S. 3. MATANZAS

LINZ, SARAH ANN, 33, F, , 10/01/1841
1. U.S. 2. U.S. 3. MATANZAS

LLORACH, JOSEPH, 21, M, MARINER, 03/31/1866
1. CUBA 2. 3. MATANZAS

LOCKWOOD, ISAAC, 25, M, CLERK, 11/19/1831
1. U.S. 2. U.S. 3. TRINIDAD

LOCKWOOD, WILLIAM, 45, M, SEAMAN, 06/09/1830
1. U.S. 2. U.S. 3. SEA

LOVELAIN, SAMUEL B., 27, M, CARPENTER, 05/19/1825
1. U.S. 2. U.S. 3. MATANZAS

LUDEN, FREDERICK, 48, M, MERCHANT, 06/21/1822
1. BOSTON 2. U.S. 3. HAVANA

LUTHER, J., 36, M, COOPER, 05/15/1849
1. U.S. 2. U.S. 3. MATANZAS

LUTHER, JEREMIAH, 40, M, COOPER, 07/11/1854
1. U.S. 2. U.S. 3. MATANZAS

LUTHER, JEREMIAH, 26, M, COOPER, 05/09/1837
1. U.S. 2. U.S. 3. MATANZAS

LUTHER, JEREMIAH, 45, M, COOPER, 07/06/1857
1. U.S. 2. 3. MATANZAS

LYNN, WILLIAM, 29, M, MARINER, 04/10/1855
1. U.S. 2. U.S. 3. LAHAINA

MACY, CHARLES, 19, M, MARINER, 04/10/1855
1. U.S. 2. U.S. 3. LAHAINA

MAGARTT, MARY, 22, F, SERVANT, 09/18/1834
1. IRELAND 2. U.S. 3. PICTOU

MANCHESTER, ALBERT, 30, M, COOPER, 10/01/1844
1. U.S. 2. U.S. 3. MATANZAS

MANCHESTER, ALBERT, 40, M, COOPER, 05/02/1850
1. U.S. 2. 3. MATANZAS

MANCHESTER, LUTHER, 25, M, COOPER, 05/09/1837
1. U.S. 2. U.S. 3. MATANZAS

MANSONY, JOHN F., 35, M, MERCHANT, 04/08/1823
1. BOSTON 2. BOSTON 3. HAVANA

MARAINE, JOHN, 28, M, COOPER, 05/30/1853
1. SPAIN 2. U.S. 3. CARDENAS

MARR, M., 38, M, MERCHANT, 05/15/1820
1. U.S. 2. VIRGINIA 3. MATANZAS

MARSDEN, H., 28, M, MARINER, 1845
1. U.S. 2. U.S. 3. MATANZAS

MARSHALL, HERBERT, 30, M, CLERGYMAN, 06/28/1825
1. U.S. 2. U.S. 3. HAVANA

MARTIN, JOSEPH E., 35, M, COOPER, 06/16/1847
1. U.S. 2. U.S. 3. MATANZAS

MARTIN, JOSEPH P., 32, M, COOPER, 08/31/1846
1. U.S. 2. U.S. 3. MATANZAS

MARTIN, RUBY, 30, F, WIDOW, 06/25/1852
1. U.S. 2. 3. MATANZAS

MARTINEZ, MANUEL, 40, M, MARINER, 06/30/1862
1. PORTUGAL 2. U.S. 3. CARDENAS

MAYHEW, E.P., 27, M, MERCHANT, 08/23/1832
1. U.S. 2. U.S. 3. HAVANA

MCGEER, CHARLES, 27, M, HOUSEWRIGHT, 01/02/1845
1. ENGLAND 2. U.S. 3. DEMERARA

MCKENZI, JAMES M., 27, M, MARINER, 06/13/1820
1. U.S. 2. U.S. 3. MATANZAS

MCNEIL, DANIEL, 41, M, MARINER, 09/30/1857
1. U.S. 2. 3. HONOLULU

MCNEIL, DAVID, 41, M, MARINER, 07/22/1857
1. U.S. 2. U.S. 3. HONOLULU

MERRILL, RANSELAER, 20, M, CARPENTER, 06/14/1820
1. U.S. 2. U.S. 3. MATANZAS

MICHAELS, CHAS., 35, M, MERCHANT, 06/12/1822
1. PARISIAN 2. 3. HAVANA

MILLER, DR. CALEB, 34, M, PHYSICIAN, 06/23/1820
1. U.S. 2. U.S. 3. MATANZAS

MILLER, JOB, 63, M, ENGINEER, 06/30/1871
1. U.S. 2. 3. SAGUA LA GRANDE

MILLER, SAMUEL T., 41, M, MERCHANT, 06/30/1864
1. U.S. 2. 3. REMEDIOS

MINER, ALLEN K., 29, M, MECHANIC, 04/26/1834
1. U.S. 2. U.S. 3. MATANZAS

MINOT, ANTONET, 11/2, , , 08/01/1822
1. U.S. 2. U.S. 3. TRINIDAD

MINOT, CHARTHREN, 35, F, , 08/01/1822
1. U.S. 2. U.S. 3. TRINIDAD

MINOT, JR., CHARTHREN, 6, F, , 08/01/1822
1. U.S. 2. U.S. 3. TRINIDAD

MINOT, JR., JAMES, 4, M, , 08/01/1822
1. U.S. 2. U.S. 3. TRINIDAD

MITCHELL, J.W., 37, M, MERCHANT, 06/12/1822
1. ENGLISH 2. 3.

MITCHELL, JOSEPH B., 31, M, SEAMAN, 02/13/1837
1. U.S. 2. U.S. 3. ST. CATHARINE

MONTEL, JAMES, 24, M, CLERK, 10/03/1831
1. ST. THOMAS 2. U.S. 3. TURKS ISLAND

MOON, LEWIS, 22, M, MARINER, 01/29/1852
1. U.S. 2. 3. LAHAINA

MOONEY, MICHAEL, 28, M, CARPENTER, 06/20/1824
1. QUEBEC 2. U.S. 3. HAVANA

MOORE, SAMUEL S., 21, M, MARINER, 05/21/1824
1. U.S. 2. U.S. 3. HAVANA

MOORFIELD, JAMES, 45, M, MERCHANT, 06/27/1824
1. U.S. 2. CUBA 3. HAVANA

MORE, WILLIAM C., 23, M, COOPER, 07/05/1848
1. U.S. 2. U.S. 3. ST. HELENA

MORGAN, CHARLES W., 19, M, , 07/05/1848
1. U.S. 2. U.S. 3. ST. HELENA

MORRIS, BENJ. B., 49, M, MARINER, 04/01/1865
1. U.S. 2. 3. MATANZAS

MORRIS, JR., BENJ., 23, M, PHYSICIAN, 04/14/1827
1. U.S. 2. U.S. 3. MATANZAS

MULICIN, JOHN H., 31, M, MERCHANT, 04/27/1837
1. U.S. 2. U.S. 3. HAVANA

MUNRO, GEORGE, 30, M, COOPER, 05/11/1827
1. U.S. 2. U.S. 3. MATANZAS

MUNRO, HARRIET, 40, F, , 05/03/1845
1. U.S. 2. U.S. 3. CARDENAS

MUNRO, HARRIET, 1, F, CHILD, 05/03/1845
1. U.S. 2. U.S. 3. CARDENAS

MUNRO, MARY, 11, F, CHILD, 05/03/1845
1. U.S. 2. U.S. 3. CARDENAS

MUNRO, THEODORA, 9, F, CHILD, 05/03/1845
1. U.S. 2. U.S. 3. CARDENAS

MUNRO, THOMAS, 25, M, SEAMAN, 07/05/1848
1. U.S. 2. U.S. 3. ST. HELENA

MURDOCK, MISS, 7, F, SERVANT, 06/27/1824
1. CUBA 2. CUBA 3. HAVANA

MURRAY, 4 MONTHS, F, CHILD, 09/06/1832
1. NEW BRUNSWICK 2. NEW BRUNSWICK 3. NEW YORK

MURRAY, JOHN Y., 35, M, GENTLEMAN, 09/06/1832
1. NEW BRUNSWICK 2. NEW BRUNSWICK 3. NEW YORK

MURRAY, MRS., 22, F, LADY, 09/06/1832
1. NEW BRUNSWICK 2. NEW BRUNSWICK 3. NEW YORK

NEWCOMB, H.J., , , U.S. NAVY, 05/26/1822
1. 2. 3. HAVANA

NEWMAN, WILLIAM, 50, M, MARINER, 07/22/1857
1. U.S. 2. U.S. 3. HONOLULU

NICILAU, OCTAVIO, 24, M, COOPER, 05/28/1824
1. U.S. 2. U.S. 3. HAVANA

NICKLYE, OCTAVIO L., , M, MECHANIC, 05/19/1829
1. U.S. 2. U.S. 3. HAVANA

NOLTE, HERMANN, 35, M, MERCHANT, 06/12/1822
1. GERMAN 2. 3.

NORRIS, CHARLES H., 16, M, , 05/02/1850
1. U.S. 2. 3. MATANZAS

NORTHAM, WILLIAM S., 22, M, MARINER, 06/08/1825
1. U.S. 2. U.S. 3. MATANZAS

NYE, NATHAN, 25, M, MARINER, 04/10/1855
1. U.S. 2. U.S. 3. LAHAINA

O'WILSON, LOCH-, 47, M, PLANTER, 06/05/1833
1. CUBA 2. 3. MATANZAS

OAKES, JOHN HENRY, 26, M, GENTLEMAN, 06/20/1820
1. U.S. 2. U.S. 3. MATANZAS

OLIVER, ANDRES M., 28, M, MARINER, 07/03/1822
1. BRISTOL, R.I. 2. 3. MATANZAS

OLIVER, ANDROS M., 28, M, MERCHANT, 07/01/1821
1. SPAIN 2. U.S. 3. MATANZAS

OSBURN, DAVIS C., 28, M, SEAMAN, 07/05/1848
1. U.S. 2. U.S. 3. ST. HELENA

PABODIE, HENRY, 7, M, SHOEMAKER, 04/23/1821
1. U.S. 2. U.S. 3. HAVANA

PACKARD, AUGUSTA, 18, F, SEAMSTRESS, 04/08/1823
1. NEW YORK 2. U.S. 3. HAVANA

PACKARD, ISAAC, 45, M, MERCHANT, 04/08/1823
1. NEW YORK 2. U.S. 3. HAVANA

PANS, LUSANI, 18, M, STUDENT, 04/11/1836
1. CUBA 2. 3. HAVANA

PANTARO, JUSTICE, 11, M, GENTLEMAN, 07/17/1827
1. CUBA 2. 3. TRINIDAD

PANTARO, PETER, 16, M, GENTLEMAN, 07/17/1827
1. CUBA 2. 3. TRINIDAD

PATRICE, HENRY, 7, M, , 05/09/1821
1. U.S. 2. U.S. 3. HAVANA

PEARSE, SANFORD, 22, M, MARINER, 06/23/1820
1. U.S. 2. U.S. 3. MATANZAS

PERKINS, STETSON, 24, M, MARINER, 02/12/1856
1. U.S. 2. U.S. 3. ST. HELENA

PERRIN, CARTINA, 4, F, , 08/09/1838
1. NOVA SCOTIA 2. OHIO 3. PICTOU

PERRIN, CATTRINA, 7, F, , 08/09/1838
1. NOVA SCOTIA 2. OHIO 3. PICTOU

PERRIN, CHARLES, 16, M, FARMER, 08/09/1838
1. NOVA SCOTIA 2. OHIO 3. PICTOU

PERRIN, CHRISTOPHER, 14, M, , 08/09/1838
1. NOVA SCOTIA 2. OHIO 3. PICTOU

PERRIN, CLERNDUDAY, 12, F, , 08/09/1838
1. NOVA SCOTIA 2. OHIO 3. PICTOU

PERRIN, ELINORE, 45, F, , 08/09/1838
1. NOVA SCOTIA 2. OHIO 3. PICTOU

PERRIN, ELISABETH, 44, F, , 08/09/1838
1. NOVA SCOTIA 2. OHIO 3. PICTOU

PERRIN, ELISABETH, 6, F, , 08/09/1838
1. NOVA SCOTIA 2. OHIO 3. PICTOU

PERRIN, FREDRICK, 46, M, FARMER, 08/09/1838
1. NOVA SCOTIA 2. OHIO 3. PICTOU

PERRIN, FRIDRICK, 17, M, , 08/09/1838
1. NOVA SCOTIA 2. OHIO 3. PICTOU

PERRIN, ISABELLA, 1, F, , 08/09/1838
1. NOVA SCOTIA 2. OHIO 3. PICTOU

PERRIN, JAMES, 49, M, FARMER, 08/09/1838
1. NOVA SCOTIA 2. OHIO 3. PICTOU

PERRIN, JAMES, 19, M, , 08/09/1838
1. NOVA SCOTIA 2. OHIO 3. PICTOU

PERRIN, JANE, 15, M, , 08/09/1838
1. NOVA SCOTIA 2. OHIO 3. PICTOU

PERRIN, JISSY, 22, F, , 08/09/1838
1. NOVA SCOTIA 2. OHIO 3. PICTOU

PERRIN, JOHN, 11, M, , 08/09/1838
1. NOVA SCOTIA 2. OHIO 3. PICTOU

PERRIN, JOSEPHINER, 9, F, , 08/09/1838
1. NOVA SCOTIA 2. OHIO 3. PICTOU

PERRIN, MARY, 14, M, , 08/09/1838
1. NOVA SCOTIA 2. OHIO 3. PICTOU

PERRIN, MILHAB, 15, M, , 08/09/1838
1. NOVA SCOTIA 2. OHIO 3. PICTOU

PERRIN, NELSON, 8, M, , 08/09/1838
1. NOVA SCOTIA 2. OHIO 3. PICTOU

PERRIN, RHUBIU, 10, M, , 08/09/1838
1. NOVA SCOTIA 2. OHIO 3. PICTOU

PERRIN, WILLIAM, 3, M, , 08/09/1838
1. NOVA SCOTIA 2. OHIO 3. PICTOU

POOL, G., 45, M, MASTER MARINER, 09/16/1848
1. ENGLAND 2. ENGLAND 3. HEBERT TOWN

PRATT, JOHN A., 19, M, CARPENTER, 06/22/1820
1. U.S. 2. U.S. 3. MATANZAS

PRIEST, GEORGE H., 27, M, ENGINEER, 06/25/1852
1. U.S. 2. U.S. 3. MATANZAS

QUELLEC, ALEXANDER, 22, M, MARINER, 02/13/1821
1. U.S. 2. U.S. 3. HAVANA

RAGEN, GEORGE, 30, M, ENGINEER, 05/12/1856
1. U.S. 2. 3. SANTIAGO

RAMIRES, FRANCIS, 2 1/2, M, CHILD, 05/03/1845
1. U.S. 2. U.S. 3. CARDENAS

RAMIRES, RACHEL, 21, F, , 05/03/1845
1. U.S. 2. U.S. 3. CARDENAS

RAMSEY, WILLIAM, 25, M, MARINER, 08/13/1850
1. U.S. 2. 3. CAPE HAYTIEN

RAY, THOMAS, 30, M, MACHINIST, 01/14/1858
1. U.S. 2. 3. HAVANA

READ, SAMUEL, 37, M, CARPENTER, 07/27/1849
1. U.S. 2. U.S. 3. MATANAZAS

REED, JOHN, 30, M, CARPENTER, 08/20/1832
1. TRINIDAD 2. U.S. 3.

REED, LYMAN, , M, SEAMAN, 07/07/1829
1. U.S. 2. U.S. 3. RIO DE JANEIRO

REMICK, ENOCH, 60, M, MARINER, 02/22/1854
1. U.S. 2. 3. MATANZAS

REMIERS, RACHEL, 23, F, , 06/16/1847
1. U.S. 2. U.S. 3. MATANZAS

REYNOLDS, WILLIAM, 30, M, MARINER, 1845
1. U.S. 2. U.S. 3. MATANZAS

RICHMOND, ATWELL, 30, M, MARINER, 06/23/1820
1. U.S. 2. U.S. 3. MATANZAS

RICHMOND, WILLIAM, 40, M, SEAMAN, 04/23/1821
1. U.S. 2. U.S. 3. HAVANA

RILEY, JAMES, 24, M, JEWELLER, 04/19/1821
1. U.S. 2. U.S. 3. MATANZAS

RILEY, JAMES, 22, M, MERCHANT, 12/18/1820
1. U.S. 2. U.S. 3. MATANZAS

RILLEY, SAMUEL, 27, M, MARINER, 07/22/1857
1. U.S. 2. U.S. 3. HONOLULU

RING, JOSEPH, 25, M, SEAMAN, 07/01/1848
1. U.S. 2. U.S. 3. ST. HELENA

RING, MARTIN, 45, M, COOPER, 04/26/1850
1. U.S. 2. 3. MATANZAS

ROBERTS, TOBIAS, 37, M, ENGINEER, 06/25/1850
1. U.S. 2. 3. CARDENAS

ROBINSON, WILLIAM, 20, M, SEAMAN, 07/01/1848
1. U.S. 2. U.S. 3. MATANZAS

ROCHMOND, WILLIAM, 40, M, , 05/09/1821
1. U.S. 2. U.S. 3. HAVANA

ROOLRIDGE, JOHN, 22, M, GENTLEMAN, 07/17/1827
1. CUBA 2. 3. TRINIDAD

ROSE, JESSE, 42, M, MARINER, 03/31/1864
1. U.S. 2. 3. MATANZAS

ROSS, WILLIAM, 19, M, MARINER, 07/22/1857
1. U.S. 2. U.S. 3. HONOLULU

ROWLINGS, CHARLES, 28, M, MARINER, 1824
1. BRISTOL 2. U.S. 3. HAVANA

SAFFORD, ALDEN, 35, M, MECHANIC, 06/30/1864
1. U.S. 2. 3. MATANZAS

SALISBURY, MARTIN, 34, M, COOPER, 05/31/1820
1. BRISTOL 2. BRISTOL 3. SALISBURY

SALMOND, SAMUEL, 35, M, GENTLEMAN, 05/10/1824
1. U.S 2. U.S. 3. MATANZAS

SALSBURY, MARTIN, 36, M, COOPER, 05/18/1823
1. WARREN 2. U.S. 3. MATANZAS

SANTOS, JUAN, 40, M, , 04/27/1837
1. SPAIN 2. 3. HAVANA

SAVAGE, ARTHUR, 30, M, MERCHANT, 06/21/1822
1. BOSTON 2. U.S. 3. HAVANA

SAVAGE, WILLIAM, 42, M, MERCHANT, 06/12/1822
1. U.S. 2. U.S. 3.

SAYER, WILLIAM, 50, M, MERCHANT, 02/27/1828
1. U.S. 2. U.S. 3. HAVANA

SAYMORE, CHARLES, 20, M, CARPENTER, 05/09/1837
1. U.S. 2. U.S. 3. MATANZAS

SCHULTZ, JOHN, , M, SEAMAN, 07/07/1829
1. U.S. 2. U.S. 3. RIO DE JANEIRO

SCOBIE, GEORGE, 40, M, MECHANIC, 10/04/1845
1. U.S. 2. U.S. 3. MARIEL DE CUBA

SCOTT, BETSEY, 28, F, , 06/20/1824
1. U.S. 2. U.S. 3. HAVANA

SCOTT, JAMES, 20, M, MARINER, 08/13/1850
1. U.S. 2. 3. CAPE HAYTIEN

SEINAL, PETER, 42, M, MARINER, 02/13/1821
1. U.S. 2. U.S. 3. HAVANA

SERGEANT, JOHN, 43, M, SHIP MASTER, 1845
1. U.S. 2. U.S. 3. MATANZAS

SEYMORE, CHARLES, 23, M, CARPENTER, 08/01/1838
1. U.S. 2. U.S. 3. MATANZAS

SEYMOUR, ANN, 19, F, CHILD OF JOSEPH, 06/25/1850
1. U.S. 2. 3. MATANZAS

SEYMOUR, CHARLES, 22, M, CARPENTER, 08/23/1839
1. U.S. 2. U.S. 3. MATANZAS

SEYMOUR, GEORGE, 16, M, CHILD OF JOSEPH, 06/25/1850
1. U.S. 2. 3. MATANZAS

SEYMOUR, J., 15, M, , 05/15/1849
1. U.S. 2. U.S. 3. MATANZAS

SEYMOUR, JAMES, 13, M, CHILD OF JOSEPH, 06/25/1850
1. U.S. 2. 3. MATANZAS

SEYMOUR, JOSEPH, , M, MERCHANT, 05/17/1825
1. U.S. 2. U.S. 3. MATANZAS

SEYMOUR, MANUEL, 7, M, CHILD OF JOSEPH, 06/25/1850
1. U.S. 2. 3. MATANZAS

SEYMOUR, SUSAN, 45, F, WIFE OF JOSEPH, 06/25/1850
1. U.S. 2. 3. MATANZAS

SHANKE, JOHN, 32, M, ENGINEER, 01/02/1845
1. ENGLAND 2. U.S. 3. DEMERARA

SHEARMAN, LEVI, 25, M, COOPER, 05/31/1820
1. BRISTOL 2. BRISTOL 3. TRINIDAD

SHEELOCK, MARTIN C., 45, M, ENGINEER, 07/05/1832
1. U.S. 2. U.S. 3. HAVANA

SHEPPARD, JOHN, 18, M, MARINER, 04/10/1855
1. U.S. 2. U.S. 3. LAHAINA

SHERMAN, ABRAHAM, 28, M, CARPENTER, 06/14/1827
1. U.S. 2. U.S. 3. MATANZAS

SHERMAN, EBENEZER, 19, M, GENTLEMAN, 05/10/1824
1. U.S. 2. U.S. 3. MATANZAS

SHERMAN, LEVI, 34, M, COOPER, 07/13/1826
1. U.S. 2. U.S. 3. MATANZAS

SHEUTHING, JAMES, 28, M, LABOURER, 09/18/1834
1. IRELAND 2. U.S. 3. PICTOU

SHORT, ANNE, 17, F, WIFE OF ALBERT P., 08/02/1852
1. ENGLAND 2. U.S. 3. BAY OF ISLANDS

SILVER, JOHN, 39, M, MERCHANT, 01/02/1845
1. MADEIRA 2. MADEIRA 3. DEMERARA

SILVER, JOSEPH, 24, M, , 04/24/1852
1. AZORES ISLANDS 2. U.S. 3. LAHAINA

SILVEY, JOHN, 28, M, MARINER, 12/31/1865
1. BRAVO 2. 3. HAVANA

SIPON, FREEBORN, 50, M, MERCHANT, 06/05/1830
1. U.S. 2. U.S. 3. HAVANA

SIVILLU, J., 30, M, , 05/15/1849
1. SPAIN 2. U.S. 3. MATANZAS

SMITH, BENJAMIN R., 26, M, CARPENTER, 04/30/1821
1. U.S. 2. U.S. 3. HAVANA

SMITH, DANIEL, 25, M, TAILOR, 05/08/1837
1. U.S. 2. U.S. 3. MATANZAS

SMITH, HENRY B., 29, M, MARINER, 09/06/1853
1. U.S. 2. U.S. 3. LAHAINA

SMITH, JAMES ARNOLD, 26, M, ENGINEER, 06/11/1849
1. U.S. 2. U.S. 3. CARDENAS

SMITH, MRS. JOHN, 50, F, , 05/20/1837
1. U.S. 2. U.S. 3. MATANZAS

SMITH, SAMUEL C., 29, M, MECHANIC, 05/17/1823
1. RHODE ISLAND 2. AMERICA 3. MATANZAS

SPALING, ANDREW, 37, M, MARINER, 07/22/1857
1. U.S. 2. U.S. 3. HONOLULU

SPINK, JR., SAMUEL, 22, M, CARPENTER, 06/30/1823
1. PROVIDENCE 2. U.S. 3. MATANZAS

STAFFORD, JAMES, 32, M, BRICKLAYER, 04/19/1821
1. U.S. 2. U.S. 3. MATANZAS

STALL, ISAAC, 40, M, COACHMAKER, 06/23/1821
1. NEWPORT 2. NEWPORT 3. HAVANA

STARKEY, CHARLES C., 20, M, CARPENTER, 06/14/1820
1. U.S. 2. U.S. 3. MATANZAS

STEERE, JOHN, 40, M, MERCHANT, 03/31/1866
1. U.S. 2. 3. MATANZAS

STEVENSON, DAVID, 35, M, MERCHANT, 02/26/1822
1. CANADA 2. CANADA 3. ST. THOMAS

STEWART, JAMES, 28, M, GENTLEMAN, 08/14/1843
1. SCOTLAND 2. SCOTLAND 3. BAY OF ISLANDS

STOREY, CHARLES, 46, M, MERCHANT, 06/27/1824
1. U.S. 2. CUBA 3. HAVANA

STUDSEN, MON. J., 18, M, CARPENTER, 06/14/1820
1. U.S. 2. U.S. 3. MATANZAS

STUDSON, JEREMIAH, 28, M, CARPENTER, 04/20/1823
1. PROVIDENCE 2. U.S. 3. MATANZAS

SWAN, THOMAS, 40, M, MARINER, 06/04/1823
1. BRISTOL 2. U.S. 3. MARTINIQUE

SWEET, S., , M, CARPENTER, 06/30/1826
1. U.S. 2. U.S. 3. MATANZAS

SWEET, S.E., , M, CARPENTER, 06/30/1826
1. U.S. 2. U.S. 3. MATANZAS

SWITZER, ANDREW, 25, M, CARPENTER, 06/14/1827
1. U.S. 2. U.S. 3. MATANZAS

SWITZER, JOSEPH, 27, M, CARPENTER, 06/14/1827
1. U.S. 2. U.S. 3. MATANZAS

SYLVIAH, J.N., 30, M, MARINER, 03/31/1866
1. U.S. 2. 3. MATANZAS

TABER, JOHN, , M, SEAMAN, 07/07/1829
1. U.S. 2. U.S. 3. RIO DE JANEIRO

TALMAN, FRANCIS, 26, M, CARPENTER, 06/22/1833
1. U.S. 2. U.S. 3. MATANZAS

TAYLOR, CARRY, 27, M, SEAMAN, 03/31/1860
1. U.S. 2. U.S. 3. MATANZAS

TERRILL, ABIJAH B., 40, M, MARINER, 05/16/1823
1. BALTIMORE 2. U.S. 3. MARTINIQUE

TEW, WILLIAM, 38, M, MARINER, 02/13/1821
1. U.S. 2. U.S. 3. HAVANA

THOMPSON, E.A., 34, M, ACCOUNTANT, 05/08/1851
1. U.S. 2. 3. SANDWICH ISLANDS

THOMPSON, JAMES, , M, COOPER, 07/07/1829
1. U.S. 2. U.S. 3. HAVANA

THURBER, WILLIAM H., 25, M, CARPENTER, 06/16/1831
1. U.S. 2. U.S. 3. TRINIDAD

TILTON, JONATHAN, 27, M, MERCHANT, 09/26/1828
1. U.S. 2. 3. HAVANA

TOBEY, ALBERT, 26, M, MARINER, 1845
1. U.S. 2. U.S. 3. MATANZAS

TOMLEY, DANIEL, 26, M, CORDWAINER, 10/20/1820
1. U.S. 2. U.S. 3. HAVANA

TORY, OTTO, 32, M, MUSICIAN, 08/17/1827
1. HOLLAND 2. BOSTON 3. GOTHENBURGH

TOWN, JAMES P., 25, M, CARPENTER, 06/05/1834
1. U.S. 2. U.S. 3. HAVANA

TOWNSEND, BENJAMIN, 24, M, GENTLEMAN, 05/10/1824
1. U.S. 2. U.S. 3. MATANZAS

TUCKER, GEORGE, 25, M, ENGINEER, 07/01/1861
1. U.S. 2. 3. SAGUA LA GRANDE

TUFTS, MRS., 20, F, , 05/31/1824
1. U.S. 2. U.S. 3. HAVANA

TUFTS, WILLIAM, 24, M, MERCHANT, 05/31/1824
1. U.S. 2. U.S. 3. HAVANA

TUMMA, JOSEPH, 28, M, MERCHANT, 1846
1. MALTA 2. MALTA 3. DEMERARA

TURTTLE, ZUREL, 23, M, CLERK, 06/16/1831
1. U.S. 2. U.S. 3. TRINIDAD

TYLER, JOHN, 38, M, MERCHANT, 02/27/1828
1. U.S. 2. U.S. 3. HAVANA

VALENTINE, JOHN, 41, M, ENGINEER, 06/20/1851
1. U.S. 2. 3. CARDENAS

VALENTINE, JOHN, 40, M, ENGINEER, 06/14/1850
1. U.S. 2. 3. CARDENAS

VAN HORTEN, CORNELIUS, 30, M, MARINER, 07/22/1857
1. U.S. 2. U.S. 3. HONOLULU

VAN RENAN, FREIDRICH, 23, M, CLERK, 05/08/1837
1. U.S. 2. U.S. 3. CAPE TOWN

VARIEN, P., 35, M, MARINER, 12/31/1865
1. BRAVO, C.V. 2. 3. HAVANA

VAUGHAN, WANTON, 22, M, MECHANIC, 05/17/1823
1. RHODE ISLAND 2. AMERICA 3. MATANZAS

VAUGHN, BOWEN, 24, M, MECHANIC, 05/17/1823
1. RHODE ISLAND 2. AMERICA 3. MATANZAS

VAUGHN, BOWEN, 60, M, COOPER, 06/04/1849
1. U.S. 2. U.S. 3. CARDENAS

VAUGHN, CHRISTOPHER, 25, M, MECHANIC, 05/17/1823
1. RHODE ISLAND 2. AMERICA 3. MATANZAS

VAUGHN, GEORGE, 26, M, MECHANIC, 05/17/1823
1. RHODE ISLAND 2. AMERICA 3. MATANZAS

WALKER, DAVID, 13, M, MARINER, 06/22/1820
1. U.S. 2. U.S. 3. MATANZAS

WALKER, GILBERT, 34, M, MERCHANT, 04/27/1837
1. U.S. 2. U.S. 3. HAVANA

WALL, ROBERT, 35, M, CORDWAINER, 05/05/1821
1. U.S. 2. U.S. 3. HAVANNA

WARDWELL, ELISHA M., 23, M, PAINTER, 03/31/1852
1. U.S. 2. 3. MATANZAS

WARNER, JAMES M., 28, M, GOLDSMITH, 03/08/1821
1. U.S. 2. U.S. 3. HAVANA

WATSON, JOHN, 50, M, MARINER, 03/15/1850
1. U.S. 2. U.S. 3. CARDENAS

WATSON, MARY M., , F, , 04/23/1832
1. U.S. 2. U.S. 3. HAVANA

WEST, ENOCK, 26, M, CARPENTER, 06/14/1827
1. U.S. 2. U.S. 3. MATANZAS

WHITE, WM. M., 21, M, MARINER, 07/03/1822
1. BORDINGHAM, D.M. 2. 3. MATANZAS

WHITMAN, D., , M, CARPENTER, 06/30/1826
1. U.S. 2. U.S. 3. MATANZAS

WILBOUR, THOMAS, 37, M, BRICKLAYER, 04/19/1821
1. U.S. 2. U.S. 3. MATANZAS

WILBOUR, WILLIAM, 33, M, CARPENTER, 04/19/1821
1. U.S. 2. U.S. 3. MATANZAS

WILKIE, WANTON, , M, MECHANIC, 05/19/1829
1. U.S. 2. U.S. 3. HAVANA

WILMARTH, M., 22, M, ENGINEER, 05/15/1849
1. U.S. 2. U.S. 3. MATANZAS

WILMARTH, MARCUS, 26, M, ENGINEER, 06/25/1850
1. U.S. 2. 3. MATANZAS

WILSON, ALEXANDER, 33, M, MARINER, 04/24/1852
1. U.S. 2. 3. LAHAINA

WILSON, CHARLES C., 27, M, AGRICULTURALIST, 07/13/1826
1. U.S. 2. U.S. 3. MATANZAS

WILSON, JOHN S., 10, M, SCHOOL BOY, 06/13/1827
1. U.S. 2. U.S. 3. MATANZAS

WINE, BARNEY A., 48, M, MILLER, 06/11/1852
1. U.S. 2. 3. TALCAHUANO

WITTS, JOHN, 45, M, MERCHANT, 12/18/1820
1. U.S. 2. U.S. 3. MATANZAS

WOLF 3RD, JOHN, 20, M, GENTLEMAN, 06/13/1827
1. U.S. 2. U.S. 3. MATANZAS

WOOD, JOHN, 52, M, MARINER, 07/03/1822
1. RHODE ISLAND 2. 3. MATANZAS

WOOD, PELEG, 24, M, MERCHANT, 05/21/1824
1. U.S. 2. U.S. 3. MATANZAS

WOOD, TIMOTHY, 29, M, CARPENTER, 04/19/1821
1. U.S. 2. U.S. 3. MATANZAS

WOOD, WM. B., 23, M, LANDMAN, 05/31/1820
1. PHILADELPHIA 2. PHILADELPHIA 3. TRINIDAD

WOODBURY, J.H., 28, M, MERCHANT, 07/01/1821
1. U.S. 2. U.S. 3. MATANZAS

WOODLEY, JAMES, , M, SERVANT, 04/23/1832
1. U.S. 2. U.S. 3. HAVANA

WOOSTER, CHAS. H., 24, M, MARINER, 04/24/1849
1. U.S. 2. U.S. 3. SAN SALVADOR

WRIGHT, JR., HENRY, 34, M, MARINER, 09/09/1823
1. BRISTOL 2. U.S. 3. HAVANA

YOUNG, WILLIAM, 40, M, MASON, 05/21/1830
1. IRELAND 2. U.S. 3. MATANZAS

APPENDIX

The following passenger manifest, titled *List of Passengers on board the Cartel Ship Rising States from the West Indies to the U.S.* was found with the Providence Custom House Papers for 1820. It appears to be an impressment list from the War of 1812. The only date on it is a date of impressment of June 30, 1813. It is unclear whether this manifest was originally part of the Custom House Papers or was removed from the Rhode Island Historical Society Manuscript collection at the time the papers were organized.

KEY: NAME, PLACE OF BIRTH, STATION (OCCUPATION),
    CAME ON BOARD
    (1) WHEN TAKEN
    (2) BY WHOM
    (3) ON BOARD WHAT VESSEL

ABRAHAM, RALJOH, BOSTON, SEAMAN, FEBRUARY 1
    1. JANUARY 19 2. DASHER 3. SANTA MATILDA

AMES, SEARS, NEW YORK, SEAMAN, FEBRUARY 2
    1. JANUARY 13 2. ELIZABETH 3. GREYHOUND (SLOOP)

BAILEY, RANSFORD, EAST RIVER, VA, MATE, FEBRUARY 2
    1. JANUARY 13 2. PIQUE 3. BURNT (SLOOP)

BERRY, JEREMIAH, BATH, PASSENGER, FEBRUARY 3
    1. JANUARY 9 2. ELIZABETH 3. MARY & ELIZABETH

BIZARD, BERNARD, FRANCE, PASSENGER, FEBRUARY 3
    1. DECEMBER 31 2. VENERABLE 3. JASON (BRIG)

BUCK, HENRY, WEATHERSFIELD, MATE, FEBRUARY 2
    1. JANUARY 13 2. WEATHERSFIELD 3. GREYHOUND (SLOOP)

BURNS, PETER, BOSTON, SEAMAN, FEBRUARY 2
    1. JANUARY 13 2. PIQUE 3. BURNT (SLOOP)

COULON, P., FRANCE, PASSENGER, FEBRUARY 3
    1. DECEMBER 31 2. VENERABLE 3. JASON (BRIG)

CURTIS, WM., MARBLEHEAD, SEAMAN, FEBRUARY 1
1. JANUARY 19 2. DASHER 3. SANTA MATILDA

DEVALE, JOHN, FRANCE, PASSENGER, FEBRUARY 3
1. DECEMBER 31 2. VENERABLE 3. JASON (BRIG)

DIEGNAE, P., FRANCE, PASSENGER, FEBRUARY 4
1. DECEMBER 31 2. VENERABLE 3. JASON (BRIG)

DUNBAR, JASRIS, PENOBSCOT, MAINE, MATE, JANUARY 27
1. JANUARY 19 2. ECLIPSE 3. MARIA CASTINE

DYER, ELISHA, CASTINE, PASSENGER, JANUARY 28
1. JANUARY 19 2. ECLIPSE 3. MARIA CASTINE

EVERT, WM., NEW YORK, SEAMAN, FEBRUARY 1
1. JANUARY 19 2. DASHER 3. SANTA MATILDA

EVERY, H., NEW YORK, SEAMAN, FEBRUARY 1
1. JANUARY 19 2. DASHER 3. SANTA MATILDA

FERRIERE, A., FRANCE, PASSENGER, FEBRUARY 4
1. DECEMBER 31 2. VENERABLE 3. JASON (BRIG)

FIELDS, JOSEPH, BOSTON, PASSENGER, FEBRUARY 3
1. JANUARY 9 2. ELIZABETH 3. MARY & ELIZABETH

FREEMAN, H., PORTLASND, SEAMAN, FEBRUARY 1
1. JANUARY 19 2. DASHER 3. SANTA MATILDA

GAREY, (CHILD), LOUDON COUNTY, VA, PASSENGER, JANUARY 27
1. 2. 3.

GAREY, (CHILD), LOUDON COUNTY, VA, PASSENGER, JANUARY 27
1. 2. 3.

GAREY, JAMES, LOUDON COUNTY, VA, PASSENGER, JANUARY 27
1. 2. 3.

GAREY, MRS., LOUDON COUNTY, VA, PASSENGER, JANUARY 27
1. 2. 3.

GIFFORD, SML., NEW BEDFORD, SEAMAN, FEBRUARY 1
1. JANUARY 19 2. DASHER 3. SANTA MATILDA

GREEN, RATHBUN, WESTERLY, RI, SEAMAN, FEBRUARY 2
1. JANUARY 13 2. ELIZABETH 3. GREYHOUND

GRIFFIN, WM., BOSTON, MATE, FEBRUARY 2
1. JANUARY 8TH 2. PIQUE 3. ELLEN

HARRISON, JOHN, BOSTON, COOK (BLACK), FEBRUARY 2
1. JANUARY 8TH 2. PIQUE 3. ELLEN (BRIG)

HICKLEY, ELNATHAN, BRUNSWICK, SEAMAN, FEBRUARY 4
1. JANUARY 9 2. COMET 3. MARY & ELIZABETH

JAHONNAGE, J., FRANCE, PASSENGER, FEBRUARY 4
1. DECEMBER 31 2. VENERABLE 3. JASON (BRIG)

JAMISON, GEORGE, CHARLESTON, MASTER, FEBRUARY 1
1. FIVE MONTHS AGO 2. ROVER BRIG 3. EMPRESS OF NEW YORK

LAFONTAINE, F., FRANCE, PASSENGER, FEBRUARY 4
1. DECEMBER 31 2. VENERABLE 3. JASON (BRIG)

LAMBERT, SOLM., PHILADELPHIA, SEAMAN (BLACK), FEBRUARY 1
1. JANUARY 19 2. DAHER 3. SANTA MATILDA

LINCOLN, NATHL., BREWSTER, SECOND MATE, FEBRUARY 2
1. JANUARY 8TH 2. PIQUE 3. ELLEN (BRIG)

MAY, WM., NEW BEDFORD, MASTER, FEBRUARY 2
1. JUNE 30TH, 1813 2. BRIG MARIA 3. LUCRETIA (SCHOONER)

MCFEDDEN, THOS., GEORGETOWN, SEAMAN, FEBRUARY 4
1. JANUARY 9 2. COMET 3. MARY & ELIZABETH

MOULTROSS, DAVID, PORTLAND, SEAMAN, JANUARY 25
1. JANUARY 19 2. DASHER 3. SANTA MATILDA

MURRAY, JAMES, PORTLAND, STEWARD, FEBRUARY 1
1. JANUARY 19 2. DASHER 3. SANTA MATILDA

ORCUTT, GALEN, CASTINE, PASSENGER, JANUARY 28
1. JANUARY 19 2. ECLIPSE 3. MARIA CASTINE

PENDILET, E., FRANCE, PASSENGER, FEBRUARY 4
1. DECEMBER 31 2. VENERABLE 3. JASON (BRIG)

PERRY, EBENEZER, BOSTON, COOPER, FEBRUARY 2
1. JANUARY 8TH 2. PIQUE 3. ELLEN (BRIG)

PETERS, FRANCIS, FRANCE, PASSENGER, FEBRUARY 4
1. DECEMBER 31 2. VENERABLE 3. JASON (BRIG)

PETERS, WM., PORTLAND, COOK (BLACK), FEBRUARY 1
1. JANUARY 19 2. DASHER 3. SANTA MATILDA

PLAPIARD, A.S., FRANCE, PASSENGER, FEBRUARY 3
1. DECEMBER 31 2. VENERABLE 3. JASON (BRIG)

PLAPIARD, E., FRANCE, PASSENGER, FEBRUARY 3
1. DECEMBER 31 2. VENERABLE 3. JASON (BRIG)

SAWYER, JOHN, CAPE ELIZABETH, FIRST MATE, FEBRUARY 1
1. JANUARY 19 2. DASHER 3. SANTA MATILDA

SMITH, JESSE, NEWBURYPORT, SEAMAN (BLACK), JANUARY 26
1. FIRST OF WAR 2. SURINAM BRIG 3. MARIA NEWBURYPORT

SMITH, JOSHUA, SEDGEWICK, SEAMAN, JANUARY 28
1. JANUARY 19 2. ECLIPSE 3. MARIA CASTINE

STACEY, B., MARBLEHEAD, PASSENGER, FEBRUARY 4
1. DECEMBER 31 2. VENERABLE 3. JASON (BRIG)

STANLEY, SIMON, SHAPLEIGH, SECOND MATE, FEBRUARY 1
1. JANUARY 19 2. DASHER 3. SANTA MATILDA

WATKINS, ASA, FRENCHMAN'S BAY, COOK, FEBRUARY 2
1. DECEMBER 4 2. CLEOPATRA 3. SANTA MARIA

WORREL, ISAAC, KENNEBECK, SEAMAN, FEBRUARY 4
1. JANUARY 9 2. COMET 3. MARY & ELIZABETH

www.ingramcontent.com/pod-product-compliance
Lightning Source LLC
Chambersburg PA
CBHW071855270326
41929CB00013B/2234

* 9 7 8 0 8 0 6 3 8 0 1 4 8 *